PRAISE FOR *SELLING BASEBALL*

"In *Selling Baseball*, Jeffrey Orens provides his readers with a new perspective of the sport and the sports equipment industry through the long-overlooked relationship between Albert Goodwill Spalding and George Wright. The more than fifty-year friendship of these two on-the-field stars, Baseball Hall of Fame inductees, and sports equipment pioneers, transcended competition and launched baseball and other athletics to the status that we take for granted today. Thought provoking, instructive, and enjoyable—a must read."— **Peter Mancuso**, co-chair, Nineteenth Century Research Committee, Society for American Baseball Research

"*Selling Baseball* tells how the then-new game of baseball grew into the "National Pastime"—a big business complete with fanatic fans and professional teams—via the joint stories of two of baseball's most impactful pioneers, Hall of Famers George Wright and Albert Spalding. Whether on the ball field or in management, the duo helped shape the game as we know it today. Jeffrey Orens's *Selling Baseball* gives readers a grand tour of 19th-century baseball, as well as of 19th-century America."— **Bruce Allardice**, baseball historian and author

"Orens brings a fresh perspective and lively writing to the early years of professional baseball."— **Richard Hershberger**, baseball historian and author of *Strike Four: The Evolution of Baseball*

"Orens's book invites us on a journey through American and baseball history from the 19th into the early 20th centuries. Through the eyes of two early baseball icons, Al Spalding and George Wright, we witness the evolution of the game, from the fun of under-handed pitching to its formation as a national economic enterprise. Along the way, we crisscross America with the famous Cincinnati Red Stockings; follow the game overseas; watch the rules, equipment, and economics of the game transform; and appreciate how American sports became big business. A must read for anyone fascinated by the interplay of sports and American society."— **Bob LeMoine**, author of *When the Babe Went Back to Boston: Babe Ruth, Judge Fuchs and the Hapless Braves of 1935*

"In his fine book, *Selling Baseball*, Jeffrey Orens offers a uniquely sliced view: how Al Spalding and George Wright, superstars on the ball field, came to dominate its mer-chandising, building empires that extended to tennis, golf, and, yes, roller polo. Highly recommended, even to those who may know a thing or two about sports."— **John Thorn**, official historian of Major League Baseball and author of the critically acclaimed *Baseball in the Garden of Eden*

"In *Selling Baseball*, Jeffrey Orens makes a compelling case that two early superstars went far beyond the ball field to change the face of sports in America. All fans of early baseball and American cultural history owe Orens a debt for his entertaining and deeply sourced account of the remarkable rise of George Wright and Albert Goodwill Spald-ing."— **Edward Achorn**, Pulitzer Prize finalist and author of *Fifty-nine in '84* and *The Summer of Beer and Whiskey*

1874 Boston Red Stockings. *Standing, l to r:* Cal McVey, Albert Spalding, Jim "Deacon" White, Ross Barnes. *Seated, l to r:* Jim O'Rourke, Andy Leonard, George Wright, Harry Wright, George Hall, Harry Schafer, Tommy Beals. *Courtesy of Byron Museum of History, Byron, Illinois*

Selling Baseball

How Superstars George Wright and Albert Spalding Impacted Sports in America

Jeffrey Orens

ROWMAN & LITTLEFIELD
Lanham • Boulder • New York • London

Published by Rowman & Littlefield
An imprint of The Rowman & Littlefield Publishing Group, Inc.
4501 Forbes Boulevard, Suite 200, Lanham, Maryland 20706
www.rowman.com

86-90 Paul Street, London EC2A 4NE, United Kingdom

British Library Cataloguing in Publication Information Available

Library of Congress Cataloging-in-Publication Data

Names: Orens, Jeffrey, author.
Title: Selling baseball : how superstars George Wright and Albert Spalding impacted sports in America / Jeffrey Orens.
Description: Lanham, Maryland : Rowman & Littlefield, 2025. | Includes bibliographical references and index. | Summary: "Selling Baseball breathes fresh energy into baseball's origin story with this captivating tale of two vibrant personalities whose rivalry cum friendship was integral to the rise of the professional game. It's a fascinating look back on the sport's humble beginnings and its rapid transformation into the national pastime"—Provided by publisher.
Identifiers: LCCN 2024027781 (print) | LCCN 2024027782 (ebook) | ISBN 9781538189269 (cloth) | ISBN 9781538189276 (epub)
Subjects: LCSH: Wright, George, 1847–1937. | Spalding, A. G. (Albert Goodwill) | Baseball—United States—History.
Classification: LCC GV865.W746 O74 2025 (print) | LCC GV865.W746 (ebook) | DDC 796.357092/273—dc23/eng/20240715
LC record available at https://lccn.loc.gov/2024027781
LC ebook record available at https://lccn.loc.gov/2024027782

To my wonderful daughter Rebecca,
who shares with me an addiction to the Yankees.

Contents

Introduction
Play Ball!

The game of "base ball" was initially designated by these two words to show it was a game of ball that included bases as opposed to other ball games that did not have this feature. At first these bases were wooden stakes or even holes in the ground, eventually replaced by flat stones or sacks stuffed with hay or dirt and finally canvas bags of specific dimensions. During most of the 1800s, the game was designated with these two words, and since this story's events mostly take place during this period, "base ball" will be used to refer to the sport until the epilogue.

Origins of the game lie well beyond the scope of this book. Some claimed that base ball evolved from English sports of ball and bat such as rounders or cricket. However, continuing research up through the present day, by numerous base ball historians, firmly discounts these hypotheses, pointing out many distinctions that make it truly American in derivation.

The game itself has come far since its recognized days of more formal organization during the 1830s and 1840s. By the mid-1840s, a group of players in the New York City area who were attracted to it decided to develop and codify a set of principles on how to play the sport. Their team was called the Knickerbockers, and as such the guidelines they wrote down were known as the Knickerbocker Rules. These rules and regulations, as opposed to some that were being developed by a few other teams at that time, were generally adopted by the sport and have been altered over the years, often being modified to make the game more equitable and exciting for the participants to play as well as enjoyable for the spectators to watch.

Today's version differs markedly from those original rules. From pitchers whose role was to deliver a ball underhand to the striker to hit into the playing field and initiate the game, we now feature hurlers who can routinely fire the ball overhand one hundred miles an hour with the intent of denying the batter a chance to hit it at all. We've evolved from strikers who waited until just the right pitch to deftly put the ball into play to batters who unleash gargantuan swings at the ball with the intention of smacking it out of the ballpark, anything less than a home run often seemingly not worthy of their efforts. Still, the game as played after the Civil War is, for the most part, recognizable as the precursor of today's sport.

The first professional base ball league began in 1871 with the organization of the National Association of Professional Base Ball Players (NAPBBP or NA for short). After the Civil War, the sport exploded in popularity across the country, with people willing to pay a dime or quarter, sometimes even fifty cents, to see it played firsthand. It had previously been composed of clubs that stressed amateurism as a founding principle, but, in relatively short order, as a portion of the mounting gate receipts were offered as enticements to star players for their participation, this became an untenable position. It gave way to this new league whose clubs openly paid all their players.

The famed Cincinnati Red Stockings of 1869 were the first club to overtly pay salaries to everyone on the team, while others still clung to some form of amateur status for a few years. The Red Stockings were so overwhelmingly successful that year, not losing a single contest of the scores they played, that it was a foregone conclusion that base ball would have to embrace this change in the game. Cincinnati disbanded at the end of the following year, after losing their first game in almost a season and a half, and the NA was formed before the beginning of the next season of play.

The disbanding of the Cincinnati club and the formation of the new professional league were twin engines of creation in the sport. Both led to the formation of a new team in 1871, a professional club composed largely of a number of former Cincinnati players wearing its nationally known hosiery and taking up shop as the Boston Red Stockings. This team has gone through multiple transformations of name and location over the years, today being called the Atlanta Braves. The Boston Red Sox are a completely different animal, formed initially in 1901 as the Boston Americans, a charter member of the American League. But the heritage of both clubs has instilled in Boston, as in many locations across the country where the sport has sunk deep roots, a fanatical support of the game.

From the Civil War to the founding of the NA, Harry Wright and his brother George established themselves as the leading manager and initial superstar of the sport, respectively. Harry was a valued ballplayer as an outfielder and pitcher. However, his real talent lay in managing a group of men who were individually skilled at playing the game and molding them into a unit that saw the winning ways of teamwork. George was the prototypical player that Harry was delighted to have on his team: athletic, inventive, exuding positivity as he participated in each game with a smile. Of course, it also helped that George was almost universally recognized as the best player in the land.

By 1869, when Harry assembled the team in Cincinnati that was to take the country by storm, he knew that George must be part of it. Uniting the two brothers with other talented ballplayers, under Harry's tutelage they were invincible that season. After the 1870 campaign, the club disbanded, having lost a handful of games and with them the support of its sponsors. Harry took George and a few other teammates to Boston, also bringing Albert Spalding, the best pitcher of the day, along with some of his Forest City of Rockford teammates to create the team that was to become the Boston Red Stockings dynasty of the 1870s.

The fusing of the baseball talents of George, Albert, and Harry resulted in more than a dominant team with George the star infielder, Albert the stellar pitcher, and Harry the inventive manager. It immersed the three in the sport in a manner that allowed their thoughts on the game to mingle, producing novel situations. Innovative play was often the result, as when George and Albert concocted a scheme to have George catch an infield pop-up in his hat, freezing the runners at the oddity of the action before initiating a double play. This forced the umpire to rule on the legality of their antics, quickly overruling them altogether. But it showed the ever-churning minds of these teammates, creating as they went along at a time when the sport was rapidly developing.

Harry took Spalding under his wing in making him a promoter of the game, charged with negotiating the terms, conditions, and logistics of Harry's planned venture to introduce base ball to England by taking the Red Stockings and Philadelphia Athletics there in 1874. As well, during their time together the Wrights and Spalding undoubtedly exchanged views on the sale of sporting goods to an eager American marketplace. George had established a fledgling sports equipment business in Boston and Albert was intent on learning how to financially capitalize on the sport. Both were planning ahead for life after base ball.

By 1875, Spalding could see that the dominance of Harry's team, though personally satisfying for them all, was doing a disservice to the organized sport. It had become an association of "Boston and the rest," and was beginning to wear on the patience of the sporting public. The league focused on the Northeast of the country, with little room for the growing Midwestern appetite for base ball. Surreptitiously, Spalding and three others on the Red Stockings were approached by a moneyed individual from Chicago who proposed that they come to that city as the centerpiece of the White Stockings club, soon to become part of a new professional league. In the following year, with the "Big Four" of Spalding and these three other teammates announcing their desertion of the Red Stockings for greener pastures, the NA collapsed and was replaced in short order by this upstart organization, the National League.

At the same time, Spalding launched a sporting goods venture. In 1879, George Wright brought a new partner into his own sporting goods business and formed Wright & Ditson, leaving base ball a few years later to devote his full efforts to its operation. Both Spalding and Wright were to make this their future vocation, although Spalding retained his management and ownership role in the Chicago White Stockings through the end of the century. The business of base ball had been launched on two fronts, both of which sold products that Americans clamored for in ever-increasing numbers: the game itself and the equipment to play it.

Spalding and Wright would expand the equipment facet of this business model to include other sports as well such as tennis, golf, ice hockey, football and basketball. In addition to sporting goods, they sold guides on the rules and regulations of these organized sports and provided detailed statistics that could be employed in evaluation of individual and team performances. These journals also contained explanations on how to play each game, essential for many who were new to America and desired an understanding of how to participate in these activities and in doing so fit into the cultural mainstream. Wright and Spalding supported league play in these sports, sponsoring events at different organizational levels and donating trophies for superior performance. They participated in two international base ball tours, first to England and then later around the world, touting the game to curious audiences, in the process igniting a deep sense of pride in the sport back home. They loved the part they played in stirring the enthusiasm of the country for base ball and other team games.

These early superstars of base ball had become instrumental in feeding the country's expanding appetite for sports, teaching America how to "play ball" in the process. This book is not intended to represent complete biographies of these two but, rather, to show the development of sport in America, especially baseball, through their intertwining careers. Yet, while Spalding retains a familiar ring to many in this country, mention of George Wright is invariably met with a blank stare. Such is the power of branding in the marketplace. While the name Spalding may be vaguely remembered as that of a ballplayer, it has been successfully fixed within collective American consciousness as synonymous with a sporting goods empire. George, along with his brother, if recognized at all, might be mistakenly confused with the illustrious Wright brothers from the field of aviation a generation later. "Smiling" George Wright, the charismatic infielder who revolutionized the position of shortstop and in doing so became the first professional superstar of the sport, is but a twinkle in the eye of only the sharpest baseball aficionado.

1

East Meets West

Albert Spalding had come to town with his friend Ross Barnes and the others, a group of bright-eyed ball players, the Forest City team traveling ninety miles east from their homes in Rockford, Illinois, to the big city of Chicago. They had been invited there for a tournament, a celebration of base ball in late July 1867. The powerful team from Washington, DC, the Nationals, was the main attraction, traveling from St. Louis to complete the last leg of their so-far-undefeated tour of the West and to showcase their prowess among the "Lilliputians" of the country's ballplaying hinterlands.

Earlier in July, the Forest City club had played two games against Chicago's best, the vaunted Excelsiors, narrowly losing both in closely contested matches, 45–41 and 28–25. In so doing they had demonstrated their growing talents. These competitions had earned Spalding and his teammates a much sought-after spot in the tournament to take place at the end of July. Not only that, but they were to be one of the three teams, besides Chicago's Excelsiors and Atlantics, to take on the famous Nationals' nine.

Spalding and Barnes had been playing base ball together for a number of years in Rockford. Initially, they were members of the town's sixteen-and-under club, known as the Pioneers. When they joined they were no more than boys, but a precocious duo. Albert was a gifted pitcher and Ross an already-accomplished second baseman and short fielder, the early term for what was soon to be known as shortstop. They both performed their roles bare-handed, the standard of the day, palms and fingers often bruised and swollen as marks of a game fearlessly played. Barnes was a

1

little above medium height and weight for the times, about five feet eight inches and 145 pounds. As for Spalding, he was already a tall, long-armed lad, destined to be solid of frame and sprouting to six feet one inch, a perfect combination of physical attributes to leverage into the dynamics of pitching a ball with speed and finesse.

The two thought highly of their developing skills at the game. The role of pitcher was evolving quickly into a more important part of the action, and Albert was intent on being part of this transformation. Originally, from forty-five feet away, a pitcher served the ball up to the striker in an underhand fashion, straight-armed with no wrist break, delivering the ball so that the striker might initiate the main focus of the game. This was to hit the ball and run to first base, or further to other bases if possible, before the fielders could catch the ball on the fly—or on one bounce if a foul ball—for an out or retrieve it from the ground and throw the runner out.

The striker had the luxury of dictating to be pitched to in either a "high" or "low" zone, high being waist to shoulder, waist to a foot off the ground being the low zone. Either choice gave the striker a good indication of where the ball would be, all the easier to ready his efforts to hit the ball and begin to get the game moving. The striker would wait to swing at a pitch that was in his indicated zone, sometimes letting an inordinate number of pitches go by until swinging at just the right one.

This slowed down the game so much that by the mid-1860s, strikes and balls were being called, though infrequently, by the lone umpire. His position was in foul territory, usually a bit off to the right side of the infield, which presented some difficulties in properly calling balls and strikes. Even then, it took nine balls for the umpire to award the striker a walk to first base, but only three strikes for an out. As Richard Hershberger describes it in his detailed book on the rules of the game,

> The called strike was meant as a small expansion of the existing swinging strike, added [to the rules] in response to some batters seeking advantage by not swinging at hittable pitches. The base on balls was meant as a penalty for pitchers wasting time by violating the existing rule that they deliver the ball where the batter wanted it. The unintended result was that the pitcher could aim to force the issue by delivering a strike that wasn't what the striker actually wanted.[1]

Pitchers were beginning to add speed to their delivery and to vary this speed from one pitch to the next. And they could pitch to specific spots of the striker's indicated zone, trying to catch the striker off guard and receive an umpire's called strike as the reward for this effort. Spalding, in his mid-teens, was quickly becoming a master of these techniques. As he grew to his imposing adult height, with the ball cradled in the palm of his hand on his long pitching arm, he could harness a significant amount of force to propel the ball at various speeds. This, coupled with his accuracy in pinpointing different parts of the striker's chosen zone, enabled his pitching to become a weapon rather than just a meek offering that the striker could wallop.

Albert remembered that one day in the fall of 1865, "[Ross] and I conceived the idea that we could 'do' the Mercantiles, whose players were for the most part salesmen in the several stores of the city. A challenge was therefore sent, but the tradesmen at first regarded it as a joke: they were not in the game to play with children."[2] However, players from the other adult ball club in Rockford, the Forest Citys, teased and taunted the Mercantiles into a match with the Pioneers. The boys proceeded to thrash the men, routing them by a score of 26–2.[3] Several Forest City players attended the contest, heckling the hapless merchants but also noting the abundant base ball talents on display by both Spalding and Barnes.

By the coming spring, the two boys were wearing Forest City uniforms, both at the age of fifteen. That year, 1866, Forest City of Rockford lost only one game of the seven they played, the single loss by one run, 14–13. Their competition was not fearsome, but challenging battles ensued nonetheless with skilled teams of the surrounding communities in Illinois and Wisconsin. They opened the 1867 season with two convincing victories before succumbing to the Excelsiors in those tightly fought battles of early July. Now, here were the base ball farmers from Rockland, about to be the leading act of a great tournament. Not unexpectedly, Albert was developing a bit of stage fright for the forthcoming day and the potential embarrassment it might hold for him as the pitcher against the acclaimed Nationals.

The humidity had not dissipated as heavy purple-gray rainclouds spread across the breaking dawn of July 25. Showers came and went throughout the morning, threatening the playing of the Nationals' much-awaited debut game in Chicago with Forest City. Still, many were anxious to see the spectacle, taking the train to the ball grounds on the southern edge of the racetrack at Dexter Park. Some struggled to get there in horse-drawn carriages, buggies, or wagons slogging through the mud-clogged roads. By the time the game began at two o'clock that afternoon, the Chicago newspapers reported that over five thousand spectators had arrived, more than 10 percent being ladies. This latter fact was important enough that the next day's *Chicago Tribune* waxed rhapsodic in its opening paragraphs covering the tournament,

> One of the strongest inducements to the popularity of our American game is that it is an out-door sport, and almost the only one which ladies can countenance and witness. Our ladies have hitherto been shut out from all the pleasures incident to [other] such games by the low character and association of the sports men indulge in. In base ball there is an exception in their favor which the fair sex have not been slow to take advantage of. If our national pastime had no other advantage than this, the fact would suffice to give it a popularity no other recreation could compete with.[4]

This emphatic endorsement of base ball as a recreational pastime fit for observation, if not participation, by women as well as men certainly envisioned the widening of the sport's future appeal. While it welcomed the presence of women at a ball game, it omitted the fact that a small but determined number of women in America had actually begun to organize clubs to play the sport themselves. The previous year, at Vassar College in New York, a newly opened all-women's institution of higher learning in America, namesake founder Matthew Vassar had promised that the curriculum would include mandatory time for recreation and exercise, which at the ladies' insistence included base ball. This was certainly a different approach to physical activity for women during the Victorian age, when strict parents and learned medical professionals agreed that vigorous exertion was not only unsuited for ladies but potentially damaging to their ability to reproduce.[5] The childhood allure of base ball, in which both boys *and* girls had fondly taken part in mid-nineteenth-century America, attested to the powerful, youthful connection that had taken shape in the form of a sport that was maturing as it spread throughout the land.

The Nationals were known far and wide as playing a brand of base ball practiced by only the elite clubs in the Northeastern part of the country, the cradle of the game. Among others, their roster had recently been beefed up to include arguably the best player in the sport, twenty-year-old infielder George Wright, from the champion Unions of Morrisania (later part of the Bronx) in New York. He was a sparkling playmaker at shortstop or second base who was also a consummate ball striker. Like a majority of his teammates, he was "technically" employed by the government in Washington, DC, as a clerk, receiving a salary for his official desk job while his only actual work encompassed playing base ball. This was the convenient ruse of the day for clubs that desired to fill their ranks with top-notch talent while still claiming amateur status. George's place of employment was listed as 238 Pennsylvania Avenue, a vacant lot about fifteen blocks from the White House.[6]

Wright was an athlete, plain and simple. The kind who excelled at most every sport in which he participated. He was not overwhelming physically, standing a bit over five feet nine inches and weighing about 160 pounds. But his body provided strength and agility that few others of his size possessed. He ran with abandon, could spring into the air with ease, was ambidextrous, and had uncommonly good hand-eye coordination. And he had a quick mind that loved to examine options, the possibilities presented by each game that he played, to devise clever strategies to employ his many capabilities. Chances are that if you provided George with a ball, for cricket or base ball (and later in his life, golf or tennis), and a stick with which to manipulate it, he could outperform most anyone else in executing what was intended to be done with each. With these overwhelming natural abilities, it's no wonder that George Wright excelled at, and loved, base ball.

George had been born on January 28, 1847, into a sporting family, to be sure. His father Sam, an Englishman who emigrated with his young family to New York City in the mid-1830s, made the game of cricket his professional calling with St. George's Club in the City. George and two of his brothers, especially older sibling Harry, George's senior by a dozen years, followed suit. They all grew up learning the intricacies of the game at their father's knee, listening to his instruction, guided by his strategies, playing whenever they could. Eventually, Harry and George became as fascinated by the newly developing American sport of base ball as they were at elevating their game of cricket.

Their burgeoning love of base ball soon superseded their interest in their father's sport. In this regard, Harry was to become famous for his inspired, inventive approaches to the game as well as his deft managerial abilities versus his solid but relatively unspectacular performance in the field. George, on the other hand, with his superior talents matched with rakish good looks, a gleaming smile, and accompanying personality, was destined to be professional baseball's first superstar. Both would eventually be enshrined in the game's Hall of Fame, only one of two pairs of brothers ever to be so honored.

For the monetary compensation of his clerkship in Washington, George had been induced to leave the Unions and join the Nationals to spread the gospel of base ball out "west." It was the first time an Eastern base ball team had ever ventured to this part of America. The group wanted to bring the excitement of the game to a larger segment of the population and demonstrate their superior skills to what they considered a provincial audience. Prior to sweeping into Chicago, they had left in their wake the demolition of a half-dozen clubs in Ohio, Kentucky, Indiana, and Missouri, topping them by anywhere from thirty to eighty runs, even winning one contest in Indianapolis 106–21 (Wright hit five home runs in the game) and another in St. Louis by the score of 113–26.[7] Certainly, bare-handed play accounted for many errors and resulted in inflated scores versus inferior teams, but the heavy-hitting Nationals were not a club with which to trifle.

At not quite seventeen, Spalding had followed with growing apprehension the preceding days of newspaper reporting of the Nationals' touring successes. He was genuinely shaken as he considered the championship team he was about to face. On the day of Forest City's confrontation with the Nationals,

> [I] experienced a severe case of stage fright when I found myself in
> the pitcher's box facing such renowned players as George Wright . . .
> and others of the visiting team. It was the first big game before a large
> audience in which I had ever participated. The great reputations of the
> Eastern players and the extraordinary one-sided scores by which they had
> defeated clubs [in the West] caused me to shudder at the contemplation of
> punishment my pitching was about to receive. A great lump arose in my
> throat, and my heart beat so like a trip-hammer that I imagined it could be
> heard by everyone on the grounds . . . The fact is, we were all frightened
> nearly to death.[8]

Such was the state of affairs as the umpire called the teams together to begin the game promptly at two that afternoon. Forest City started well enough, scoring two runs in the first inning and holding the Nationals to three tallies. Spalding settled down rather quickly and provided both solid pitching and timely hitting, contributing a double to drive in two runs to highlight a Rockford eight-run second inning. The Nationals countered with five of their own in their half of the second, and so began a match in which each team scored their share of runs.

Wright, playing second base rather than his customary shortstop position, made dazzling leaps to secure the ball and steal away sure hits. The strikers on both sides sent several shots heavenward into the outfield. These lofty efforts, though only amounting to long outs, were admiringly termed "sky-scrapers" well before buildings bore that name. The spectators were in awe of the action, cheering on each play, exhorting every striker to take as many bases as possible with each hit.

By the end of the fifth inning, Forest City had built up a lead of 16 to 11. Intermittent showers made the ball slippery and soaked the participants and many of the onlookers, even halting the proceedings for half an hour, but the game continued. Wright stroked the contest's only home run in the Nationals' half of the sixth inning, "a beautiful hit far beyond left field."[9] Still, the Forest City team was on top by 24 to 18. Another inning trading blows, and the Nationals had fought back to within three runs, 24 to 21.

Ross Barnes poked a single to left field, driving in a run in the Forest City eighth. Then Spalding and his teammates made a stand. They held the mighty Nationals scoreless in their half of the inning with some flawless defensive play, rare when the ball and the field had become slick with rainwater. Wright, leading off with a single in the bottom half of the inning, became the front end of a double play executed perfectly by Spalding. He fielded the next batter's ball, wheeled to the second baseman with a sure throw to force Wright at the bag, the ball then being flung on to the first baseman to get the striker hustling down the basepath in vain. The Nationals' right fielder drove a two-out single to left field but overplayed his hand, being caught between the bases and tagged out on his way to second. As reported in the press, "The crowd fairly yelled their delight at the beautiful manner in which the Forest City nine had put out their three men."[10]

Rockford had literally weathered the storm. Four more runs for their team in the ninth sealed the deal when the Nationals could only respond with two runs in their half of the frame. Final score: Forest City 29, Nationals 23. David had hit a perfect line drive up the middle, smiting Goliath right between the eyes.

No doubt in most everyone's mind, including the stunned group of nine Forest City teammates, the improbable, nay, the impossible, had occurred.

Excuses would be forthcoming the next day from the defeated Nationals as well as most everyone who had thought their losing to the team from Rockford was inconceivable. Many said the Nationals' play was not up to their usual standards, probably due to fatigue from the long tour across the country coupled with the oppressive, strength-sapping summer heat. This, along with the unexpectedly sterling play of the Rockford nine, had tilted the day toward the locals. Still, the precise pitching of Spalding, the infielders' wonderful efforts and the unrelenting hitting of Forest City, all combined to make this a team effort that set a new level of performance for the group.

Yet, not a few felt there might be something odd behind this unexpected turn of events. And two days later, when the Nationals summarily destroyed the highly regarded hometown Excelsiors on the same playing field, 49–4, the humiliating defeat of the Chicago team added fodder to the narrative. For this was the beating that was expected of the Forest City club at the hands of the Nationals two days prior. Remembering that these same Excelsiors had defeated Forest City not once, but twice, earlier in July, most felt that the Nationals would administer an even stronger thrashing of the Rockford team. Now the Excelsiors, considered superior to the Rockford team, were thoroughly demolished by this same Nationals squad that had lost a close but convincing competition only two days prior. As an Iowa newspaper speculated in the aftermath of the contests, "During their western swing . . . the Nationals were victorious, except in the game with the Forest City Club of Rockford, and it is generally inferred that some 'shenanagan' [*sic*] as well as base ball was played by the former club. It looks a little that way."[11]

Gambling was a significant part of the game at mid-century, especially betting on which team would emerge the winner. Players routinely put money on their own team to win, and many of the spectators did the same with wagers on their hometown favorites to be triumphant. But almost unheard-of was the case where it could be proven that players were paid by gamblers to actually "throw" the game, through their own poor play, resulting in a win for the other team and a payday for the gamblers, who had bet on this very outcome.

In fact, the first such documented case for the organized sport had occurred only two years before, in the fall of 1865, when two elite teams from New York City, the Mutuals and the Eckfords, played a game that the latter won 23–11. The two clubs were in a close battle until the fifth inning, when an extended series of poorly pitched, fielded, and thrown balls by the Mutuals resulted in the Eckfords scoring eleven runs, eventually leading to their victory.[12] Shortly after this match, one of the Mutual players admitted that he and a few of his teammates had "fixed" the game, purposefully playing in a shoddy manner in exchange for compensation from gamblers who were betting on the other team. Three players involved in this travesty were banned from the sport for a number of years, eventually returning to play after the commotion over the incident had died down. But at the same time, the public exposure of the situation actually added to the temptations of the mostly unpaid ballplayers who might seek compensation for their efforts through various covert alternatives.

Given this highly publicized precedent, it was not surprising that some people thought the Nationals had lost to Forest City on purpose to increase the betting odds that the stronger Excelsior team would handily defeat them a few days later. Those betting in support of the Nationals, which would certainly include some of their players, would then reap a significant windfall if their team could beat the Excelsiors, which they easily did two days after their loss to Rockford.

A Washington, DC, newspaper reported accusations printed in the *Chicago Republican*, which the Washington article referred to as "a foul-mouthed fling at the Nationals." The Chicago paper opined,

> The [Forest City-Nationals] game on Thursday last was a "play off" on the part of the Nationals in order that they might more profitably 'speculate' upon the [Excelsior-Nationals] game yesterday. While we have no evidence that such was the fact, and would wish, for the honor of those interested and the interests of the game, that this is not true, we are reluctantly compelled to the acknowledgement that the gains of our Eastern visitors in "greenbacks" certainly equal their gains in honor.

The Washington paper then went on to quote another Chicago paper, the *Journal*, which took the opposite viewpoint.

> In regard to the complaints of numerous disappointed gentlemen—some of whom, it is said, have lost money—insisting that dishonorable means have been employed by the Nationals to win money; in short, charging them with having "played off" in their game with the Rockford Club for the

purpose of securing heavy bets on the Excelsiors—we do not believe it or any part of it. . . . Until we have something more tangible as an argument than mere rumor . . . we shall believe the National Club to be composed of gentlemen whose honor is as fair as their skill in playing is inimitable.[13]

Arguments would be made on both sides of the issue, which could be seen as an outgrowth of professionalism in base ball. George Wright and his team composed of Washington clerks could be thought of in something of a "pay for play" manner, the giving of their best efforts secured by a team through under-the-table salary inducements. For a few players, it might be just a short next step to be influenced as well by money that could be had from gamblers' pressure to throw a game, a much riskier option for a ballplayer's reputation and career.

Albert Spalding would be drawn into the professionalism issue as well later that fall, when he was approached by a team in Chicago that offered to pay him a weekly salary as a billing clerk in a wholesale grocery business in exchange for his services on the ballfield.[14] The game was quickly evolving from gentlemanly exercise and an amateur contest of athleticism into a money-making proposition with all its attendant vices as well as virtues.

But one thing was certain when it came to base ball. It had been proven by the gallant struggle on the rain-soaked diamond out in Dexter Park that July afternoon in Chicago when the Forest City nine defeated the heavily-favored Nationals. On paper, the winner of the game was a foregone conclusion. The newspapers had predicted as much. Young Albert Spalding was going up against the accomplished veteran who was the best in the game, George Wright. The Nationals had outscored all seven opponents they had faced on their tour to that point by a total of 460 runs (586 to 126), almost 66 runs per game more than the competition.[15] Yet when the two teams met to play the contest, to the shock and excitement of most everyone, the reverse had occurred. As John Thorn, the current official historian of Major League Baseball, noted when he designated this game, in his opinion, the most important game in baseball history, it "points to one of the game's glories, routinely on exhibit every day. You just don't know who's going to win."[16]

And this, at its core, is the attraction of base ball, then as now—the playing of the game itself. The pitcher's speedy delivery of a spinning sphere, the striker's crack of the bat against ball, the mad dash of the fielders to catch it or retrieve it to put the other team's players out. All accompanied by the fervent urgings of the crowd as they observe events unfold in real time before their very eyes, injecting themselves into the unfolding action of the moment, imploring the players on their team to use every ounce of their strength and abilities to make the unlikely happen.

George Wright and Albert Spalding would play starring roles in this drama, both on the field and off, as two of its earliest superstars. During 1869 and 1870, they would meet on the field of play many times as adversaries, each exhibiting the capabilities they had shown as ballplayers in their initial encounter that rainy summer's day in 1867. George's reputation would continue to grow as the top talent in the game, fielding with grace and athleticism, hitting with power as well as craftiness, all the while beaming with delight at playing the game. Albert was fast developing into the dominant player he would become as he matured into the sport's winningest pitcher in the first decade of professional base ball. They eventually became teammates as part of the championship club Harry Wright assembled in the early 1870s, the Boston Red Stockings. During this time together, the team was the most consistently victorious squad in the professional sport. It was during this period that they brought the game of base ball to international attention with a groundbreaking tour overseas that introduced the sport to an English audience.

Later, as luminaries in the larger world of sports as a business, they would both compete yet again, this time as owners of rival companies that brought the equipment of base ball, and other games as well, to an eager sporting public. Eventually, as in their playing days, they became associates once more as they merged their companies into a sporting goods empire in the early 1890s. But in every case, whether as competitors or as colleagues, George Wright and Albert Spalding brought their love of sports, and their knowledge of how to best play these games, to an American public intent on embracing base ball as its national pastime.

2

Base Ball after the War

On April 12, 1861, a cannon was fired on the order of Captain Abner Doubleday, second-in-command of the Federal troops at Fort Sumter in Charleston Harbor, South Carolina. It was the Union's first armed response to the shelling of the fort by the Confederate Army that had commenced earlier in the day as the formal, opening confrontation of the Civil War.

Doubleday would go on to rise in the ranks of the Union Army, ultimately becoming a major general commanding forces in a string of some of the most well-known battles of the war. He and his troops fought determinedly at the Second Battle of Manassas (Bull Run), Antietam, Fredericksburg, Chancellorsville, and Gettysburg. Doubleday received multiple wounds over the span of these engagements, each time dodging death, surviving to fight again. He was one of many unsung military heroes of the day on both sides of the conflict. In Doubleday's case, he was a staunch abolitionist, resolute officer, and brave soldier. But, as would be incorrectly asserted over forty-five years later and then eventually dismissed altogether, he was not the inventor of base ball. In fact, at the moment he was supposed to have devised the game in Cooperstown, New York, in 1839, Doubleday was actually at West Point Military Academy learning the skills that would serve him so well as a dedicated officer during and after the Civil War.[1]

On the very same day that Doubleday initiated the defense of the Union, the front page of a newspaper in Richmond, Virginia, detailed the intricate negotiations taking place within its State Convention. Members were struggling to come to grips with the hotly debated, to some almost unfathomable, step of secession from the United States. Yet, in an article sharing this same front page, the paper's editor found time to energetically extoll the virtues of base ball. His piece was especially envious of the sport as played slightly over one hundred miles away in Washington, DC, in what was still the capital of the United States for Virginians until five days later, when the convention members finally decided to join the Confederacy.

> The season for out-door sports begins this month, and in Washington and Baltimore the base-ball clubs have commenced play for the season. This game of base-ball is a fine, healthy exercise, and a manly and exciting pastime. . . . We rank ourselves with those who are desirous of encouraging these invigorating games [base ball and cricket] among our too-little-exercised citizens. . . . How many admirable practical lessons on descipline [sic] and good behavior—both very requisite among the majority of our boys—might be imparted by the teachers of our academies every Saturday afternoon, if they were to organize a ball club among their scholars and accompany the players to the field, and there guide and admonish them as occasion might require![2]

Shortly, the suggested organizing of boys into ball clubs to provide lessons in discipline would be replaced by the gathering of young, raw military recruits to train for a more dangerous activity. But during the ensuing four years of deadly national conflict the game of base ball survived, with contests played by troops on both sides. These competitions were held either for exercise or enjoyment during lulls in early spring or late fall, mainly outside the time of major battle during the summer months.

Often, matches were also held within camps of prisoners of either army, some version of a game of base ball periodically occurring as a popular pastime. Images exist of ballgames in these camps, attesting to the fondness for them among the inmates. A lithograph from 1863 recorded a game from the previous summer in the Confederate camp of Union prisoners in Salisbury, North Carolina. It depicts the action of the contest itself, a runner attempting to steal second base as the pitcher is about to deliver the ball to the striker while onlookers congregate in groups along the sidelines and in the outfield, a town visible outside the prison walls, all in a wooded setting.[3] The overall effect is one of pastoral serenity rather than the cruelty of war. Within two years, the camp was overcrowded with prisoners, food and medicine were in short supply, and living conditions had deteriorated such that men were dying of mass starvation and disease.[4] By then it was the same in most prison camps, especially in the South, and base ball was an activity that required too much energy to be attempted with any regularity, if at all.

The sport as played during the war was more often than not the "New York game," with rules as established in the mid-1840s by the Knickerbocker Base Ball Club and destined to become the official game of the organized sport; sometimes the soldiers chose the "Massachusetts game" or a related precursor called "Town Ball."[5] The Massachusetts version was governed somewhat differently than the New York style of play. It allowed overhand pitching versus the Knickerbocker's stipulation of an underhand delivery, and it dictated that fly ball outs must be caught in the air only, not permitting a catch for an out to be made after one bounce as played by the New Yorkers. The infield of play was actually in the shape of a square rather than a diamond, and there was no out of bounds, which brought balls into play hit behind the striker as well as toward the square infield and beyond.[6] And the New England version of the sport stipulated that the base runner could be "soaked"—called out—if one of the fielders hit him with the ball as he ran from base to base.

In addition to base ball having been popular in the Northeast and Midwest well before the war, it was also being played in pockets of the South previous to the conflict. On February 20, 1860, the *New Orleans Daily Crescent* noted that the "base ball championship of New Orleans" had been played the prior day, the Empire club handily beating the Southern team by twenty runs.[7] Three weeks before, in keeping with the festive, genteel atmosphere of the Crescent City, the same newspaper reported that the Orleans Base Ball Club would host a Mardi Gras masquerade ball, stating, "As the ball games of the Orleans [team] are in the field well-conducted, lively and pleasant, so will be this extra Mardigras [sic] ball or hop."[8] In fact, prior to the war, New Orleans had over twenty base ball teams, more than many major cities in the North, including Detroit, Pittsburgh, and Cincinnati; other Southern locations hosting clubs included Houston, Augusta, Georgia, and Norfolk, Virginia.[9] Base ball was indeed rising in popularity as a healthy, athletic endeavor for people across much of the country prior to the war.

One such individual who sang the praises of a good ballgame was a young Walt Whitman. Before he subsequently became famous for his poetry, Walt was a strapping lad, "a muscular young man at the time—very strong," remembered his brother George, who went on to note that "he was inclined toward vigorous exercise and play" and although "He cared little for sport . . . he was an old-fashioned ball-player and entered into a game heartily enough."[10]

Whitman believed in the invigorating power of a game of base ball. He felt it relieved the stress and strain of a day's work in an office or a factory by providing some outdoor exercise with cleaner air and refreshing physicality. As the industrial revolution brought more people into the urban confines of city life, where factories could be run more efficiently, recreation was being viewed by many as more essential than ever before.[11] Office workers could emerge from a day of physical inertia sitting behind their desks to join with their colleagues in energetic pitching, hitting, and fielding a ball and running the bases. Employees on shop floors or in the mills found great enjoyment in shaking off the often-stultifying monotony of their work with the activity of base ball.

In 1858, Whitman actually reported on a contest while editing a Brooklyn newspaper. He told of a game between the championship Atlantic club and the Putnam team, the former winning 17–13. The account was as notable for its details of numerous Putnam players being injured, especially two catchers one after the other, as it was in praising the superior play of the Atlantics.[12] He knew the game and its finer points, enough to provide a more than credible summary of the action. Throughout his life, Whitman's continuing interest in the sport ebbed and flowed. Shortly after the war had ended, when Whitman was in Washington, DC, he was still an avid observer, commenting to friends about his attendance at various ballgames as part of his routine.[13]

For George Wright and his brother Harry, the Civil War, though traumatic for the country, occurred at a period in their lives that allowed them to conveniently focus on their enjoyment of playing ball. George was only fourteen when the fighting began, well below the minimum recruiting age of eighteen. By the time he turned eighteen in 1865, the war was all but over. To the contrary, Harry, twelve years older, was of prime fighting age. But, like his father, Harry had been born in England and was still a registered alien, not yet a citizen of the United States.[14] He was also a family man in 1861, with a wife and infant son. Living in New Jersey, the Wrights were geographically insulated from immediate exposure to any actual military battles of the day. They were free to follow their love of base ball and cricket, pursuing each with great gusto.

And just as they relished these sports and played them often, so too did knowledgeable local ballplayers notice their dedication and skills and offered them opportunity. This was especially so for the teenage George with his obvious talents. Stephen Guschov, in his book on the storied Cincinnati Red Stockings of 1869, said of George, "He easily made the transition from cricket to baseball and in 1863, while only sixteen years old, latched on with the New York Gothams club and competed against ballplayers twice his age."[15] As George himself described it in an interview many years later, "I became a regular member of the Gothams. First I was their catcher, but one day a foul tip struck me in the throat and it hurt me so much that I never afterward was able to muster up sufficient courage to catch, and so I went to left field, eventually going to second base and then to shortstop."[16]

Catching was the most dangerous position in the game, even when customarily stationed ten to twenty feet or more behind the striker. Protective gear of any sort was unheard of at the time, perhaps just an inkling of a thought for those bravely playing the game bare-handed, let alone unmasked as a catcher. George had learned his lesson the hard way, one that would ultimately land him in the shortstop position where his talents could best be utilized and where he would have a lasting impact on how the sport was played.

In a newspaper article after his retirement from the field, George recalled that, before base ball, he had first learned cricket from his father, who taught him how to bat and bowl (pitch) when he was ten. He was a quick study, eager to emulate his father and brother Harry in this sport. Playing in his first club match of juniors cricket by thirteen, he told of being awarded a silver quarter dollar for each of five wickets he had captured; by sixteen he was known as "little Georgie" while playing for the senior St. George's Club. At that time, the team visited Boston for a cricket match, where George remembers he "bowled well, for which I was presented with a silver mug. After the match I threw a cricket ball one hundred fifteen yards, which was considered a very long throw in those days. The Boston cricketeers [*sic*] took my cap and placed in it many silver dollars."[17] George was steadily experiencing the adulation heaped upon superior athletes as well as the profitability that might ensue based on exceptional performance.

In addition to base ball and cricket, the brothers became involved in a new variation of base ball, played on ice. The popularity of the sport had expanded into the dreary winter months as the players and spectators couldn't get enough of the game. The first matches of this type had previously been inaugurated in the Northeast in Rochester, New York in the winter of 1860. On January 16, 1860, players from four local clubs made up the two teams that strapped on ice skates and competed on Irondequoit Bay, one hundred people taking in the sight of the participants slipping, sliding, and more than occasionally crashing into each other as the eight-inning affair was decided by a close score, 27–25.[18] The contest had such appeal that another formal match was played on New Year's Day the following year, this time attracting several thousand spectators, who no doubt were interested to see what collisions would take place as the competitors skated across the frozen bay in pursuit of the elusive ball, the Lone Star team beating the Live Oak club, 21–8.[19]

Not to be outdone that year, the ballplayers in Brooklyn quickly followed suit. The Atlantic and Charter Oak teams staged a similar contest on what was known as Litchfield's Pond in South Brooklyn on February 4. The novelty of the game was not lost on the crowd, estimated to be twelve thousand, far higher than most base ball contests. Atlantic beat Charter Oak, 36–27. Newspaper coverage was quite detailed, providing a summary of the action that noted the exhilaration of the game and asked the question "When will our New York Clubs treat our citizens to a similar exhibition at the skating pond of the Central Park?"[20]

A second match occurred in 1863, but the next contest in 1864 was halted due to the "breakup of the ice" on Sylvan Lake in Hoboken, New Jersey, where the February game between the Empire and Gotham clubs was being played.[21] This location had been chosen because of its proximity to nearby Elysian Field, where the Gotham team and other New York clubs had often practiced and played their regular ball games dating back to before the war.

In 1865, the brothers participated in the third organized match of base ball on ice in the greater New York City area. Although it had not yet been staged in Central Park, on January 12, 1865, the Gotham squad took on the defending base ball champions of the sport, the Atlantic club, on the ice of the Capitoline Skating Lake in the Bedford section of Brooklyn. George and Harry were part of the regular nine of the Gotham team, with George being just a few weeks shy of his eighteenth birthday. Harry was the catcher, with George positioned at short stop, each playing well but their Gotham club losing to Atlantic 22–5. In a return match held four days later in frigid, windy conditions on Sylvan Lake, the Gothams turned the tables, winning 39–20 as both Wright brothers hit two home runs each.[22]

The game on ice proceeded with the same rules as base ball, modified somewhat for the field conditions. Bases were etched onto the frozen surface, and "over-running" them was allowed simply because it was next to impossible to skate to a sudden stop squarely on the designated location. The pitcher, balanced carefully on his skates, fed the ball underhand toward the striker, who steadied himself and took a determined swing to propel the ball into play. If it was hit into the air, fielders skated quickly to catch it; if it was stroked onto the ice, the ball had a tendency to skid and bounce randomly away, sending the defense frantically chasing after it. Unavoidably, some players plowed violently into others in their haste to corral the slippery sphere. Still, it was base ball, and that was all that mattered to the players and their adoring crowds, all infatuated with the sport. As such, it flourished for a while, over the years being played in various frigid climates by a dwindling but dedicated number of hearty participants until finally disappearing in the early decades of the twentieth century as hockey became the more-established winter team sport on ice.

Now, with the war over, the New York and Brooklyn clubs burst forth with renewed spirit for a regular game of base ball, as did teams across the Northeast, including in Philadelphia and Washington, DC. The mushrooming assembly of organizations to play the sport offered outstanding ballplayers a variety of choices as to where to play and for which team. And, with increasing frequency, cities that desired to field championship-caliber squads lured a star player or two to their clubs with financial incentives. These included under-the-table payments such as a portion of the receipts from spectators or wages for nonexistent jobs of the kind George Wright had held when he played for the Washington Nationals in 1867.

Both George and Harry found legitimate financial incentive to leave the Gotham club in 1865, but the temptress was cricket, not base ball. George became the professional at the Philadelphia Cricket Club, while Harry moved to Cincinnati in a similar position with the Union Cricket Club. In addition to playing for their team, they were paid to make the arrangements for games with other organizations and give lessons to club members. Harry would stay only a short time, moving on to join the Cincinnati Base Ball Club in 1867 for the same salary as his cricket position, a tidy sum of twelve hundred dollars per year.

George, on his off day from his Philadelphia Cricket Club role, still played base ball for a local team, the Olympics. He also kept up his connections with the Gotham ball club in New York, moonlighting under an assumed name to play a few games for them as well.[23] This practice of playing for two teams simultaneously was frowned upon by the base ball community, so George was intent on keeping this situation private, assuming an alias to play for the Gotham team. But he formally returned to the New York area the following year.

The Unions of Morrisania brought George back in what would become a series of annual moves that took him to Washington in 1867, back to the Union club in 1868, and finally to Cincinnati in 1869. This was termed "revolving" from one club to the next, sometimes even playing for one club while still contractually committed to another as he had done while in Philadelphia, all for successively higher remuneration for his much-coveted base ball–playing abilities.

Upon returning to the Unions in 1868, George was to embark on a venture related to base ball, one that would become his sole occupation after retiring from the game. He joined with brother Harry as they augmented their earnings by going into the sporting goods business together. In March of that year, in the well-read sports publication the *New York Clipper*, they took out a small advertisement with just a few lines of copy: "Wright Brothers, Importers and Dealers in BASE BALL, CRICKET, CROQUET, And all other Outdoor Sporting Materials, Parlor Games, etc."[24] Listed with both brothers' names was a downtown Broadway address, though Harry was still in Cincinnati. They were responding to what they saw as a developing need in the marketplace, that of supplying sports equipment to a growing enthusiastic customer base. It was the first such effort by George to capitalize on his sports celebrity in a commercial manner of this kind, a business venture that would lead to George's bringing a wide variety of sports to the public's interest, generating equipment needs that he would profitably fill.

For base ball, initially these goods were few in nature, basically balls, bats, bases, and team uniforms. Before the sport became organized, the ball had been a homemade sphere of yarn or string and some stuffing wrapped around a solid core, all held in place with a piece of leather or cloth stitched together in an X pattern. Sometimes "an old rubber overshoe would be cut into strips a half inch wide, and the strips wound together in a ball shape," providing the elastic center of the ball; the strips were often boiled in water to form a gummy mass of solid rubber. A particularly interesting variation of this situation was notable for its ingenuity in using materials at hand.

> In the lake regions and other sections of the country where sturgeon were plentiful, base balls were commonly made of the eyes of that fish. The eye of a large sturgeon contains a ball nearly as large as a walnut. It is composed of a flexible substance and will rebound if thrown against a hard base. These eyeballs were wound with yarn and afterward covered with leather or cloth. They made a lively ball.[25]

Generally, balls varied in size and weight, being mostly smaller and softer than its future versions. As the game became more organized, it was relatively easy for a local tradesman specializing in leather goods to sew a piece of animal hide in a pattern over a plug of an ounce or two of rubber wound with yarn to make a ball more suitable for the game. The two-piece, figure-eight sewn ball came shortly thereafter, a more uniform, tightly-stitched product that would eventually be standardized and machine made.

Only one ball was used for each contest, the team challenging another club to a match furnishing the ball as per organization convention, it being awarded to the winning team as a simple trophy for their efforts. Since there were not many games played each year, demand for balls was relatively low. But after the war, organized base ball was addressing such basics as standardized circumference, weight, and especially the composition of the base ball. The times when a "lively" ball or a "dead" ball could be used in different contests, mostly determined by core composition and size, were beginning to fade from the scene as regulations covering various elements of the game were developed.

Similarly, a wood turner could churn out a few bats from his stock of ash, maple, hickory, or even willow, which was already the chosen material for cricket bats due to its stiffness and light weight. Teams carried several of their own bats, but they were used for the season, even over multiple seasons, so again demand was not large. Initially, these bats were longer and heavier than in later years, each striker able to choose something that suited him in taking aim with a hefty swing at a ball that was pitched underhand to his preferred zone of contact. By the late 1860s, the bat length was regulated to no more than forty-two inches, still a prodigious club by modern standards.[26] And as pitching became swifter, strikers found that swinging lighter bats helped them make more consistent contact with the ball.

The uniforms were hand sewn with care by local seamstresses, one to a player. With only ten or eleven players per team—nine regulars and a few substitutes—the need for these items was very specific and rather negligible. But all of this was rapidly changing as organized base ball proliferated across the country. The swelling number of teams, the number of games they played, and their needs for base ball goods grew dramatically over a short period of time.

A slightly larger notice in the *Clipper*, two below the Wrights, proclaimed "Geo. B. Ellard, WESTERN BASE BALL AND CRICKET DEPOT" and carried a Cincinnati location.[27] A companion of Harry's on the Union Cricket Club and then the Cincinnati Base Ball Club of 1867, as well as an influential administrative member of both organizations, George Ellard had recently opened his own sporting goods venture. Harry and Ellard would go on to design the unique Cincinnati uniform for the team, a departure from the more workmanlike long-legged apparel of cricketers that was also the standard for base ball players. In 1868, the team would become known as the Red Stockings, wearing white flannel trousers shortened almost to the knee with accompanying crimson hosiery, topped with a white flannel shirt sporting a red old-English capital C in the middle for Cincinnati.[28] With the conservative sensibilities of the Victorian era, it was said that women spectators would often blush when they saw the players in their red-stockinged outfits displaying their muscular calves. The men in attendance didn't quite know what to make of it all, teasing Harry and his teammates for wearing what amounted to boys' knickered shorts while perhaps being inwardly jealous of the looks the players drew from the ladies.

There was one more advertisement in this section of the paper, between those of the Wright brothers' and Ellard's. It was for the Base Ball Emporium of A. J. Reach of Philadelphia. This purveyor of base ball goods, as well as other sporting equipment, was yet another ball player, Al Reach. He was the well-known star second baseman of the Brooklyn Eckfords who had moved to the Philadelphia Athletics a few years before for a higher wage. Money, and how to make it, was not surprisingly on the minds of these and most other ballplayers. It was fueling a juggernaut that was soon to turn what remained of the simple pleasure of an amateur game into the business it was to become, for the teams and players as well as those who would supply them with a mushrooming demand for the tools of their trade.

The reality of professionalism in base ball became more of an issue after the Civil War. Before the conflict, the sport had evolved from barely more than a children's game into an organized affair of recreation and exercise. It was a pleasurable activity for amateur groups of middle- and upper-class gentlemen of varying athletic abilities who sought a break from the burdens of their staid workdays. For laborers it was a stimulating competition, a physical diversion from the grind of their burdens. Often, teams were formed based on a common occupation or ethnic background.

As its popularity grew, rivalries arose between various clubs within a city or between cities of different geographies that demanded more skilled players be part of each team in order to vanquish the competition and claim superiority for themselves and their citizens, at least in the sporting world. Thus, though the vast majority of those playing the game were unpaid, the practice of secretly compensating a few exceptional ballplayers on most teams developed before and during the early war years, payments made in various ways, from free drinks and meals to cash from gate receipts and salaries for phantom jobs.

A few players on Brooklyn teams, Jim Creighton of the Excelsiors and Dickey Pearce of the Atlantics, were two of the early discretely paid professionals before the war. Creighton was one of the first and perhaps the best double talent in the sport, both a phenomenal pitcher and a tremendous striker, winning universal fame in the early 1860s before his tragic death of an intestinal rupture at the young age of twenty-one.[29] And many claimed that no one played the infield like Dickey Pearce. Only a shade over five feet three inches tall, he was built like a fire plug yet had marvelous fielding capabilities, helping to define the short field position into what would later become known as shortstop. His deft handling of the bat contributed to his invention of the bunt as well as the general concept of strategic hitting.[30] Both delivered championship seasons to their organizations, which heartily agreed that each player's performance was more than worth the compensation provided.

It was an obvious next step to openly pay ballplayers, though this occurred only on a very select, non-publicized basis. Supposedly, Al Reach had been paid under the table in the early 1860s by the Brooklyn Eckfords. The Athletic Club of Philadelphia brought him to their city in 1864, followed a few years later by a young, heavy hitter from the Atlantics, Lipman Pike. They had both been lured by a steady wage of twenty to twenty-five dollars a week. Pike and a few other teammates were soon charged by organized base ball's governing body, the National Association of Base Ball Players (NABBP), with being paid ballplayers, but the whole matter was abandoned when a scheduled formal hearing never materialized.[31] Pike, a prodigious striker whose home runs were legendary, was also an anomaly of a different sort: he was the first Jewish star of the game. His services, like those of Creighton, Pearce, Reach, and George Wright were increasingly available for a price, secret or not. There was no doubt that the NABBP, charged with enforcing the game's rules, one of which was amateurism, needed to address the matter before it spun out of control. The burning question was: How?

Albert Spalding tackled the issue of professionalism in his autobiography. In 1867, after first joining Rockford's Forest City Club as an amateur, he told of being introduced to "the business end of the game. . . . I was approached one day by a Chicago man with an offer of $40 per week to take a position as bill clerk with a wholesale grocery house of that city, with the understanding that my store duties would be nominal, and a chance given to play ball frequently [for the Excelsiors]."[32] He discussed the offer with others and decided to take it, though he wasn't able to follow through with the plan because the wholesale grocery concern with which he had agreed to "work" went out of business shortly after, leaving him to return to play for Forest City. But the offer had caused him to consider professionalism in baseball and the value he felt he brought to his team and those paying to see him play. He concluded,

Most clubs of prominence, all over the country, had players who were either directly or indirectly receiving financial advantage from the game . . . I believed that I foresaw the day soon coming when professional Base Ball players would be recognized as legitimate everywhere. I was not able to understand how it could be right to pay an actor, or a singer, or an instrumentalist for entertaining the public, and wrong to pay a ball player for doing exactly the same thing in his way.[33]

Although certainly justified in his equating a ballplayer with a thespian or musician as an entertainer of the public, rightfully due to be paid for his or her efforts, Spalding's thoughts seemed to skip over consideration of one very important aspect that dramatically complicated the matter. Those others entertaining a paying audience were doing so simply to provide the spectators with a pleasurable experience. In the case of the ballplayer, an added dimension was the possibility that those attending the game, as well as those actually participating in its playing and so affecting its outcome, might be gambling on its conclusion. This subtext was the knife's edge on which sports performed for a paying public was to attempt to balance well into the future.

Historically, in most events or competitions that had a definite win or lose outcome, betting on the result was invariably a significant part of the proceedings. It represented a stimulating facet of the match for the spectators, perhaps to some as exciting as the competition itself. As Daniel Ginsburg emphatically stated in his book on the history of gambling in baseball, "If clubs were willing to pay players secretly to assure victory, it was not too great a leap for gamblers to pay players secretly to assure defeat!"[34] But because money was made simply on who won, the policing of the contest to make sure it was not fixed in any manner would become a difficult problem to solve. This would hold true from the beginning of professionalism in the sport through to the present day. Different eras have seen different approaches to this thorny issue with varying degrees of success. In the end, if caught in the act of gambling on the sport in any manner, expulsion for lengthy stretches of a player's career, up to a lifetime ban, appears to have had the greatest effect in subduing the practice.

Albert Spalding was only ten years old when the Civil War began, an impressionable youngster through much of the conflict. It's fair to say that professionalism and gambling in base ball had not even crossed his mind

at that age. But even then, a specific incident about the sport left its mark
on him in 1863. In a weekly journal publication of 1909 describing base
ball during the Civil War, a writer notes,

> Whenever, in summer or fall, the Federal armies rested for a week, some
> one was sure to take a Base Ball out of his haversack and start a game. . . .
> They played it in Confederate prisons, where they taught it to their
> captors. . . . A volunteer private returned invalided to Rockford, Illinois,
> in 1863. He saw the boys batting up flies, and he told them that he knew a
> better game. He had learned it in the army. One tall, wiry boy took a special
> interest. It was Al Spalding, great pitcher, great manager, great organizer—
> prime figure in Base Ball from that day to this."[35]

According to Spalding's own account, he did indeed learn of baseball
from a returning army veteran. His interest intensified while watching the
sport as he grew up in Rockford. He had been born on September 2, 1850,
in nearby Byron, Illinois, but when his father died in 1858, Albert was
sent to live with his aunt in Rockford until the rest of the remaining family
joined him.[36] A newspaper article at the time of his death in 1915 gave
a condensed version of his reminiscences on the subject from his own
autobiography. In it, Spalding told of how he actually went from being a
rather shy youth, a lonely observer of the game, to playing it.

> I was boarding at the home of a relative at Rockford—it was my first
> prolonged absence from home—and memories of the homesickness at
> that period haunt me like a nightmare to this hour. The only solace I had
> was when I could go back to the common to watch the other fellows play
> baseball. And then my diffidence was so great that I would go away down
> the outfield, take a seat on the turf and watch the boys have fun.
>   On this particular day, I was occupying my usual place [as a spectator],
> far out beyond centerfield, when one of the boys hit the ball square on the
> nose. It came soaring in my direction. Talk about special Providence! That
> ball came to me straight as an arrow. Impulsively, I sprang to my feet,
> reached out with my right hand, held it a moment and then threw it home
> on an airline to the catcher. When the game was over, one of the boys
> came over to me and said: 'That was a great catch you made; wouldn't
> you like to play tomorrow?' I did, and that was my start in baseball.[37]

Albert would join in with the other youngsters of this ball club, the
Pioneers of Rockford, subsequently meeting future close friend Ross
Barnes on the team. There they both perfected their skills, moving on to

the Forest City club and eventual base ball stardom with the Boston Red Stockings.

As the war ended and soldiers took their passion for base ball back home, the game's popularity soared across all classes of society. In the wake of the devastation of the war, it was a way to help bind the wounds of a nation in tatters. In fact, it was on the road to becoming America's game, the "national pastime," especially appealing to the working class and immigrants as an enjoyable way in which to simultaneously engage in recreational sport and show their love of country.

Among these were African American communities, who desired to become an integral part of a reunited nation. To "play ball" was not only to participate in the growing excitement for the game, but it was also to demonstrate the very inclusion in American society that the Black community yearned for after the Civil War and its end to slavery. As professor of sports history Michael Lomax commented in his book *Black Baseball Entrepreneurs*, "Baseball became a vehicle to assimilate within the fabric of mainstream America and simultaneously elevate the status of African-Americans."[38] Various progressive African American thinkers of the time viewed the formation of base ball teams in this manner, bringing together youthful athleticism and patriotic spirit in a fusion that was both vigorously healthy and openly proud. "In other words," says Lomax, "baseball would be a catalyst to 'elevate the race.'"[39]

African American teams, a few of which had begun to organize even before the war, now became more evident across much of the Northeast. Philadelphia and Washington, DC, were particularly notable in their efforts to field competitive clubs. In 1866, the first all-Black team in Philadelphia, the Excelsior, was formed. Later that year, Octavius Catto, a young Black educator, reformer, and major in the Pennsylvania National Guard, founded the Pythian Base Ball Club. The name came from a fraternal order, the Knights of Pythias, to which many team members belonged.

Matches were organized between the two clubs as well as other African American organizations. In Washington, two sons of ex-slave and abolitionist Frederick Douglass, Frederick Jr. and Charles, were pioneering team organizers and players. By 1867, a Washington newspaper was reporting that "two colored base ball clubs," the Mutuals of

Washington and Catto's Pythians of Philadelphia, had played on July 19 in Philadelphia, the Mutuals eking out a victory, 44–43.[40] The games were not only invigorating competitions, but they also provided opportunities for the Black community to socialize, with dinners and dances planned around the contests. These gatherings gave Octavius the chance to develop his network of contacts throughout the Northeast, exchanging ideas on political and social issues and strategies to expand the Black communities' civil rights, which he himself prominently championed in such efforts as helping to desegregate the street cars of Philadelphia in 1867.[41]

Beyond African American teams playing each other, Catto believed that by participating in base ball and competing against "our white brethren," blacks in America could demonstrate credibility and acceptability.[42] But with no white organizations willing to accept any challenges by Black clubs to play them, the African American teams in 1866–68 were confined to compete amongst themselves. Still, Catto continued to lobby for the Pythians to be given the chance to play against white clubs. "Regardless of whether a black team won or lost, a championship [series of games] between blacks and whites would serve to eliminate racial barriers and establish a sense of equality in the minds of blacks."[43]

In 1867, representatives of Pennsylvania's baseball teams met to charter the Pennsylvania Association of Amateur Base Ball Players. These state organizations were the outgrowth of the NABBP, which had governed the amateur game with rules and regulations on a national level since its formation in 1858. Starting at that time from an association that encompassed only teams from the Five Boroughs of New York, it now had hundreds of clubs as members. As base ball expanded geographically as well as in popularity, state associations representing their region's clubs rather than the individual clubs themselves became members of the NABBP. The Pythians were intent on becoming part of the Pennsylvania contingent, but white baseball on the state level was not ready for integration. Despite a determined effort, the convention refused to admit the Pythians into the league.

Representatives of the Pythians next brought the issue of African American team membership to the national level that same year, but with similar results. As reported in *The Ball Players' Chronicle* of December 17, 1867, the NABBP's Nominating Committee rejection was an even broader dismissal of the notion of integrated baseball involving African Americans in general, stating it would not admit "any club which may be composed of one or more colored persons."[44] The organized sport had decided that, for better or worse, in order not to politicize this issue, they would effectively take it off the table going forward. This effectively drew the first formalized color line in baseball on a national level. It would largely remain intact, most strictly enforced in the major leagues of the sport, until eighty years later when Jackie Robinson finally integrated baseball in 1947. Until then, African American baseball would continue on a parallel path with the segregated, all-white sport, developing its own history and heroes, and with it players who would eventually tear down the entrenched barriers that had artificially been erected in the sport's infancy.

In September 1869, Catto's Pythians did succeed in integrating baseball, if not interracially on a team then at least in initiating interracial play between teams. In their loss to the all-white Philadelphia Olympics on September 3 they gained grudging respect from the opposing players as well as the public. Two weeks later their victory over another white ball club, a convincing 27–17 win over the Philadelphia City Items, proved that African Americans really did belong, at least on an integrated baseball field. Catto hoped the victory would help open the eyes of a racially prejudiced city to the potential for equality of the races from this tiny sliver of social perspective, and a few similar matches proceeded to take place. But, for the most part, segregated ball continued.

Tragically, Octavius Catto's life was cut short when on October 10, 1871, he was gunned down in broad daylight on Municipal Election Day in Philadelphia. Political friction combined with racial prejudice and exploded into violence by Democratic operatives against the black voters who were overwhelmingly casting their ballots for the Republicans, the party of Lincoln. Catto was well known in the city as an activist for African American equality. He was on his way home that day when a Democratic party operative, Frank Kelly, recognized him, drew his pistol and shot Catto in the back multiple times. Octavius died from his wounds shortly thereafter. Kelly escaped from the city but was apprehended six years later and brought back and tried for Catto's murder. He was acquitted by an all-white jury.

Certainly, base ball was coming of age in tumultuous times. But even so, its grip on Americans of all cultural and social backgrounds was fast becoming an overwhelming force. The game was no longer the province of those well-to-do gentlemen seeking lively exercise and comradeship. It had been embraced by the working class as well as the elite, by different races and ethnicities. It was a game that was spanning the multitudes, played in an empty lot or an open field with simply a ball, a bat, and some bases. In the process, this widely shared activity might even help in the healing of a badly shattered nation, certainly across formerly warring regions of the country. At the same time, its progress was painfully slow in accepting African Americans within its larger organized framework.

Spalding in the West and the Wright brothers in the East were emblematic of its possibilities. Amateurism was fading fast in the face of blatant violations of the NABBP's feeble attempts to administer its rules and guidelines. As a responsive organization attempts in its struggles to survive, it tried to adapt to its surroundings. The result was a radical change in policy for the upcoming 1869 season, a jettisoning of the untenable by allowing any team to become a professional club, paying its players above-board rather than clandestinely. Now the issue shifted, no longer focused on whether or not a player should be paid but rather on how to control open professionalism within its midst.

The first such club to take full advantage of this sea change was to become the most well known of its kind, the Red Stockings of Cincinnati. Proudly declaring themselves the first openly professional base ball club, Harry Wright assembled and led a band of completely salaried ballplayers, headlined by his all-everything brother George at shortstop. In 1869, this team embarked upon the most successful season to ever take place in the history of the sport.

3

Two Wrights Can't Be Wrong

The red, white, and blue ribbon suspending the medal had a pin at the top that allowed it to be affixed easily to George Wright's shirt. He wore the ornament around the house often the first few weeks after receiving it, bursting with pride every time he put it on. His play since he had returned from the Washington Nationals to the Unions of Morrisania for the 1868 season had been brilliant. The medal meant George was being recognized as the best shortstop in the game that year, some said the best player of them all, to which he somewhat smugly agreed. Sometimes he projected an air of superiority related to his base ball prowess, bordering on arrogance, which caused resentment in some, but the simple fact was that he had few, if any, equals in the game.[1]

So proclaimed the *New York Clipper*, which had concocted the idea of presenting a fancy medallion to each of nine players deemed the best at their positions for the year 1868, the "Clipper Gold Medal." The item itself was valuable in its own right as a piece of finely fashioned jewelry. It was a gold Maltese cross engraved with base ball imagery on the four wings. A single base ball shoe was pictured on each of the two arms, a uniform cap on the top appendage, and a base on the bottom. An enameled ring lay in the middle, labeled CLIPPER PRIZE and supported by two crossed base ball bats behind the ring, which contained a blue stone, the whole affair topped with a gleaming gold wreath surrounding the year "1868."[2]

It was a stunning award for the times, nothing quite like it ever crafted before as an individual base ball trophy. It became one of George's most prized possessions through the years, six decades later still prominently gracing a wall in the office of his Boston sporting goods establishment.[3] Certainly, it added credence to the view that George was an elite performer in the sport.

Around the same time, over six hundred miles away in Cincinnati, Ohio, George's brother Harry sat at his desk in the clubhouse of the Union Grounds, speculating about the task before him. Over the course of the past few years, almost since the founding of Cincinnati's ball club in 1866 and its sharing of the grounds with the Union Cricket Club, Harry had shifted his position from being the professional of the cricket organization to becoming the manager of Cincinnati's base ball team. He had left behind his apprenticed trade of jewelry manufacturing in the East as he focused solely on cricket, then base ball.

As 1868 wound to a close, Harry was firmly established as the base ball club's manager and captain. The job encompassed not only providing direction to the players but being the team's pitcher or occasionally patrolling center field, sometimes even manning second base. Additionally, he scheduled their games with other clubs, made travel and hotel arrangements for the team, and was watchdog over the team's expenses. Harry's organizational skills, his civility and his base ball talents were succinctly captured in a set of verses that honored each member of the team, lustily delivered in song by his players to themselves and their followers after their many victories that season:

> Our Captain is a goodly man
> And Harry is his name;
> Whate'er he does, 'tis always "Wright,"
> So says the voice of fame.
> And as the Pitcher of our nine,
> We think he can't be beat;
> In many a fight, old Harry Wright
> Has saved us from defeat.[4]

In his managerial capacity, as well as his playing capabilities, Harry had brought winning ways to the Cincinnati club, which had compiled a dominant record of forty wins against only seven losses during the 1868 campaign. Management had instructed Harry to bring in a few strong professional ball players on a covertly paid basis to bolster the team's prospects. Accordingly, he, along with the club's president, Aaron

Champion, and a few other senior club officials, had secured some top-shelf talent.

Asa Brainard, who had played second base for the Brooklyn Excelsiors and then become their pitcher after the tragic death of the incomparable hurler Jim Creighton in 1862, was hired away from the Washington Nationals in 1868 in exchange for "employment" at a Cincinnati legal firm that gave him unlimited time to play ball. Brainard was a powerful pitcher with an unpredictable fastball that often rose or dipped, generally overwhelming the opposition. His first name would become corrupted by the press, from Asa to "Acey," then to just "Ace," eventually this moniker becoming commonplace in describing the leading pitcher of any base ball team.[5] Fred Waterman, an outstanding third baseman from the Mutuals of New York who was also a consistent hitter, came to Cincinnati at the behest of Champion and Wright. Like Brainard, Waterman was provided with a phantom "job," a part-time position with an insurance company that paid him, in effect, to play base ball.[6]

Charlie Gould was the only Cincinnati native on the team. He was a sturdy six-footer with long arms, nicknamed "The Bushel Basket" for his exceptional ability to catch most any ball thrown in his direction. Harry had hired him away from the cross-town rival Buckeyes ball club. And Doug Allison, a Philadelphia bricklayer and player who fearlessly manned the position of catcher up closer to the striker rather than the customary ten to twenty feet behind, was recruited to corral the speedballs served up by Brainard.

These, along with the rest of the team, became Harry's assembled band of red-stockinged warriors fighting for the glory of Cincinnati. The city had its own labels, known as the "Queen City" for its relative cultural refinement in the midst of a rough-and-tumble Midwest. Derisively, it was also called "Porkopolis" for its growing hog-butchering and processing industry. Designated in either fashion, the team was proud to represent its citizenry as an emerging base ball powerhouse.

Now, as Harry contemplated the upcoming 1869 season, he was intent on building upon the club's previous success. The NABBP, the sport's governing body, had finally succumbed to the immense pressures of professionalism, covertly practiced by a growing number of ball clubs seeking to find a competitive edge versus their rivals. In early 1869, they grudgingly gave their official blessing to allow teams to openly pay individuals to play the game, offering the teams the option of becoming professionals or to stay as amateur clubs. The floodgates had burst, and Cincinnati was determined to ride this new wave of proud professionalism as 1869 unfolded, becoming the only club that year to overtly claim the mantle of an all-paid professional base ball team.

Harry already had the nucleus of a strong squad. Brainard, Waterman, and Allison had been offered compensation to lure their talents from the East. These men had shown during the 1868 season that they could be counted on to perform consistently at a high level, as reliably as he himself was in pitching or playing the outfield. He had a problem, however, with their star left fielder and catcher John Hatfield. In the controversial tradition of a "revolver," Hatfield had signed contracts with both the Red Stockings and the New York Mutuals, a flagrant rules violation that Harry couldn't countenance.[7] He knew he needed to replace Hatfield, as well as amass greater talent at a few other positions if Cincinnati was to contend for a national championship.

Content for the most part to flesh out the team by plucking gems he could unearth in his own backyard, he brought in second baseman Charlie Sweasy, left fielder Andy Leonard, and substitute Dick Hurley from the cross-town rival Buckeyes. Sweasy and Leonard, stellar fielders and good strikers, had tested Eastern base ball backgrounds, coming to the Buckeyes from the Irvingtons of New Jersey. Harry then took a chance on an eighteen-year-old, heavy-hitting Iowa farm boy by way of Indianapolis named Cal McVey to play right field. As was often the case, Harry's jeweler's eye had judged this diamond in the rough correctly; Cal would become a powerful batsman and dependable outfielder. All that remained to make this team truly special was to set in place the keystone of success by bringing to the Queen City its own base ball royalty, arguably the best all-around player in the sport, Harry's brother George. By early 1869, he had succeeded in gaining George's commitment to become a Red Stocking.

As Harry perused the pages of the *New York Clipper* in the first few weeks of 1869, he saw confirmation of his decision to sign his brother to a Red Stockings' contract. On January second, this sports journal announced the recipients of the unique awards they had offered to the individuals deemed the best offensively by each position for 1868. This was calculated by determining those with the lowest averages for outs made in a game and highest averages for runs scored per game at each of the nine positions over the course of the season. To no one's surprise, George had won this coveted "Clipper Medal" at shortstop.[8] If fielding had been included in the determination, the result in George's favor would have been even more pronounced.

The Red Stockings had won three of the other eight prestigious awards as well, Waterman at third base, Hatfield in left field, and William Johnson in right field. Now Harry was in the process of dismissing Hatfield for deceitful dealings, a move that many were already second-guessing due to Hatfield's obvious exceptional ballplaying capabilities as signified by winning a Clipper Medal. But Harry felt he had no real choice in the matter, his moral compass unwavering in the direction to follow. And Johnson had decided to "retire from active play, on account of business engagements."[9] Fred Waterman was the only remaining awardee of the three Red Stockings winners. Obtaining brother George's services became Harry's top priority.

One could plainly see why. Contemporaries lauded the star player, and continued to do so long after their playing days with him were over and they had the chance to compare him to other top base ball talents. Future Hall of Famer Jim "Deacon" White, a superb catcher and teammate of George's on the Boston Red Stockings of the mid-1870s, stated as he surveyed the game in the early 1900s,

> There isn't an infielder in the game today who had anything on George Wright when it came to playing shortstop, and certainly there was none during his time. George fielded hard-hit balls bare-handed, gathered them up or speared them when in the air with either hand. He was an expert and accurate thrower, being able to throw with either hand.[10]

In 1915, another former teammate of George's, Hall of Fame to-be outfielder Jim O'Rourke, assessed things even more completely,

> George Wright never had any equal as a fielder, base runner, and batsman, combined with heady work of a quality never accredited to any ball tosser. All his qualifications taken together, he was really in a class by himself, and I do not know of a ball player today who ever was entitled to be considered in the same breath with him.[11]

Harry's twenty-first-century biographer, Christopher Devine, noted, "George had developed into the best base-ballist in the country [by

1869]."[12] One decidedly biased tome on Cincinnati base ball history, written by Harry Ellard, the son of one of the original Red Stockings of 1868, George Ellard, put it this way, "George Wright was the model ballplayer in the United States."[13]

Of course, Harry knew his brother and his capabilities better than anyone. Twelve years George's senior, Harry had grown up with him as a youngster sometimes tagging along at his side. "Little Georgie" had quickly evolved into a splendidly capable athlete, eager to learn everything there was to know about playing cricket, then base ball, flashing his trademark broad smile in the process. Their father, Sam, was a professional cricketer of great renown in the Northeast, a proud, transplanted English sportsman who had taught his sons the finer points of what was a revered, exacting tradition.

One of George's treasured memories of his early days learning cricket from his father was studying a text titled *Felix on the Bat*. It was an instructional on the game by a well-known English cricketer in which the boy had immersed himself during his formative sporting years to glean the secrets of stellar play. Undoubtedly Harry had done the same, but Sam eventually had given the book to George in 1865 when he was eighteen.[14]

George often recalled playing cricket and base ball while growing up as one of four active boys living next to the Dragonslayers of St. George's Cricket Club grounds at the Elysian Fields in Hoboken, New Jersey. His older brothers, Harry and Dan, who was two years younger than Harry, were just as addicted to games of ball and bat as were their younger siblings George and Sam Jr. The family had moved from George's birthplace in Harlem, New York, to Hoboken in the late 1850s when he was not yet in his teens, his father being the professional of the St. George's club, which had relocated to these more expansive grounds. By then, a baby girl had incongruously joined the already-large family. As George would relate of the boys,

Harry, Dan, Sam, and my self [*sic*] would get up mornings early and play—Dan and Harry before going to New York City on business, and Sam and I before going to school. Oftentimes in the winter we have swept away the snow to play, while our hands, with gloves on, would stick to the bat from the frost. Most of the time we played with a rubber ball. This is where our early knowledge of cricket and base-ball came from.[15]

Sam Jr., a year younger than George, would also become a proficient cricketer and base ball player as an adult, a good fielding shortstop who never attained the success of his brothers due to his meager ball-striking capabilities. Little is known of Dan, who drifted from New Jersey to the West Coast over the years, settled in San Jose, California, and was lost to history.[16]

Despite the lofty pedestal on which the men in the Wright family placed it, during the 1860s cricket was beginning its slow decline in popularity as a sport in America. Granted, the activity had certain similarities to base ball, just by being games of bat and ball. The orbs were pitched, or bowled in the case of cricket, to the strikers who initiated play by hitting it with sticks. These were long, rounded clubs much like a thick broom handle for base ball or shorter, flat-faced bats if playing cricket. If these hits were successful, the ball would bound away from the fielders, allowing the strikers to try to achieve a score. In base ball the striker scored runs by circling the four bases that comprised the diamond to reach home and tally a point. In cricket, the running was back and forth on a narrow path between wickets to accumulate a score.

In cricket, the game itself might take days to complete, a contest between teams that cared as much about formalities and etiquette in accomplishing the goal of winning as about victory itself. On the other hand, a game of base ball was over in a matter of hours, suffused with speedy action and sheer excitement that made each play a possible deciding factor in the game. By the time the Civil War had ended, both Harry and George knew they could make a living as cricket professionals, as their father had done before them. But deep inside each burned a passion for this lively sport of base ball that could not be replaced by a polite, protracted game of cricket.

Though quite proficient in both sports, even touted as an exceptional base-ballist during mid-century playing the outfield for New York City clubs, Harry could not compare as an athlete with his brother, who was stronger, quicker, and more agile. He was a fine ball player, but would never be what his brother was, a pure natural at the game. George ran with seeming effortless speed and his reflexes were cat-quick, fielding with wide range and throwing with deadly precision. These capabilities allowed him to redefine how the position of shortstop was played, enabling him to move further back from the baseline toward the edge of the outfield grass, thereby extending the ground he could cover while roaming more freely between second and third base. At the plate, he could strike the ball with ferocious power in one at bat and employ subtle skill in poking it through the infield the next time up.

George had first come to Cincinnati as part of the Washington Nationals' tour of the West in the summer of 1867. The initial segment of the journey took them through Ohio, where they dismantled the Capitols of Columbus by a score of 90–10. Then they triumphantly entered the Queen City, beating Harry's team, 53–10, Cincinnati's only loss of their eighteen-game campaign that year. For good measure, the next day the Nationals proceeded to demolish the city's Buckeye club, 88–12.

Harry had initially pitched well in the loss to George's team, holding them to a 6–6 tie through the first three innings with his tricky change-of-pace deliveries before the Cincinnatis' fortunes sank.[17] According to a report on the game in *The Brooklyn Union*, when George first came to bat against Harry,

> It was amusing to see the brothers face to face. "There you are, are you?" said Harry. "I am here," replied George, knocking the home base with his bat, "and I don't want any of your nonsense; so just give us a ball, will yer?" Whereupon Harry sent him one, and away it was sent along the ground in cricket style, as Harry expected, and George secured his first.[18]

Perhaps this was an apocryphal account of their verbal exchange, but it certainly was plausible. Two siblings good-naturedly gibing each other, the twenty-year-old phenom needling the thirty-two-year-old veteran. Here were two superior cricketers turned base ball standouts, both knowing what to expect from the other based on years of honing their skills together dating back to their family play in Hoboken. George clubbed a home run in his next at bat, a few Cincinnati fielding mistakes set up an eleven-run inning for the Nationals, and the rout was on. Harry could only watch in frustration as George's team soundly outplayed Cincinnati. But the Brooklyn paper had some encouraging words for the Porkopolites:

> The chances are that [the Nationals] have played the strongest club they are likely to meet with on their tour; certainly they will encounter no such difficult pitching as that of Harry Wright's, who only wants well-trained support in the field to be the most troublesome pitcher in the country. . . . No club in the West will [beat] the Cincinnati Club if they only back up their pitcher well in the field.[19]

Over the next few years, Harry would come to agree with this assessment. He now felt that bringing George to the Red Stockings completed the set of talented players he had assembled that, under his guidance, could rise to the pinnacle of the sport. This was because Harry, not the equal of George as a player, had something that his brother did not. It was a mind that saw not only the game and its ever-exciting possibilities as the ball was struck and the fielders set in motion. Harry's genius lay in his ability to devise strategies for situations even *before* they occurred so he could coach each individual on the club to be ready for these possibilities. He conceived of how each player could work with the others, as part of a cohesive team, to produce results that invariably would win ball games. By 1869, Harry knew that with George's superior play, Brainard's pitching wizardry, and his own steadying presence on the field, he could mold Waterman, Allison, Gould, and the others into a championship team of ballplayers.

After the Nationals had won their games in Cincinnati in 1867, they traveled further west to continue their winning ways until they suffered their only loss of the tour, shockingly succumbing to the underdog Forest City Club of Rockford and their boy pitcher, Albert Spalding. By the next year, George had left Washington, DC, to reunite with his old Union of Morrisania teammates while Harry continued his mission to transform the Red Stockings into champions.

It was during this year of 1868 that the brothers participated in a sporting goods venture together. George handled the business in New York while Harry lent his name to the fledgling operation. The company sold just a few items, mainly balls, bats, bases, and cricket goods. At the same time, George was beginning to devise a tangential piece of equipment that he would eventually call the "Catcher's Mouth Protector," a molded piece of rubber that fit inside the mouth to bite on and guard the teeth from damage while catching the ball. It was the first piece of protective equipment devised specifically for the game, a mouth guard for base ball. As George noted, "I invented a rubber plate to be held in a catcher's mouth. . . . That saved teeth and dentists bills for some of the boys."[20]

This piece of equipment would be, throughout the 1870s even after the catcher's mask was invented in 1877, a simple, useful item of which ballplayers could avail themselves while playing the sport. It was fitting that it be especially helpful for those playing the most dangerous position on the field, that of catcher. Being hidden inside the mouth, unseen by spectators, was a benefit of the product that wouldn't detract from the rugged image the catchers wanted to publicly project. Other players could use it as well, and certainly George was one, being careful to protect one of his most important physical features, his sparkling, well-known toothy grin.

The fearless catcher of the 1869 Red Stockings, Doug Allison, regularly employed George's "tooth protector," as it was called at that time. A number of treasures from that famous team were sold at auction in 1916 after the death of Harry Ellard, the son of Harry Wright's old teammate on Cincinnati's original cricket and base ball clubs of the mid-1860s. He had carefully preserved these pieces of Cincinnati base ball history, now being sold as part of the estate's liquidation. Game ball trophies, splintered bats, faded uniforms and old photographs were all part of the memorabilia. Allison's original mouth guard was an oddity among the forty-seven-year-old items.

The auctioneer described the device in this manner, "Look at this chunk of rubber, scored deep with marks of gripping teeth. They had no masks in 1869—this is the 'tooth-protector' that Doug Allison wore to save his handsome face when up behind the bat."[21] One can only image the fierce pressure Allison exerted as he clenched his jaw tight while playing his position, teeth digging into the piece of molded rubber. It was the first protective equipment he had ever used, the insert attempting to keep his mouth intact as he snared the lightning deliveries of batterymate Asa Brainard or gamely dodged the screaming foul tips coming off the bats of strikers who had only nicked the ball as it blazed by.

Gloves were beginning to be thought of as useful equipment, but no self-respecting ballplayer would regularly employ them in the "manly" game of base ball, the participants preferring to submit their hands to continual doses of bruising and swelling, often accompanied by jammed, split, or broken fingers. As George remembered it, his ritual to protect his hands was simple, "Before a game, I used to harden up my hands with cold water and paint them with iodine . . . sometimes they would get so puffed up I could hardly throw to first. When our fingers would get split, we would just tape them together and go ahead."[22] Of course, gloves would eventually become welcomed parts of the players' gear, but that was still many years in the future.

For now, selling the basic goods for the game seemed to the Wrights like a good money-making idea. Only a handful of such competitors existed in this business, dotting the major ball-playing urban landscapes. The largest was an establishment in New York City on Nassau Street founded in 1866 by Andrew Peck and Irving Snyder as Peck & Snyder's Sporting Goods Company. They offered base ball goods and other sports equipment, eventually to include uniquely invented footwear such as "rubber-soled and canvas tennis shoes as well as the two-wheeled inline skate."[23] In 1869, to promote their entry into providing an expanding range of base ball items, Peck & Snyder is often referenced as inventing the first mass-produced base ball cards. These were advertisements for their goods in the form of a picture of ballplayers, choosing as their first image the "Red Stocking B. B. Club of Cincinnati."[24] The starting nine plus a substitute were photographed arranged sitting and standing in two rows of five each, a rough-looking bunch posed in their natty uniforms, a few with bats propped upon their knees.

A significant contribution of Harry's to the Wrights' venture, besides his name, was an item for sale noted in the last line at the bottom of their sparse advertisement in the *New York Clipper*. "P. S.—Wright's Patent Base Ball Telegraph supplied."[25] Although as yet unheard of in the sport of base ball, its designation as a *telegraph* was in reference to the game of cricket, of which the Wrights were of course well-acquainted. It referred to a crude scoreboard that cricketers had used for years in keeping track of the runs tallied in the game for all to see. It employed "telegraph" plates, metal sheets each emblazoned with a figure which could be used on a board to display the number of runs scored.

In 1866, the *New York Clipper* sports journalist Henry Chadwick had mentioned the idea while reviewing one of the Washington Nationals' games and commenting on the need for a separate section in the stands for the scorers to shield them from spectators constantly asking about the score of the game. "We are surprised that our ball clubs do not adopt the cricketers' style of having a telegraph announcing the state of the game each innings [*sic*], so that all on the field can see."[26] By the following year, Chadwick noted that Harry Wright had introduced such an item in Cincinnati.[27] Now, in the Wrights' new sporting goods store, it was part of the slowly expanding offerings for sale, along with the mouth protector a stroke of ingenuity from the ball playing brothers. To their way of thinking, the famous name of the Wright's was hopeful to draw an interested clientele, especially in the hotbed of base ball activity that was New York City.

In fact, it appears from advertisements in the *New York Clipper* as far back as at least 1857 that there was involvement of the Wright family in the promotion and sales of sporting equipment. An advertisement in the April 25, 1857, issue of the paper noted H. Lillywhite Jr., as an agent for Lillywhite & Wisden, London, Eng., supplying "everything necessary for the game of Cricket."[28] The Lillywhites were an English family with deep cricket roots, mainly planted in England but more recently spread to America with H. Lillywhite Jr., the professional to the New Brighton, Staten Island cricket club. Lillywhite and Wisden was the London business partnership of sports outfitter Frederick Lillywhite and famed cricketer John Wisden, supplying cricket gear as well as annual guides to the game itself. Noted at the end of the advertisement is that orders should be addressed to H. Lillywhite Jr., in New Brighton, Staten Island, or Sam'l Wright, Hoboken, NJ.[29] There can be little doubt that this reference to "Sam'l Wright" is to none other than Harry and George's father, the professional of the St. George's Cricket Club based in Hoboken.

By the early 1860s, Harry appears to have followed not only in his father's cricket-playing footsteps, but his association with supplying cricket equipment as well. The May 10, 1862, edition of *The Clipper* contains an advertisement placed by Harry to sell "cricket or base ball material of the best quality, at the most reasonable rates."[30] It's a companion item to a short paragraph found in the same edition of the newspaper that states Wright's expertise in supplying the best cricket materials, and "who, from his long connection with cricket and base ball, knows just what is what."[31] No doubt the family's familiarity with sporting goods marketing, coupled with their well-known skills in both base ball and cricket, provided a good business basis as George and Harry established their new partnership.

Now, the first step down the path of openly salaried professionalism for the Red Stockings in 1869 was to pay their members handsomely for their efforts, especially George. To entice this superstar to come west, the Red Stockings gave recognition to his stature within the game. They contracted with George for a year at fourteen hundred dollars, Harry graciously supporting the payment of a premium for his kid brother's services, himself receiving an annual salary of twelve hundred dollars. Years later, at least one report indicated George might actually have been paid as much as eighteen hundred dollars that year, with Harry getting a fifteen-hundred-dollar, twelve-month contract. Brainard's contract was for eleven hundred dollars and Fred Waterman's one thousand dollars, while the other five were to receive eight hundred dollars and the substitute six hundred. Again, other information suggests these players all received between six and eight hundred dollars for a seven-month commitment.[32] Whatever the case, compared to unskilled laborers at that time, who earned about two to two and a half dollars per day, or roughly seven hundred dollars on average per twelve-month year, or farmhands, whose pay was half as much, being paid to practice and play a game of base ball for seven months wages for the Red Stockings appeared to be a relatively lucrative proposition.[33]

Contracts were inked by the end of winter, allowing a month or so for practice before the first of the matches was to take place that year. All signees were immediately subjected to the principled nature and firm guidance of their leader, Harry Wright. He was a teetotaler with a staunch conviction that alcohol weakened the body as well as the mind. He never wavered in admonishing his charges toward a life of aversion to drink as an important pillar of athletic performance. Sometimes he even succeeded in his pleas, but he was speaking to a skeptical crowd.

It was an era of free-flowing alcohol consumption in the United States. Partaking in the consumption of beer, wine, or hard spirits equated to approximately three and a half gallons of pure ethanol per person annually, roughly 50 percent more than today.[34] Historically across the country, frequent bacteria-tainted water and milk supplies in many communities led some people to prefer to consume much of their liquids in alcoholic forms of fermented or distilled fruits, grains, and starches. This was especially true among many of the ballplayers, who were traveling out of town to play their games in unfamiliar places with unknown sanitation conditions. Then, too, they were often under the usual temptation of drinking and carousing after a hard-fought ballgame, a point of contention while under Harry's leadership. But throughout his life, he held strongly to the view that temperance, coupled with exercise, a wholesome diet and regular hours, were the keys to consistent physical success in sports.

Harry had a mild temperament, virtually never swearing, preferring to express himself in calm, measured tones when vexed. If he was displeased with the effort being given by a player, one of his favorite expressions, "You need a little more ginger," could be more effective than a strong oath coming from him, his players knowing that this was his way of conveying disappointment in their performance and demanding more from them.[35]

Beyond all this was Harry's steady mantra of practice to develop superior performance in hitting, fielding, base running, throwing and catching. This was his expected standard of preparation for developing the teamwork and coordinated efforts that Harry sought as he strove to instill a consistent approach to each game. He invented new schemes of play, teammates shouting instructions or signaling to each other, outfielders backing each other up on fly balls, shifting players in the field to account for individual strikers' batting tendencies, bringing in himself as primarily a "slow ball" pitcher in the late innings of a game in place of fireballer Brainard to change the pace and catch the strikers off guard.

Of course, achieving the ideal comportment of the team would be far from easy. After all, the group he had assembled had widely varying personalities and proclivities. Asa Brainard, known as "The Count," for his fashionable manner, refined dress, moustache, and prominent muttonchop side-whiskers, was Harry's opposite in temperament, a man unaccustomed to restrictions.[36] As such, he could easily slide into the role of a wayward Pied Piper, leading like-minded or just curious teammates into the wee hours in mischief and sometimes drunken revelry, often resulting in missed practice sessions the next day. More often than Harry liked, Brainard would conduct a tour of the nightlife of the city in which the squad found themselves after a ball game, a few teammates in tow, returning from their escapades as the sun's first rays crept from behind the horizon. The Count, potentially followed by Fred Waterman, sometimes referred to as "Innocent Fred" for his guileless demeanor, or adventurous Charlie Sweasy and his pal Andy Leonard, were often his companions on these adventures. Add to this the fact that Brainard was a hypochondriac of the first order, taking to his bed at the first sign of illness, real or imagined, or from aches caused by an especially physical game or practice, and it was a wonder that Harry was able to coax the extensive amount of playing time he did from the Count during the season.

Some players resented being told how to play the game that they felt they already had mastered over the years, even if this guidance was offered in an almost avuncular manner from their manager, who had a decade or more base ball experience than most of his players. A few had tempers that flared when confronted with mistakes or differences of opinion. Looking back, Harry told a reporter, "It was not a hard team to handle," then providing a bit more detail that indicated otherwise, "although Sweazy [*sic*] and Leonard would at times be hard to manage. Allison had to be handled very carefully, as he was subject to stubborn spells."[37] And the youthful McVey often bristled when Harry would reposition Cal in the field as different strikers came to the plate.[38] Harry was nothing if not persistent, and they could see the benefits of his instruction and innovation. But it would always be a struggle to take a group of mostly young men, playing a boy's game, and make them toe the line as might be expected of a mature adult.

Many of the players actually knew each other as teammates from previous clubs. In addition to Brainard, Waterman, Gould, and Allison playing for Harry the year before and being acquainted with their skills and personalities, Sweasy and Leonard had played together on both the Irvingtons of New Jersey as well as the Cincinnati Buckeyes. George and Asa had spent time together when Brainard joined the Nationals before their tour of the West in 1867 and through the remainder of that season. George would play shortstop or catch, sometimes alternating with Asa at second base when the latter wasn't pitching. Getting to know each other as they traveled, George was well aware of the Count's inclination for nighttime partying—he usually good-naturedly sidestepped the temptation when offered an invitation to join. For, though affable with a ready grin and somewhat mischievous in his own way, George was more of a quiet type when not performing on the field.[39] As such, he was mainly content to follow Harry's direction when it came to skipping an evening's entertainment while preparing for the next day's coming ball game. However, George was only human, and he too sometimes missed practice to explore a new locale with his teammates.

In fits and starts, the teammates began to slowly gel as a group. Practices led to identifying the rough edges in need of polishing if this assembly of talented individuals was to learn to work together in becoming a well-oiled championship machine. A mid-April exhibition match against a "picked nine" of various other accomplished local ball players represented an inauspicious beginning for the club. About all that could be positively said was that the Red Stockings won 24–15, but it was reported that the game showed the team "hardly working well together, and the members being evidently rusty for want of practice."[40]

The Red Stockings still plainly lacked the cohesiveness that had been expected by the manager as well as the players themselves. That would need to change quickly, and the next exhibition match with another picked nine yielded better results with a 50–7 victory. Promising improvement, indeed, but did it signal the coalescing of the team around its innate abilities in their quest to beat the best in the sport, led by George Wright's superior skills and guided by Harry Wright's unparalleled strategic planning and tactics? The next few months would prove a revelation to themselves as well as the game of base ball, bringing unprecedented prominence to both.

4

Invincible

The regular season of 1869 now began in earnest. The Red Stockings played and won seven games in Ohio and Indiana over the course of the next six weeks, conquering their foes by anywhere from nineteen to seventy-eight runs. The game with the widest margin of victory was largely due to George's dominant performance as a striker, collecting three home runs and five doubles in eleven hits in an 86–8 demolition of the Kekiongas of Ft. Wayne, Indiana.[1]

The last two of these games in Ohio initiated four weeks of continuous travel in June that would bring them to the "Cradle of Base Ball" in the Northeast, home of the best teams the sport had to offer. Club president Aaron Champion and Harry Wright had decided that the only way in which the Red Stockings would become nationally known was to bring their brand of base ball right to the gates of the established champions of the game. Challenging these clubs on their own grounds was a sure means to gather large crowds willing to pay good money to see their hometown heroes flex their muscles in expectation of defeating the upstarts from the West. The Cincinnati organization was anxious to make a profit and refill the war chest they had emptied to sign their professional players.

During this journey the Red Stockings participated in nineteen contests, a punishing schedule in which they played almost every day and often took exhausting train rides in the early morning or late evening to their next stop. Sometimes, to lighten the mood while on these trips, George would exhibit his penchant for practical jokes. At one point he hovered over a few unsuspecting teammates with a device that resembled a long-legged wire spider and delicately grazed the faces of those who were trying to get some rest. The close-eyed victims invariably brushed the intrusion away with a sleep-deadened hand like a horse might do with its tail to shoo away a bothersome fly, eliciting gentle laughter from those not yet sleeping players.[2]

The sporting public was indeed curious as to how this unproven group of westerners would fare versus the entrenched powers of eastern base ball who made New York, Philadelphia, and Washington, DC, their homes. Newspaper coverage was abundant and detailed, most games being parsed as part of the Red Stockings "Tour of the East." Within the month, any base ball enthusiast who cared to know would understand just where this band of crimson-hosed Porkopolites ranked in base ball's hierarchy.

The Red Stockings won the first eight games against upstate New York and Massachusetts clubs in ten days of competition, mostly by wide margins of twenty runs or more. The major exception was a tight contest with a recognized powerhouse, the Unions of Lansingburgh, on the outskirts of the city of Troy, New York, a team commonly referred to as the "Haymakers of Troy." The score was close until the fourth inning, when Cincinnati scored ten times and kept the Unions at bay for the remainder of the contest, winning the heavy-hitting tussle 37–31. The Haymakers "felt sore at being beaten by a country club," a rural team as opposed to one from the urban Northeast. A newspaper gave an opinion that would become a more common refrain as the month progressed, noting "[the Unions] should not [feel sore], considering that most of the Cincinnatti [*sic*] players are men who have held positions in the first nines in this neighborhood [the Northeast] for some years."[3]

This was the beginning of a line of reasoning to which the defeated clubs of base ball's birthplace could cling, repeated often as the Cincinnatis methodically thumped every team in their eastern tour. The thinking went something like this: we haven't lost to an inferior team of country bumpkins but rather to a club composed mostly of players who had originally earned their base ball pedigree in the Northeast before moving west. It certainly had some logic to it, on the surface intimating that the defeated teams hadn't actually lost to players from the "primitive" West at all, but rather to some of "their own," making the losses easier to swallow.

Employing similar reasoning, the British shouldn't have been stunned because they were defeated by the upstart United States and its army in the Revolutionary War because, after all, those troops were really made up of recently British citizens, making the defeat more palatable, almost acceptable. Or, conversely, just *perhaps* it was time for the plainly superior British Army to ask why these losses had occurred and what lessons could be learned from the defeats.

Those adopting this excuse for the continual drubbing of the crack eastern ball clubs by the Red Stockings were overlooking a few important points about the professionalization of the game. Winning teams no longer needed to have players with hometown roots. In fact, relocation of some top ball players for covert compensation had become somewhat commonplace since the mid-1860s. A club from any location now need not be tied to its immediate surroundings to field a squad that could compete against the best. And over the next few years, the desire for a city to stick to its homegrown, skilled ballplayers would become virtually nonexistent if other talented individuals could be signed to a contract. Rather, the increasingly practiced capabilities of the players and the honing of strategic teamwork for game-time competition appeared to be more overriding factors in producing championship-caliber play going forward.

Base ball was moving quickly down the path from being just a game of sociable enjoyment and exercise among neighbors and colleagues to becoming a business. The fungible commodity of this industry was the capability that an individual brought to striking the ball, running the bases, and playing his position, rather than his geographical location. A player was now akin to a sports mercenary, ready to go to war versus others just like him, all for whichever team gave him his price to represent them. Paying spectators were more than willing to support this shift if it allowed them to claim bragging rights of civic pride or gambling winnings.

Now, onward marched this paid militia from the West into New York City. Cincinnati newspapers had shouted the early triumphs from their pages, their readers beaming with the team's achievements. Base ball's championship clubs from the Northeast were now consumed with their own desires of bringing the Red Stockings to heel. The first team from New York City to attempt to derail them came the closest.

On June 15, the Mutuals, a club deeply respected and feared by all for its winning ways, fought the invaders to a standstill through eight and a half innings. Cincinnati tallied once in the first inning and once in the third, the second run courtesy of George Wright's double to left field and subsequent score on a passed ball by the Mutual's catcher. Each team was fielding everything that the other club hit at them until the Mutuals managed to tie the score with a run in both the top of the eighth and ninth innings.

Perhaps more could have been expected of the Mutuals in the ninth. But with runners on second and first, crafty Cincinnati third baseman Fred Waterman executed what appears to have been the first recorded instance of the "trapped ball" play, a deception that would be outlawed in later years with the institution of the infield fly rule, eliminating what transpired next to the runners on base. A Mutual striker hit an infield pop-up that should have been an easy catch for Waterman, both runners holding their places at second and first, waiting for Waterman to grab the ball. "Innocent Fred" then pulled an unexpected surprise when he "let the ball drop from his hands, and then passed it to George Wright, on the third base, who promptly sent the ball to Sweazy [*sic*] at second, and the result was that [the Mutual base runners] were both out."[4]

With the game still knotted at two runs apiece, the Red Stockings were able to score twice in the bottom of the ninth, claiming a 4–2 victory and what would be reported in the press as "the smallest known [score] in the history of the game in a first-class match."[5] This low combined tally signified the magnificence of the teams' fielding at a time when putting the ball in play, bare-handed errors, and the high scores that followed were typical of the game. The sport was, indeed, changing.

A telegram arrived at the Red Stockings' hotel from Cincinnati that evening. It summed up the hopes and dreams for the ecstatic supporters of the team in the formal language of the times: "On behalf of the citizens of Cincinnati, we send you greeting. The streets are full of people, who give cheer after cheer for their pet club. Go on with the noble work. Our expectations have been met."[6] In fact, it might be more accurate to say that Porkopolis was delirious from a very particular strain of swine flu termed "base ball fever."

Over the following few days, the Atlantics and the Eckfords of Brooklyn, became Cincinnati's next victims. The Red Stockings produced convincing wins over these two teams, clubs that were as sainted as the Mutuals in the annals of 1860s base ball in the New York City region. Next came the defeat of the Irvingtons of New Jersey, near Newark. The

New York papers struggled to make sense of the losses. One thing was certain though. All agreed that the Red Stockings had shown everyone the value of fielding, teamwork, and a coordinated approach to the game that only a manager like Harry Wright seemed to be able to instill in his charges. Writing of the totality of the effort put forth by the Cincinnatis, a New York paper commented presciently about the week's activity and how it augured well for base ball as a whole.

[The] three Brooklyn matches, and the game at Irvington, on Friday, were witnessed by an aggregate of 25,000 people, showing the rapidly extending popularity of the sport. . . . It requires no great stretch of the imagination to see in the future enclosed grounds of vast extent, surrounded with seating accommodations for twenty-five or thirty thousand people where the public will gather to witness the play of athletes trained and skillful to a degree not yet reached.[7]

The next portion of the commentary could have been a paid advertisement by Harry Wright for the benefits of the program he espoused for turning his team into a consistent winner. Better yet, some of it was even true.

The Cincinnati Club is probably the only organization in the country that has been properly and thoroughly trained and disciplined, and to this fact we attribute wholly their extraordinary success. The members are required to be strictly temperate in their habits, to eat none but wholesome and nutritious kinds of food, and to retire to rest at a certain and reasonable kind of hour. Here we see the secret of their being able to play matches day after day without apparent fatigue; and we insist that no club in the country will be able to compete successfully with them whose members will not adhere strictly to the rules of health, and in addition exercise daily and constantly with ball and bat on the green field.[8]

With this take on the inevitability of Cincinnati victory, maybe the remaining ball clubs should have just waved the white flag of surrender. But the matches continued. To make their triumphal tour complete after the beatings administered to the teams from New York and New Jersey, the Red Stockings met and defeated clubs from Philadelphia, Baltimore, Washington, DC, and Wheeling, West Virginia, before returning home. In Washington, President Ulysses S. Grant met the team at the White House to pay his compliments under the blue haze of the nonstop chimney-like emanations from his cigar-smoking.[9] From his Civil War days, he was particularly familiar with leading a determined group of warriors from the West on an extended, victorious march eastward, destroying everything in its path.

While in Washington, they also paid a visit to the shop of Mathew Brady, the famous photographer of Civil War carnage as well as prominent Americans. Here Brady made a historic image of the team. Harry Wright is standing in the middle of the group, arms folded in a seemingly contented assessment of his club's efforts. George is positioned on Harry's immediate right in the picture, angled to the side somewhat, preening a bit with one arm folded behind his back as he gives a rather stern look into the camera. Unique for the times, he is the only one of the nine players who is clean-shaven, with no moustache, beard or muttonchop sideburns. His bearing, his glaring, his dehairing; it all made him stand out among the other ballplayers, which perhaps was his intention.

On July 1, the Red Stockings returned to Cincinnati as the conquerors of all the Eastern ball clubs they had faced, from Massachusetts to Maryland. A parade led the returning victors through the town, the cheering nonstop. The next day the team overwhelmed a local picked nine, 53–11. Before the contest, the Cincinnati Lumber Company presented the club with what was termed the "Champion Bat," a twenty-seven-foot-long monstrosity that some said wasn't manufactured but, rather, was "grown to order for the occasion."[10] At a grand banquet that evening, euphoric speechifying was the standard, rising to its rhetorical zenith when Aaron Champion claimed he would rather be president of the Red Stockings than president of the United States.[11] At times, immersed in the political cauldron that was Washington, DC, President Grant might have felt the same way.

After this month of grueling travel and pressure-packed competition, the team felt good to be back in the friendly confines of the Queen City, at least for a few weeks. Harry's wife and young children were eager to be with him again as well as their uncle, "Smiling George," who lived with them while he was in Cincinnati. Most of the other players resided at a boarding house on Main Street, only a few minutes' walk from the Union Grounds ball field.[12]

The ballplaying, and the winning, recommenced as soon as the partying was over. For the next few months, the Red Stockings played in Cincinnati or roamed the Midwest for a few days at a time, not far from home. Twenty wins were notched from July 3 to September 10, a more leisurely schedule than the Eastern Tour, for the most part against decidedly lesser competition. The major exceptions to this were mainly Eastern foes that traveled to Cincinnati for return matches, hoping to avenge their losses in June. The Olympics of Washington lost three times to the Red Stockings within ten days in early July, while the Eckfords of Brooklyn and Alerts of Rochester fell once apiece.

The mighty Haymakers of Troy, which Cincinnati had narrowly beaten in June, almost turned the tables when they met again at the end of August in Cincinnati. It was a back-and-forth event from the start, being tied at seventeen apiece in the fifth inning when the Haymakers contested an umpire's call and were ordered by their team president to leave the field. Rumor had it that the mighty team from Troy stalked off due to massive wagers by their supporters, including one of the team owners who had thousands riding on a Haymaker victory. They feared losing it all if they played to a natural nine-inning conclusion of the game, as the Red Stockings were known for their strong finishes. Troy's desertion of the field caused the umpire to award the game to Cincinnati, per league rules. However, history records the score as a tie ballgame, a faint smudge on the otherwise pristine record of the Red Stockings that year.

The growing rivalry with the Forest Citys of Rockford continued during the summer. They played the Red Stockings in four games from mid-July to early August, the Forest Citys losing each of these matches. Cincinnati was the only club to beat them in the twenty-five games they played that season. One game was exceptionally close, a tussle on July 24 at Cincinnati's Union Field where the Red Stockings barely eked out a one run victory. After seven innings, with Cincinnati ahead by three runs, the bats of the Rockford boys came alive. They exhibited a streak of steady hitting that resulted in plating five runs to take the lead by two, 14–12. So it remained as the Red Stockings came down to their last chance in the ninth. But an indefatigable attitude and steady nerves prevailed among the Cincinnatis, along with some timely hitting of their own. Successive one-out singles by Harry Wright and Andy Leonard were followed by a well-executed and fairly novel double steal that scored Wright, and then a passed ball by the Forest City catcher let Leonard come home with the tying run.[13] Brainard smacked a double and was brought in by a Sweasy single to win the game, 15–14, a closer contest than even the victory over the Mutuals in June that had been hailed as one of the greatest matches of the sport. The other three contests between the two rivals paled in comparison, each ending with a twenty-one run margin of victory for Cincinnati.

Typical of these three losses was the initial game, played on July 10, two weeks before the one-run squeaker. Forest City hosted the event at its home field, Fairground Park in Rockford. Darryl Brock, famed base ball novelist, noted in a presentation given to a baseball convention in 1999 that an old-timer described the field simply and harshly, "'A poorer field was never known.'"[14] Brock fleshed out the issues, "Third base stood on a hill, to which you ran upward from second; you then navigated a hollow between third and home . . . a quarter-mile-long horse track cut through the outfield; it had a gutter for drainage, which caused major problems for outfielders."[15] Such was the "home field advantage" of each ball club of the day, knowing how to exploit or avoid the unique conditions of one's own park. But nothing could stop the Red Stockings from defeating their hosts. Brock commented,

> [Cincinnati's] 32 hits included 6 homers. Lead-off man and all-everything shortstop George Wright . . . set the tone as he stepped to the plate in the bottom of the first and drove the ball far over the right fielder. One reporter called it the longest ball ever hit on this field and described Wright as trotting home to score his run—a rarity in those days. Later he went the other way and hit one over the tree row in left field.[16]

In each of the four games of the series, Albert Spalding was the starting pitcher, at nineteen a seasoned veteran of the Rockford club. Some considered him already one of the best at his trade at the time.[17] To consistently lose to these Midwest rivals was a bitter pill to swallow for the young, proud star hurler of the Rockford team, but at least it was against the unparalleled champions of the sport.

Spalding was a resolute competitor, confident in his skills sometimes to the point of being brash. He was already termed a "strategic" pitcher for his combination of physical capabilities with the baseball and mental calculations of how best to mystify the strikers in delivering the ball to the plate. He would size up each opponent he faced from his pitching box only forty-five feet away, at six feet one inch an imposing sight in the batter's eyes. Then Spalding would cock his arm and let fly a cannon-shot of a pitch toward a selected target of the striker's requested hitting zone, sprinkling in an occasional change-of-pace slowball. In these matches with Cincinnati, he had not been able to unlock the secret of making them weakly strike, or miss altogether, enough of his deliveries. But, even in defeat, the Wright brothers, especially Harry, took note of his keen competitiveness and obvious abilities, filing this impression away for future reference.

Before most games, the Red Stockings would warm up the crowd of spectators as a precursor to the real action on the diamond. After fielding sharp grounders and shagging lazy fly balls, there came a special treat. The Cincinnati infielders were as agile a group of players as could be found in the game, especially when it came to handling the ball, and they were not shy when it came to showing off their skills. George Wright, the showman on the team, along with Sweasy, Leonard, and Waterman, customarily gave an exhibition before each match of juggling the ball, to the delight of the spectators, who always applauded warmly.[18] They would adroitly toss the sphere behind their backs and knees to one another, bringing the crowd alive with shouts of approval and gasps of delight as they kept it moving with increasing speed.[19] Invariably, Wright would bring the pregame demonstration to a conclusion "by throwing the ball high in the air—higher, it seem[ed], than a man could throw a ball."[20] If the game ended in victory for the club, which it always did during that magical season, outfielder Cal McVey, a strong, proficient tumbler, would conclude the festivities with a few handsprings and flips for the crowd's amusement.[21] The youthful teammates reveled in their dexterity and physical prowess, never tiring of displaying these traits to the enjoyment of those in attendance. Their actions certainly conveyed their feelings about the sport: it was great to be young and alive, playing the game of base ball as a Cincinnati Red Stocking.

Of no one on the team could this be truer than George Wright. His ball-playing skills, coupled with his personality, wavy brown hair and infectious smile, made for an engaging combination that captivated the crowds. He was the consummate entertainer, "juggling bats or balls before games . . . mesmerizing the crowd with sleight-of-hand tricks. . . . George also attracted the fairer sex to the ballpark with his good looks. . . . But, above all, he was noted for flashing his large, white teeth that earned him the nickname 'Smiling George.'"[22]

During the opening months of the season, while Cincinnati was winning the first of their ballgames, the country had witnessed the completion of the Transcontinental Railway in May. Ball clubs had previously considered Chicago "the West" as they traveled there in the 1860s to show their country cousins the cosmopolitan ways of a maturing eastern base ball. Now, the true West of America could be reached by taking a train all the way to California from Omaha, Nebraska, the previous westernmost stop on the rail line. Instead of taking five months by wagon train, it took only five days from Omaha to Sacramento via this new connection. The railroad facilitated the economic flow of goods in both directions, opening up new markets for each, as well as supporting the nation's swelling westward expansion.

Once the railroad was completed, club president Champion worked with contacts in San Francisco to arrange a trip to this profitable, untapped market. The San Francisco Recreation Grounds had opened in late November the year before, a mostly fenced-in field that boasted a large grandstand. It was a venue intended to host a wide variety of outdoor entertainment, including musical performances, running or biking races around a track, cricket matches, quoits and, of course, base ball games.[23] On Thanksgiving Day, 1868, the park was christened with a ball game between the San Francisco Eagles and the Wide Awakes of Oakland.[24] By the following September, its grounds were filled with spectators teeming with anticipation as they hosted a series of contests featuring the undefeated Red Stockings against the best of their local ball clubs.

In San Francisco, there were some who reportedly had been taught how to play base ball by a few former Knickerbocker Base Ball Club members from New York City who had gone west with the gold rush of 1849.[25] The sport had become commonplace by the early 1860s; the Eagles of San Francisco took the first state title versus the Red Rovers of Sacramento in a best-of-three series in 1860. As the Red Stockings added to their undefeated record over the summer, the excitement of them making the journey to "Frisco" was palpable, for both the Red Stockings themselves as well as their ardent admirers in the Bay area.

En route to traveling west in mid-September, Cincinnati soundly beat two teams in St. Louis. While in town, they continued to read the news of the intense skirmishes of a more deadly nature that were taking place across the western plains that summer with the Native American population. Typical was a front-page headline, "Indian Hostilities," in a Chicago newspaper in mid-September with accompanying stories that spanned the geography from Montana to Wyoming and the Dakota Territories as it detailed confrontations between soldiers or settlers and members of the Blackfeet, Sioux, Cheyenne, and Arapahoe tribes.[26] Two weeks before, this same Chicago paper had a front-page dateline story from St. Louis itself, noting a struggle between nearby railroad surveyors and Native American tribesmen.[27]

Earlier in July, the plains of Colorado had been the stage of a brutal attack the army had conducted against the Cheyenne, which came to be known as the Battle of Summit Springs. The Cheyenne and US military had been skirmishing in this region for several years. After a particularly intense series of raids the tribesmen had made on settlers in northern Kansas the month before, a reprisal by US cavalry would be the final, deadly battle fought between these warring factions in Colorado. Close to four hundred Cheyenne, including warriors, women, and children, were camped by the South Platte River in the aftermath of these raids. A force of almost three hundred army and accompanying scouts, under cover of nearby sand hills, came within a half mile of the encampment, dividing their forces into three separate attack groups and simultaneously attempting to drive the horses from the village, gallop into the center of the congregated villagers, and try to cut off any escape routes.[28] Over fifty Cheyenne were killed in the battle and many captured, but most of the women and children were able to flee the scene.

This fighting not only ended major hostilities with the Cheyenne in Colorado, but it also began the making of the legend of Buffalo Bill Cody as an Indian fighter, to be immortalized in dime-novel style over the coming years as an army scout and hero of the wars with Native Americans.[29] This was his first significant involvement in these types of military campaigns. In his later years, he created his famed Wild West show that toured the country as well as internationally, often including in his performance a reenactment of the Battle of Summit Springs, in which he mythologized himself, incorrectly, as having killed the great Cheyenne leader of the encampment, Tall Bull.[30] Buffalo Bill was a great self-promoter, never reluctant to hype his own roll in the proceedings if it helped increase interest in his ventures, another example of America's growing cultural commercialization.

The plight of the Native Americans was exacerbated by the coming of the Transcontinental Railroad. They looked down from the hills at the

Transcontinental Railway's "Iron Horse" chugging relentlessly across the prairie with its trailing railcars of ever-larger groups of interlopers. The invaders' mouths were agape at the splendor of the majestic mountains, seemingly endless plains, and their vast bounty of bison, antelope, and mineral wealth, ready for exploitation. The natives sorrowfully contemplated how they could ever be able to reclaim their homeland, yearning for a time of former independence that allowed them to freely roam in any direction, living in harmony with nature and its wonders. Inevitably, the clash of these two cultures would be decided in favor of the transgressors' overwhelming superiority in numbers, but not before much blood was shed, with dreams shattered for some and realized for others in the process.

Of more immediate concern to the Red Stockings players was how they would be able to safely cross this strange but dangerous territory. Many years later, George Wright was to recount, "The players carried pistols under their pillows and one time a report was circulated that the Indians were about to attack us. A guard of soldiers was placed on the tender of the locomotive, but the redskins did not bother the train."[31] The story of George making his pillow lumpy with a sidearm stowed nervously underneath was to be a staple of his repertoire as he regaled family, friends, and acquaintances over the years about his first-ever journey to California.

The guns, though never used in battle, were typically employed by those carrying them in target practice as their train wound its way across the prairie toward the West Coast. George remembered, "To pass the time away those players with pistols would shoot at wolves, prairie dogs and other wild animals from the car windows."[32] Fortunately for the animals, the boys' aims were better when throwing a base ball than shooting a gun.

At times he recalled the newness of entering what was to George and his companions a completely fresh world of sights, sounds, and experiences. "At several places we stopped enroute and the players got out and began digging alongside of the road for gold. . . . Many of the players bought moss agates after they had found digging for gold was not so easy."[33] It seems tales of the Forty-Niners and mining riches from that adventurous time twenty years before were firmly lodged in their heads, perhaps imagining even they themselves striking it rich at a railroad siding in the middle of the Great American Plains. How foolish it must have seemed later on, but how real the possibility at the time. It appears the players settled for the purchase of the more available moss agates found along the route as souvenirs of the journey, semi-precious stones that were a beautiful mix of turquoise, forest green, and milky white colors.

After five days on the rails, the train pulled into Sacramento. Then they took a steamship downriver to San Francisco and were greeted by more than two thousand curious locals as the vessel docked at the Broadway Wharf, anxious to see the titans of base ball in the flesh, the fabled Cincinnati Red Stockings.[34] During the team's visit, these admirers would not be disappointed.

The Recreation Grounds were overflowing the next day for the first of the scheduled contests. There was a newly constructed pavilion seating one thousand "ladies and their escorts" who had paid the princely sum of one dollar each for the privilege.[35] The hometown Eagles were the first to take on the vaunted Porkopolites, who were clothed in their trademark knickered pants and red hosiery, "which shows their calves in all their magnitude and rotundity," one local paper gushed in reviewing the proceedings.[36] Cincinnati easily won this game by a score of 35–4, and the one-sided victories would continue to mount. The next contest with the Eagles was played two days later and resulted in a larger thrashing, 58–4. Similar margins marked the subsequent defeats of the Pacifics, 66–4 and 54–5. The game with the Atlantics was mercifully halted after five innings with the score 76–5 in favor of Cincinnati.

The city's press concluded that the Red Stockings were playing a markedly more advanced version of the same game than the San Franciscans. Asa Brainard, the Red Stocking pitcher, would take a sweeping step toward home to develop momentum to speed the ball's progress, while the locals practiced an antiquated technique of delivering the ball with both feet firmly planted, requiring any velocity at all to be imparted from motion of the arm alone. At bat, the West Coasters invariably launched wonderfully lofted fly balls into the outfield where they were easily caught, versus the visitors who stung low, line drive "daisy-cutters" inches off the ground, forceful strikes that were difficult to field.[37] Once on base, the agile, aggressive Red Stocking runners got quick jumps toward the next bag even as the pitcher was winding up, nothing like the hometown boys who stayed almost on top of the base until the ball was struck. It all added up to complete dominance by the champions from the Midwest.

But through it all, the host city and its sports fans graciously took their lumps. They had gotten what they had paid for, an opportunity to witness the best in base ball in person and understand how they got there. A farewell banquet capped the celebration of the contests that had taken place, demonstrations of excellence in the field by the Red Stockings and equanimity in defeat exhibited by the San Francisco teams and their partisans. Just as quickly as they had arrived, the Cincinnati club was off to retrace their steps homeward, delivering a shellacking to a picked nine in Sacramento before leaving California for good and administering thrashings to two more teams in Omaha before journey's end.

Throughout October and early November, the winning streak was kept intact, a few more Midwestern clubs suffering losses as they unsuccessfully sought revenge for their earlier defeats as well as some Northeastern teams trying to bounce back from their debacles in the spring but failing to win a game from the Red Stockings. The Cincinnatis had accomplished what they had set out to do, taking on all comers and winning consistently and emphatically, leaving their team's name on every sportsman's lips. When all the matches were added up, the picked nine skirmishes, exhibition contests, amateur and professional games, the Red Stockings were undefeated.

As reported in the *New York Clipper*, the Red Stockings had fifty-seven wins (counting the tie as an awarded win by the umpire) against "regular" teams (amateur and professional clubs) and six wins against "picked nine" squads, equaling sixty-three wins.[38] Adding in exhibition game victories gave an overall win total for the season of sixty-nine games.[39] Somewhere close to two hundred thousand people had seen them in action across this schedule, from a high of about fifteen thousand or more spectators in Philadelphia where they played the Athletics, to a tiny gathering of forty curious individuals on a spring morning attending the Tri-Mountain club's game in Boston.[40]

George Wright had performed in spectacular fashion. In the fifty-seven "regular" games, he was almost unstoppable at the plate. George hit an amazing .623 in those games while slamming a combined forty-nine home runs, accounting for almost 30 percent of the team's total.[41] The game was meant to be initiated by putting the ball in play, and George was one of the most dependable strikers to do so, making it easy for Harry to place him in the leadoff batting position as a sure spark to ignite the offense right from the start. His fielding percentage was over .900 on fly balls caught, combined with his sure-handed corralling of grounders accompanied by deadly throwing accuracy to any base.[42] George even stepped in as a substitute pitcher when needed, tossing fourteen innings during the year. It all added up to one of the most impressive seasons of base ball ever by one of the most talented players of all time.

Meanwhile, brother Harry had played a solid role as centerfielder as well as spelling Asa Brainard in about a quarter of the four hundred seventy innings pitched in these games.[43] However, his real contribution was as the team's guiding hand, an innovative savant whose knowledge of how best to play the game, and whose ability to convince his team to trust in his direction led to what was to be a season of base ball unlike any other in the history of the game. As memorialized in a newspaper account almost sixty years later, they were

> THE INVINCIBLES
> They had no masks, they wore no gloves,
>   But with their bare, red hands,
> They took the drives amid the cheers
>   Of thinly peopled stands.
> Long years have passed—the game has grown—
>   But still admirers pine,
> To see again those ancient stars,
>   The Reds of '69![44]

The only question now was, what could they do as an encore to follow the smashing success of a season like this one?

5

Fall of the Titans

The week of June 13, 1870, was greeted with a mixture of anticipation and anxiety by a number of the residents in the New York City area. Monday's newspaper headlines were troubling, as they described the current state of affairs in Cuba and its insurrection against Spain. But even more concerning was the expected invasion of the city by a powerful, mercenary horde due to arrive in the area that very day.

The Cincinnati Red Stockings were on the rampage once again, their base ball games so far being an extension of their fabulously triumphant campaign of the previous year. Undefeated in 1869, they had carried over their winning ways well into the current season, victorious in each of their twenty-six previous encounters from mid-April through early June. Similar to last year, they had dispatched a variety of amateur and professional teams, in regulation contests as well as picked nines and exhibition matches, in the Midwest as well as Massachusetts and upstate New York. Additionally, they had included an unbeaten tour of half a dozen southern clubs in New Orleans and Memphis in their list of the vanquished. Now they were back in the city, determined to once again have their way with the eastern base ball establishment.

Not that the New York sporting public thought any differently about what would be the fate of their beloved teams in the face of this spring onslaught. The only question appeared to be not whether their clubs would lose, but by how much. A Brooklyn newspaper carried a front page advertisement from a local music store, twenty repeating lines at the top of the page blaring in all capital letters "RED STOCKINGS' MARCH," followed by the same number of lines of "RED STOCKINGS'

POLKA" and "RED STOCKINGS' SCHOTTISCHE" (a more sedate polka), highlighting the fact that sheet music of these melodies would be available for sale and "Illustrated with a correct likeness of the Red Stockings."[1] Perhaps they felt the music might assuage the agony of the expected defeats yet again at the hands of the Porkopolitans. But their advertisements of these recently penned compositions emblazoned with the names and picture of the victorious enemy only rubbed salt in the wounds inflicted the prior year.

On the afternoon of Monday June 13, the Mutuals, who had played the Red Stockings to a standstill a year ago before finally succumbing in their historically low-scoring contest, 4–2, could only muster three runs this time around, while the steamroller from Cincinnati tallied a methodical sixteen. One reporter described the Mutuals performance in a tidy manner, "They were unable to bat, while their fielding was execrable."[2] Not a promising description for the hometown crowds, to be sure.

However, the next day Cincinnati found itself engaged in a completely different type of contest. Over ten thousand spectators had grudgingly paid the exorbitant price of fifty cents each to get into the stands while thousands of others ringed the wooden fences to sneak glimpses of the action through knotholes or settle for milling in a large crowd spread across the fringes of the outfield.[3] Harry Wright had insisted on this high ticket price, expecting the crowd would be willing to part with half a dollar to see this much-anticipated contest, and he was right. This would be a fine payday for the Red Stockings as they shared the lion's portion of the gate receipts with the home club, the Atlantics of Brooklyn.

The latter had focused significant effort in preparation for this contest, coming together as a team as they had seldom done in the recent past. By the ninth inning, the surprisingly close game was tied at five apiece, with Cincinnati still in contention due in large part to the impressive hitting that day of George Wright. He had singled and scored in the first inning, then garnered hits in the third and seventh innings to drive in a few more runs and keep the game close.

With the score knotted after nine innings, the Atlantics were more than pleased to call it a day. Better this result, they felt, than an extra-inning loss to the champions, who had a knack for closing with a winning rally. The Brooklyn team captain, Bob Ferguson, received this instruction from the club's directors in attendance, and he began to lead his group off the field. Harry Wright, on the other hand, after conversing with team president Aaron Champion, held the exact opposite opinion—play on![4] Fortunately there was an easy way to settle these differing sentiments.

New York newspaperman Henry Chadwick was in attendance, acknowledged by virtually everyone in the sport as the person most steeped in the workings of the organized pastime. A transplanted Englishman who had initially covered the cricket beat for local papers in mid-century, Henry had quickly included base ball in his reporting and had embraced it as the game of America's future. He extolled its virtues as well as worked to institute its playing with a universally accepted governing set of rules and regulations. In his efforts to bring some standardization to the sport, Henry was credited with inventing the base ball box score and its accompanying shorthand notations to record the game's actions on the field and use this data to examine each individual player's contributions.

For all this and more, Chadwick would one day be characterized as "The Father of Baseball" and be inducted into its Hall of Fame, the only journalistic presence with a plaque of his own in the players' wing of honorees. In his own modest way, Henry in his later years would say of this paternal sobriquet, "I suppose they call me its father because in the day when it was attracting little or no attention, except among a mere handful, I became interested in it and did what I could to make it popular."[5] The game of base ball would eventually have many who might be called "Father," but perhaps none more appropriate than Henry Chadwick.

In addition to reporting on the game, he was a longstanding member and current chairman of the sport's rules committee. Who better to ask concerning the debate at hand than Chadwick? Harry Wright, an acquaintance of Henry's from the former's playing days in New York City years before, asked Chadwick for his advice on the matter. He affirmed Wright's opinion that, according to the rules, a tied game at the end of a regulation nine innings must continue unless there was mutual agreement by both teams to end the affair as a draw.[6] Without such unity, the game would be forfeited to Cincinnati if the Atlantics chose to retire. To this Brooklyn would not agree, bringing them back to the field to resume play.

A tie game going into extra innings ratcheted up the already-tense atmosphere of the contest. In the tenth, George Wright's fielding now took center stage as he creatively squelched a rally by the locals. With one out and Atlantics runners on first and second base, George watched as Brainard induced the striker to pop up the ball in Wright's direction. Perhaps what flashed through his mind was the eerie similarity of this situation to their year-ago historically low scoring game against the Mutuals, when in the ninth inning of the ballgame, tied at 2–2, third baseman Fred Waterman was faced with this same set of circumstances. As with Waterman, George carefully let the fly ball drop through his grasp to the ground as the runners stayed close to their bases, thinking Wright would surely catch the ball. Quickly picking it up, George passed it to Waterman on third, who sent it to Sweasy covering second base to complete a double play and end the Atlantics' threat.[7]

Now the Red Stockings came to bat, momentum having shifted their way after the dramatic trapped ball play by George Wright. With one out, Brainard doubled and moved to third base as two Atlantics outfielders collided on Sweasy's catchable fly ball, allowing it to drop and Sweasy to take first. Cal McVey hit a drive to the outfield that was caught, but Brainard scored from third, pushing Cincinnati ahead by one run. George Wright was the next batter, the deadliest striker in the game, relishing the opportunity to inflict further damage. He proceeded to scorch a daisy-cutter to the Atlantics' second baseman, who could not handle the missile, Sweasy scoring on Wright's hit to make the score 7–5.[8] The Red Stockings had mounted their comeback and were three outs from yet another victory.

However, after tossing a superb game to this point, Brainard appeared to lose control of his pitches. He allowed a lead-off single, then "by a high over-pitch" wild-pitched the runner to third base.[9] The next batter hit a long fly ball to right field, Cal McVey giving chase and grabbing the ball on the ground. It was reported that an onlooker in the outfield jumped on his back and disrupted play, preventing McVey from getting the ball back to the infield until the runner on third had scored and the striker had made it to third base.[10] Much later in life, McVey was to contradict this version of his entanglement with the crowd, insisting that he did not remember anyone deliberately flinging themselves on his back but, rather, he had "difficulty in digging the ball out of the crowd."[11] Of course, with all the milling about of the large number of spectators in the far reaches of the outfield, something like this was bound to happen. Now this intermingling of players and spectators had come at a most inopportune time for the Red Stockings.

With one run in and a runner on third, the Atlantics were determined to at least tie the game once again. After the next striker grounded out,

Brooklyn's Ferguson, a righthanded hitter, took a stance on the other side of the plate, intent on hitting lefthanded to keep the ball away from the shortstop, Atlantics' killer George Wright.[12] This was one of the first recorded instances of switch-hitting. One newspaper stated this outright, "The point was to avoid George Wright . . . [Ferguson] stood so as to hit the ball left handed, and, as he can use one hand as well as the other, by this change he drew the ball round from George's reach towards right short . . ," his single driving in the tying run.[13] A minute later, Ferguson scored the winning tally himself.

A spectator would have been hard-pressed to find a more competitive, exciting match to date in the young history of professional baseball. Even the historic 4–2 Red Stockings victory of the previous year over the Mutuals, a brilliant display of defense in the midst of high scoring contests, took a back seat to this game. The pitching had been solid from both teams until Brainard's unexpected meltdown in the last inning. Stingy fielding was on display, highlighted by the creative flair of George Wright's trapped ball escapade late in the game. Timely ball-striking was abundant, especially in the form of what was termed "scientific hitting" with Ferguson's strategic switch at the plate and flawless execution of that tactic. After almost a year and a half of continuous victory, the vaunted Red Stockings had gone down to defeat.

Once the game had concluded, heavy with disappointment but still proud of his players even in the face of this loss, the Cincinnati club president Champion wired back to the throngs of anxious followers in the Queen City, "Atlantics, 8; Cincinnatis, 7. The finest game ever played. Our boys did nobly, but fortune was against us. Eleven innings played. Though beaten, not disgraced."[14]

The next day's reporting of the contest heaped praise upon the winners as well as the losers, both being recognized for their valiant efforts. Yet, amid the hometown's victory celebration, an opinion piece appeared in a Brooklyn newspaper, raising the specter of gambling's ugly head. It reminded everyone that even the previous day's widely admired contest was subject to the devious efforts of this scourge of sports. It speculated,

> The result [of the game] . . . is only what close observers of sporting
> matters might have expected. The Red Stockings had been as successful as
> they could afford to be for the present, it must be shown that it was possible
> to beat them, or betting would be at an end. A horse that could make such

time as no other horse could approach and was dead sure to win every race, would soon become worthless for sporting purposes, no other horse would be entered with it, no bets could be had against a sure thing. . . . Base Ball has fallen under the same influences as horse racing . . . and must suffer from suspicion of the practices of the turf.[15]

No accusations were brought by anyone, nor were any expected. But, of all teams, to accuse a contingent of the esteemed, scrupulously honest Harry Wright's of selling out to gamblers would be akin to saying that the sun rose in the west each morning: it just didn't happen that way. It certainly appeared that both teams had played to win, each exhibiting athleticism, determination and creativity worthy of champions. The fact that the article was even written, and by no less than a paper of the city in which the winning team was luxuriating in its triumph, made it all the more unsettling. It just showed the tarnished backdrop against which each game was viewed by a portion of the public, gambling being a thin layer of grime clinging to the sport, ever-present despite the ongoing efforts to display its finer points.

Undaunted, the Red Stockings' tour continued. They ran off a string of fifteen victories against their eastern foes, winning the remainder of their scheduled contests in New York, New Jersey, Philadelphia, Baltimore, and Washington, DC, regaining some of their swagger in the process.

Once home, they played a series of games in Cincinnati and vicinity, as they had done the year before. Chief among their opponents was their western rival, the Forest City club. As in the preceding year, over the next few months these two teams clashed again in four contests. Only this time, rather than losing all four games, the team from Rockford showed steady progress. After succumbing in the first two matches in early July, the second game by the slimmest of margins at 14–13, they tied the Red Stockings a week later at 16–16. This game showed the fighting spirit of the Rockfords who, trailing 16–8 in the bottom of the ninth inning, came back to score eight runs and were threatening to pull ahead with two runners on base and two out. By then, darkness had overtaken the field, and the game was mutually agreed as a tie.

Finally, as the season was nearing an end, on October 15 the Forest City's beat Cincinnati on the fourth try by a solid 12–5 score. By then, Cincinnati had lost three more close games, two to the White Stockings of Chicago. Al Spalding and his Rockford teammates were justifiably proud of their victorious effort in finally defeating their western nemesis after almost two years of futility. Spalding had broken through with a sterling pitching effort in this last game, giving up only six hits during the whole affair. Granted, three of these were home runs, including one each by George and Harry Wright, while Spalding's own club collected sixteen hits, including four homers, of which he contributed one himself.[16] The local paper noted the "splendid victory was nobly earned, and [Rockford's] game, both at batting and fielding, has probably never been surpassed."[17]

Shortly before this triumph, during the previous month, the Rockford team traveled to play some exhibition matches in the region. One of these stops in mid-September was to take on a team in the little village of Marshalltown, Iowa. Though the town was small, word of the prowess of its ball club had intrigued the Forest City squad and a match had been arranged. What ensued was Albert Spalding's first encounter with a young ballplayer who would become an integral part of Spalding's base ball world for years to come as both a friend and one of the greatest hitters ever to play the game, Adrian Constantine Anson. In later years he was simply known as "Cap" for his role as the captain of the ball club on which he played.

At the time, fully a third of the Marshalltown nine was composed of players from one family, the Ansons. Henry was the founder of the town as well as father of two boys on the team, Sturgis being two years senior to Adrian. According to Adrian's autobiography, Henry was an early pioneer in an area of Iowa inhabited by the Pottawattamie tribe, building the first log cabin in the little hamlet of Marshalltown in 1852, where Adrian was "the first white child that was born [in that region]."[18]

The three Anson men were enamored with base ball. They were all powerfully built, competent in the field, and punishing as strikers. When the Forest Citys and Albert Spalding came to town to play an exhibition game as they were winding down their 1870 campaign, the village was packed with eager spectators. The local team did themselves and their followers proud, holding the score to an 18–3 loss to a team stocked with major-league talent. In fact, Forest City was so accustomed to romping over western competition by much greater scores that when they only managed to win by this relatively low margin, they promptly scheduled a rematch for the next day. The visitors won that match more convincingly, 35–5, but Adrian's father remembers that second game for an incident when Spalding "fired a vicious [pitch] straight in my direction. . . . I dropped the bat and walked out in his direction with a view of administering a little proper punishment to the frisky gentleman. He discovered what was coming, however, and meekly crawled back, piteously begging pardon and declaring it all a mistake."[19]

These games were an up-close-and-personal introduction for Albert Spalding to the no-nonsense Anson men. They made such an impression on the young star pitcher that later he recommended to Forest City club management that they offer contracts to all three Ansons. Henry and Sturgis declined, but eighteen-year-old Adrian jumped at this opportunity, signing a six-month contract with Rockford for "Sixty-Six and two third ($66 2/3) Dollars per month."[20] So, for four hundred dollars for the upcoming base ball season of 1871, Adrian Anson was to begin a career that would span twenty-seven years as a player and manager, setting handfuls of major league records and eventually becoming widely recognized as the greatest hitter of the nineteenth century.

Rockford's victories over the Marshalltown team were fully expected, but their hard-fought win over the Red Stockings was not. It capped a strong season for the Forest City club, winning fifty-one games against thirteen losses and one tie.[21] Conversely, the Red Stockings would finish the year with only six losses and one tie in seventy-four contests, an even better mark than Forest City but not nearly up to the impossible standard of perfection set the year before. The magical mantle of invincibility had been shredded, and the losses had a destabilizing effect on the players, whose tight bond that had enabled them to achieve their string of victories the previous year was coming undone. Moreover, the dedicated followers in the Queen City had seen their team's undefeated bubble burst, deflating their confidence in the prospects for the club going forward. Without the aura of all-conquering heroes that had surrounding their efforts, hometown interest dropped off rather precipitously.

Mirroring the deteriorating situation of the team was the physical condition of its star player, George Wright. Though only in his early twenties, his finely tuned musculature was often beset with a variety of ailments that sometimes sidelined ballplayers of his physicality. Lameness due to strained or pulled leg muscles happened periodically. These injuries were often caused by accelerating with blazing speed one minute, then suddenly changing direction, or churning down the basepath and stopping abruptly on first base after beating out a hit. In fact, in 1869 George suggested a rule change, accepted for the 1871 season, to allow a runner to overrun first base, in large part as an effort to avoid this muscle trauma.[22] It was indicative of the ongoing tinkering with the game's rules that persists even to the present day in attempting to make the sport safer and fairer for the players as well as more enjoyable for public viewing.

George was cursed with a series of increasingly serious leg injuries during the year. From early July through September, these issues caused him either to miss games entirely or play on a restricted basis. The three games against the Forest Citys of Rockford during July illustrated his physical ailments. On July 2, "George Wright did not play, owing to lameness; his place at short was taken by Harry."[23] Two days later, the teams met again, George playing shortstop this time, but the press noting his being "quite lame."[24] Finally, in their third meeting a week later on July 11, it was written that all the players were in good shape except "Stires [Rockford's left fielder] and Geo. Wright, each of whom nursed a game leg. They batted well, Addy running for Stires and Geo. also putting in a substitute runner."[25]

According to rules in effect at the time, a substitute could run the bases for an injured player who was batting, the substitute starting from behind home plate and running as soon as the batter struck the ball.[26] If George was able to field and hit, even in a weakened condition, his talents were of such a game-changing nature that Harry wanted him in the lineup, even if he couldn't run the bases. Harry's insistence on using his brother on July 11 in this limited capacity paid off in the seventh inning, when George came to bat with two on and two out. A newspaper captured the moment as follows, "George then took the stick and, smiling sweetly, sent the ball out into the right centre field, bringing both men home and taking his third sawdust receptacle, from whence [the substitute] came in on an over-pitch."[27] George's gimpy presence had still played a vital part as a striker in accounting for three runs in the late innings of what turned out to be a hard-fought tie ball game.

By early August he seemed to be recovering, playing shortstop and hitting three home runs in a 25–9 conquest of a team from Maryland. But the worst was yet to come for George. On August 9, Cincinnati was in the process of a surprisingly easy demolition of the powerful Haymakers of Troy. They were leading 15–4 during a thirteen-run scoring barrage in the sixth inning on their way to a 34–8 victory. While attempting to steal second base, George seriously injured his leg. Various accounts indicated he "slipped and fell, injuring his game leg"[28] or that the Haymaker second baseman "lost his balance and fell heavily onto Wright's leg"[29] as he approached the bag. George had hurt his knee so badly that he passed out from the pain and needed assistance to get off the field once revived.[30] A knee ligament had been torn during the incident, putting him on crutches for close to two months.[31]

Left fielder Andy Leonard would take George's place at shortstop in his absence, adequately covering the position, but the team felt the loss of the game's best player. It would be the beginning of recurring, often serious knee problems for Wright. In an interview with his great grandson Denny Wright, he noted that, according to family lore, due to this knee injury George began to seriously consider his long-term future beyond baseball and renewed his focus on the sporting goods business.[32]

On the field that day, watching from his position at third base for the Haymakers as George's calamity transpired, was the first Hispanic ballplayer to play professional base ball. Born Esteban Bellán in Cuba to a wealthy native Cuban father and an Irish mother, "Steve" was sent to New York City for higher education, attending a small Catholic school in the Bronx that was the precursor to Fordham University and learning the sport as a member of its sponsored club.[33] His skills at the game were readily apparent, and he left school to join the Unions of Morrisania in 1868. George was the star shortstop of the Unions that year, ultimately winning the "Clipper Award" for his efforts, while Steve was his teammate, playing right field for the majority of his tenure with the team before moving on the following year to the Unions of Lansingburgh, the vaunted Haymakers. Steve's fielding skills were quickly recognized, moving him to third base, where journalists eventually nicknamed him "The Cuban Sylph" for his graceful ability to handle most every ball hit his way.[34]

Esteban Bellán was a talented ball player. Though just average as a striker, he was a slick barehanded fielder and quick on the basepaths. But beyond his abilities, as a Hispanic what allowed him to play at all on the Unions, either of Morrisania or Lansingburgh, was his light complexion, which skirted the ban on his darker-skinned compatriots, who were barred from intermingling with white teammates on any National Association club. In fact, Bellán's career in this country lasted six years before he left for Cuba. Upon returning to his homeland, he was instrumental in accelerating a wider introduction of base ball there, turning it into a sport with a fierce following among the native Cubans as the pointed alternative to bullfighting, which was their Spanish occupiers' sporting preference.

In this country, Hispanics could now covertly claim a tiny place on a big league roster in the ever-evolving world of organized base ball, the major caveat being as long as they were fair-skinned enough not to elicit "concern." In contrast, Blacks continued to play the sport with sustained enthusiasm and proficiency, but this was invariably among themselves in intra-city contests or inter-regional matches, often resulting in the two best Black teams in an area competing for an all-Black city or state championship. On occasion, games might be scheduled against all-White teams willing to engage in this type of match, more for entertainment value than as a test of competitiveness.

In late September, one such game took place in Boston between two teams named the Resolutes, "one of them white, the other colored," the winner claiming rights to the team name.[35] As described in the newspaper, the game "resulted in a victory for the sons of Ham, who 'fought nobly' for their cherished title, out-playing their fair-faced friends at every point of the game, especially in the field."[36] The "sons of Ham" were welcome to compete versus an all-white squad for the right to be called the Resolutes, and they were praised for their ballplaying skills in the match. However, they would never be recognized in their "resolute" desire to individually be allowed to participate as teammates with white ballplayers of similar skill and purpose.

Integration of the ballfield was one thing, but the prohibition of doing so within a team's own composition was still holding relatively firm, at least on a visible basis. Interracial contests proved to be financially beneficial for both teams participating. As Black clubs became more competitive, both races "capitalized upon whites' fascination with Afro-American clubs playing on the same level as white clubs on the diamond. White baseball club owners found it to be good business to schedule games with black clubs who proved to be good gate attractions."[37] Yet it would take well into the next century for base ball to evolve into a truly competitive sport open to everyone, no matter his skin color, to play on each team in the game.

While some things seemed still to be set in stone, others were changing, and fast. The latter encompassed the very existence of the Cincinnati Red Stockings Base Ball Club. As the losses started to occur for the Red Stockings, few as they were, from a former position of invincibility they were untenable to the organization and its supporters. In mid-August, with just two losses and a tie marring their otherwise spotless record of scores of victories, team president Aaron Champion, along with the club's vice president Thomas Smith and secretary John Joyce, tendered their resignations. They claimed that they had neglected their business duties outside of base ball for too long and needed to refocus on these obligations. From recent historical research by author Tom Gilbert, it seems that one such responsibility gone awry was the political campaign that the lawyer Champion was immersed in that year for the office of county district attorney. He was in real danger of losing this election, and he and his staunch supporter, team secretary Joyce, were intent on righting this foundering effort, which ultimately failed.[38] For all the support these gentlemen had given to the team over the past few years, everyone was grateful. Still, it had all the markings of an initial wave of deserters, in this case perhaps jumping from one sinking ship to another.

By the end of the season in early November, the writing was clearly on the wall. Many years later, an article in the *New York Sun* somewhat hyperbolically summed up the feelings of the people of Cincinnati at the relative collapse of their beloved club, "Disappointment and chagrin marked the visage of every man, woman and child in Cincinnati who had the interest of the team at heart, and gloom like a pall spread over the town."[39] More measured, but no less emphatic, was Harry Ellard's description, "Public interest and enthusiasm had greatly weakened. People were no longer willing to put up the money to sustain the club in the way in which it should be. The players became dissatisfied, and it was quite evident that the nine and the club would soon be broken up. . . . The old Reds were offered increased salaries [by other clubs], much more than the people of Cincinnati would be willing to contribute."[40]

Indeed, the very fabric of the club was being torn at the seams. Accusations from all corners were hurled at the team, from mismanagement and greed of those running the club to players drinking and violating other club rules.[41] Two factions within the group were clearly forming: Harry and George Wright, Charlie Gould, and Cal McVey favored abstention from alcohol and a disciplined approach to the game, whereas the others were more liberal in their inclinations.[42] It all pointed toward an abrupt end to the short but mighty reign of the Red Stockings, the Titans of base ball. But very soon, in its place would rise a new Olympus, emanating from the East in the city of Boston.

6

Brothers in Arms

In the history of our nation, Samuel and John Adams were often confused for brothers as they fought valiantly side-by-side for the ideals of independence during the years leading up to the American Revolution as well as its aftermath. Rather, they were cousins living in the Boston area during the mid- to late 1700s, both to become signers of the Declaration of Independence and to be known as "Founding Fathers" for their tireless efforts to birth a new republic. John Adams would say of his older second cousin that he had "the most thorough understanding of liberty,"[1] while he, himself, would become the second president of the United States of America as a culmination of his endeavors. Although neither actually fought in the war that broke the chains of tyranny that had bound America to England, as philosophical brothers in arms both had struggled mightily to found and lead a country based on democratic principles.

Almost one hundred years after America declared its independence, George and Harry Wright would form a team in Boston that would be at the forefront of a league unlike anything that had gone before, eventually to be seen as a revolution within the infancy of professional baseball. Breaking away from the established National Association of Base Ball Players and its focus on amateur play, it would be dedicated to professional base ball players and the transformation of their sport from a game to a business. The demise of the Cincinnati Red Stockings Base Ball Club had left the door open for the overtures of those in Boston with an entrepreneurial spirit to seek out the Wright brothers to become the nucleus of a team to bring honor, esteem, and business opportunity to the city.

During the American Revolution, Boston had been a growing seaport and shipping hub of fifteen thousand inhabitants, the third-largest colonial city behind Philadelphia and New York.[2] Surrounding towns added another hundred thousand or so to the metropolitan population. By 1870, the number of inhabitants in the area had grown almost tenfold, to approximately nine hundred thousand, about 30 percent of whom lived in the city proper, in support of railroads shipping goods throughout the Northeast, seafaring international trade, increased industrialization, and general commerce.[3] The nearby community of Lowell had an amateur base ball team, as did Harvard University, but it was somewhat surprising that Boston itself lacked a ball club that it could proudly tout as its own versus the major centers of base ball activity in New York, Philadelphia, and Washington, DC.

Prosperous Boston businessman Ivers Whitney Adams felt it was his mission to right this wrong. Earlier in the year, he was one of several thousands who witnessed the Red Stockings overwhelm Harvard, 46–15, on the Union Grounds ballfield in the Roxbury area of Boston.[4] Adams eventually determined that to realize his ambition to have a first-rate ball club represent the city, "I should secure Messrs. Harry and George Wright first, and failing to secure them, let the whole matter drop."[5] It was plain to see that a powerhouse team could be fashioned around these two, just as had occurred in Cincinnati. Without them, Adams could not envision a reasonable path forward.

Shortly after the Red Stockings dissolved in November 1870, Adams invited George Wright to Boston to offer the opportunity to manage as well as captain a professional team.[6] As George remembered it,

> The man behind the move [Ivers Adams] sent for me to organize the team, and I was the first player to be placed under contract. They asked me to become Captain and manager, but I declined for the reason that I did not believe a man could be a successful playing manager, and upon my suggestion the Boston club secured my brother Harry from the Cincinnati Red Stockings by telegraph to become manager.[7]

George's doubting the potential success of someone simultaneously playing on and managing the same base ball team was somewhat surprising. After all, the Cincinnati Red Stockings had been undefeated in 1869 and won close to seventy games in 1870 with a manager who also played centerfield and occasionally pitched, namely his brother Harry. George had witnessed first-hand how Harry adroitly handled both tasks, in the process bringing home a winner. Perhaps George noted how much effort it took to simultaneously do both jobs well, and this might have prompted his declining the dual offer from Boston. But it also might have been his perception of how Harry had to painstakingly coax each individual on the club to work together as a cohesive unit that could have seemed intimidating to George.

Now, both George and Harry were the first players to commit to the new team. With them on board, Adams then convinced a handful of leading businessmen in the city to invest in the venture, raising fifteen thousand dollars to have on hand to allow Harry, as manager, to shop for the top-notch players needed to field a club with championship aspirations.

Harry wasted no time in this effort, immediately bringing Cincinnati teammates Cal McVey and Charlie Gould into the fold. He spurned others on the team who had chaffed at his disciplinary management style and preference for teetotalling. This included star pitcher Asa Brainard, whose heavy drinking and hypochondria were not suited to building the team Harry had in mind. In fact, over the winter the remaining Cincinnati starting nine of Brainard, Sweasy, Leonard, Waterman, and Allison all signed with the Olympics of Washington, DC. The disbanded Cincinnati club had effectively split in half, developing significant interest from most base ball observers as to which faction might triumph in their future encounters, testing Wright's disciplined approach to base ball versus a more lenient style of management.

To replace Brainard, Harry selected a hurler whom he had observed over the past two seasons maturing into a force to be reckoned with, Albert Spalding. The eight games the Forest Citys of Rockford had played against Cincinnati in that time span stuck in Harry's mind as he appraised this star-in-the-making, especially the progressively tighter contests during the past year that culminated in Spalding finally beating the Red Stockings with a sterling six-hitter only a few months prior. He traveled to Rockford to sign Spalding as well as his teammate Ross Barnes, a crackerjack infielder who also wielded a lethal bat. For good measure, leftfielder Fred Cone was convinced to join the other two. Thus, a hefty chunk of the Rockford team moved East in one fell swoop to combine with the four Red Stockings already part of the new Boston club.

According to Spalding's recounting of the meeting with Wright, he had to persuade Harry that these three Forest City players should be compensated openly as professionals rather than in an under-the-table arrangement, Wright being unsure which way to go on this point.[8] This hesitation toward overt professionalism seems rather unlikely for Harry, since he already had crossed that bridge in his well-known pay-for-play organizational development of the Cincinnati Red Stockings in 1869, and now along with his brother George had each signed a much-publicized contract with Boston for a salary of $2,500 per year.[9] But over the years, Spalding tended to stretch the truth in his recollections as he melded his superior performance and inflated ego into a rather unsubtle display of self-promotion.[10] Embellishing his organizational exploits, within the game of base ball or in expanding his sporting goods empire, would be a recurring pattern for Spalding.

Growing up on the prairie without a father, Spalding would look to Harry Wright, and in the future to other men of a commanding presence, as a paternal influence.[11] Albert already knew and respected Wright's history as the superlative leader of the Cincinnati club as well as his business exploits in the field of sporting goods, of which Spalding had actually saved newspaper clippings noting the Wright brothers' initial efforts dating to 1868.[12] He knew there was much to learn from men like Harry Wright, and Albert was intent on making the most of this association.

To round out the team, Wright selected a few lesser-known quantities. Harry Schafer, a third baseman with the Philadelphia Athletics, was valued for his slick fielding and accurate throws, but he was a modest striker, being jettisoned by the Athletics when they signed slugger Levi Meyerle to play third.[13] David Birdsall was a stalwart talent as a substitute outfielder and part-time catcher, and Sam Jackson was a young outfielder who could hit. Harry felt confident he could develop these individuals into strong, supportive cogs within the workings of his club. The Boston team now had a roster the Wrights both felt could carry them to victory.

By February, they also had a team name. Since the dismantling of the Cincinnati Red Stockings organization, Harry felt it was fair to bring with him not only a few of its players, but its uniform and associated nickname. The *Boston Journal* wrote that since "Harry Wright, now of the Boston Club, was the first person to don [the Red Stocking uniform], and now that the Cincinnati nine, which achieved such fame while wearing it, are no more, the uniform can, with perfect propriety, be selected by its originator for his new nine."[14] With the simple replacement of the old English "C" on the chest of their white flannel shirts with the lettering "BOSTON" in all capitals, the uniform was ready for repurposing in the service of a new Red Stocking team that would once again reach the heights of professional base ball.

As the winter came to a close, on March 17, 1871, representatives from the clubs intent on breaking away from the National Association of Base Ball Players met at a tavern in New York City to form an organization based on professional play. What followed that night was the formation of a group called the National Association of *Professional* Base Ball Players, led in large part by Boston's defiant stance as outlined by Harry Wright. Peaceful coexistence between professional and amateur clubs was no longer tenable under the old NABBP. As William Ryczek put it in his book on the subject, "That evening they would organize the association that would change the face of baseball forever. Henry Chadwick, the media's foremost proponent of the game of baseball, saw the meeting as a permanent parting of the ways between professionals and amateurs."[15]

Once that break was made, other details could easily be put in place. Within a few days, nine teams paid their ten-dollar entry fee to the new league, the money to be used to purchase a pennant for the league champion to display. The newcomers of Boston joined with other existing clubs, which included the Mutuals of New York, Unions of Lansingburgh (Haymakers of Troy), Philadelphia Athletics, Washington Olympics, Forest Citys of Cleveland, Forest Citys of Rockford (Illinois), Chicago White Stockings, and the Kekiongas of Ft. Wayne (Indiana).

After the professional league formed, the old NABBP simply evaporated. Amateur clubs that had shunned professionalism limped along in a loose confederation for a while, but the same issues of pure amateurism versus semi-professional play that had wreaked havoc with the NABBP caused its dissolution a few years later.[16]

To save organizational time, the new NAPBBP, subsequently just termed the NA, adopted most of the rules of base ball that had previously existed in the old league, as long as they supported the professional underpinnings of the NA. What appeared to be most needed now was a consistent system within this professional association to crown a league champion. Previously, the winner of that title was loosely determined in the NABBP when a challenge was thrown out to the existing "champion" of the previous year by a contender, usually resulting in a best-of-three game series, the winner being declared the new champion of base ball. This unofficial practice allowed for all sorts of confusion and controversy, with some title holders refusing or evading the petition to play the three-game set requested by worthy challengers, culminating in the venerated Cincinnati Red Stockings declining to play at all for the nominal championship, making it all irrelevant.[17]

What developed in the search for a new method to recognize a titlist was actually the outline of a structure for how the professional teams would play a season. The agreed-upon format required each team to play every other league team in a five-game series, one team winning three games and possibly constituting the end of the series even if all five games hadn't been played.[18] The league championship was determined by which team won the most series versus the others. Later, this shifted to awarding the pennant to the team that won the most games during the season.

The scheduling of each five-game series with every other team, including arranging travel and lodging across a geography that covered from east coast cities to western outposts, was a prodigious task that now took center stage for the new organization. Each team's secretary was charged with this effort. These individuals were often the club managers as well, as in the case of Harry Wright. Many already knew each other from past associations in the old NABBP, helping ease the strain a bit as this new process unfolded.

Since they were now on the doorstep of the 1871 season, the secretaries flooded each other with correspondence. Numerous letters crossed paths each day, which would continue throughout the year, as arrangements, revisions, postponements and other changes for various reasons developed. Squabbles over division of gate receipts between any two clubs was a major point of contention between some teams as they tried to negotiate forthcoming games together.

Harry Wright explained as much in an April letter to secretary of the Olympics of Washington, good friend Nick Young, describing his own failure to agree on the split of gate receipts with both the Eckfords and the Mutuals, resulting in not scheduling games with either.[19] In some cases, two teams had such a rancorous relationship that they preferred not to schedule games between each other at all. Such was the situation between The Haymakers of Troy and the Chicago White Stockings, where one club had tried to sign a player that the other team was attempting to get expelled.[20] In the end it was up to the nine charter members of the NA to reconcile their differences and arrange a suitable schedule of games. As Wright put it in another letter to Young, "Base ball is a business now, Nick, and I am trying to arrange our games to make them successful, and make them pay. . . ."[21]

The NA, America's first professional league, lasted only five years. Although it solved the amateur versus professional debate by its very existence, its quick embrace of virtually all the other operating procedures of the old NABBP meant the twin evils haunting the game itself in the eyes of the public persisted. These were the continuing presence of gambling as well as excessive drinking among many of the players. Gambling had been a part of the game from the very start of organized play, initially uncontrolled, then beginning to be driven underground. The sport grappled with this situation and its disruption of people's belief in what was hoped were legitimate contests between clubs. At the same time, the professionals, who had taken the place of amateurs playing the sport for healthful exercise and enjoyment, were becoming more difficult to control in their tendencies to drink and carouse after a ball game. Eventually, both would contribute significantly to the NA's demise. But while it existed, the league showcased the country's best talents in the sport for a wide variety of spectators to enjoy. And Boston would be the premier team within this realm.

The new Red Stockings had championship-quality ball players and superlative team management. Its core of relatively unmatched talent would remain with the team over the five-year existence of the NA, delivering four consecutive championships for Boston, from 1872 to 1875. Five men played on the team in all five years, four of them recognized as the best at their roles during that stretch.

Harry's raid of the Rockford club had provided half of this foursome, Albert Spalding and Ross Barnes. Spalding would come into his own as the most successful pitcher in the league, its first pitching superstar, by notching 204 victories with Boston against only 53 losses for an amazing .794 winning percentage.[22] Each year he won more games than the last, from 19 in 1871 up to an astronomical 54 in 1875, when he lost only five times. These figures constituted by far the best performance by any pitcher over the course of the existence of the league, let alone any pitcher over a five-year stretch. Just for good measure, Albert could hit the ball as well, batting above .300 in every year but his initial campaign with the Red Stockings.

As the foremost journalistic proponent of base ball with his contributions to the *New York Clipper* and other newspapers of the era, Henry Chadwick's assessment of Spalding over this time period provided an insightful view of the maturation of his skills and character. When Chadwick first observed Spalding's pitching performance, as a reporter covering Spalding's upset of the powerful Nationals of George Wright in 1867, Albert was just shy of his seventeenth birthday, a lanky teenager who had a precocious pitching talent. Chadwick later wrote that "he completely outwitted the National nine" as he pitched them to their astounding upset victory.[23]

Later, he made note of Spalding's unusual pitching style. "Spaulding [*sic*], in delivering the ball, holds it in his hands as if taking aim at the batsman with a gun; he then suddenly lowers his hands and delivers the ball quickly to the bat. One result of this movement is to bother the sight of the batsman in judging of the ball."[24] One could almost hear the gears grinding in Spalding's brain as he stared at the striker, formulating his plan to baffle him with the location and velocity of his next delivery.

More importantly, Chadwick came to appreciate Spalding as the epitome of scientific pitching, not just a hurler who threw the ball as fast as he could. By the end of 1872, he was referring to Spalding as the "most effective pitcher in the past season" for his use of various tactics to keep the hitters off balance, varying speed from fastballs to changeups, employing pinpoint accuracy and sometimes "catching a batsman napping . . . by the promptness of the return of the ball before the striker was prepared to meet it" and being rewarded with a strike for his efforts.[25] Baseball journalist and former player Sam Crane noted that the secret to Spalding's underhand fastball delivery was that "the back motion of his arm was higher than that of any other pitcher. He could get tremendous speed and also had a very deceptive change of pace."[26]

Above all, it appears the virtue Chadwick might have prized most in his assessment of Spalding was his "gentlemanly deportment and quiet demeanor" as he went about his business in a determined, focused manner.[27] At a time when base ball was subject to constant speculation about a player's wayward tendencies, here was a young man who represented the very best in what the game could offer, both in skill and behavior.[28] What better way to sell the American public on the virtues of the sport than to point to Albert Spalding and his very nature on display for all to see. With each winning pitching performance, Boston spectators embraced him as their hero.

Ross Barnes, Spalding's friend, was an outstanding ball player in his own right. He was a stellar second baseman, reaching balls that many thought impossible to field and then accurately flinging them to first base. Crane wrote that "Ross Barnes, in the opinion of the players who played on the same clubs with him, and also those who were his opponents, was the best second baseman the game had produced."[29] Crane noted that Spalding called him "one of the best all-around players the game has ever developed" and that George Wright said of Ross, "The best man I ever played along side of. He was a wonder."[30] Wright and Barnes made a formidable infield combination around the keystone sack. Upon Barnes's death in 1915, one article circulated stating "Barnes and George Wright together made the greatest pair that ever played at short and second base. . . . They were great hitters, remarkable fielders, and among the fastest of base runners."[31]

When first signed by Harry Wright for the 1871 season, Barnes was known for his outstanding play at shortstop. Harry thought so highly of him that he was willing to experiment by having his brother shift to second base while giving Barnes an opportunity to take over at short; however, this trial was extremely short-lived, Harry noting in late April "I have put George back in his old position, Barnes 2d [base], and they both play better."[32]

Barnes' capabilities as a striker were unmatched at the time, especially in what was termed "fair-foul" hitting. This skill helped him bat over .400 in three of his five seasons with the club, leading the league in 1872 and 1873.[33] Fair-foul hitting, permitted until 1877, was a technique considered the essence of "strategic" hitting at the time. Later it might simply be called a special case of "hitting 'em where they ain't," a phrase coined by turn-of-the-century outfielder and Hall of Famer Willie Keeler.[34] The fair-foul was a ground ball hit that started out fair but bounded foul across the baseline before it reached the base. With the controlled use of the bat on a pitched ball, a hitter could impart enough spin on the ball, usually by severely chopping down on it, such that when it hit the ground in fair territory the spin would take it foul, often with enough velocity to keep moving well beyond the baseline. This caused untold problems for the corner basemen as they rushed to capture the ball in foul territory and throw the hitter out. Sometimes it took the fielders so much time to corral the spinning sphere that a speedy batter might be atop second or even third base by the time it was returned to the field of play. No one mastered this hitting technique better than Ross Barnes.

For all of Barnes's outstanding capabilities, he occasionally exhibited behavior that didn't promote harmony within the team. This was something that the others on the squad just shrugged off; Ross was an amazing talent, and he and they both knew it. Yet, Harry commented in a letter to Chadwick about these disturbing traits,

> [Barnes] has provoked me time and again by his careless and indifferent
> play when the other players were trying their best. . . . If there is one player
> more than another that needs driving, it is he, . . . When playing, he is
> continually finding fault with the others, should they be unfortunate in their
> play, and he is playing well.[35]

Harry, as a manager, knew what he wanted from his players: their best efforts at all times, especially in support of the others playing the game. He needed to keep a close eye on Barnes's lackadaisical tendencies, not to mention his needling of teammates who might not be performing at their best. Barnes required periodic reminders from Wright if Harry was to obtain the teamwork and common cause for the club that he sought. From his experience, this was the only way in which a squad could remain cohesive and achieve greatness.

Of course, the other half of the "core four" were the Wrights themselves. Harry was lauded as the managerial wizard of the diamond, and George represented the very essence of what playing base ball was all about, unmatched as a shortstop, hitter, and base runner, albeit never to be the fastest man on the basepaths due to continuing knee problems. Before the 1871 season commenced, Henry Chadwick praised him as

> [combining] in himself pretty much all of the qualifications of a model
> player. . . . He is honest, the primary essential of a professional ball
> player. . . . He is good humored; then he is one of the swiftest and most

accurate throwers in the fraternity, and the fly ball he cannot get at and hold no one else can that we know of. And the way he picks up hot ground balls is a caution to the swiftest runner from home to first base.[36]

Over the course of five seasons together, Harry and these three players provided the stability as well as the spark in building a dynasty. Others would come and go, invariably Harry's eye for talent being able to spot replacements that could meet or exceed the performances of those who chose to move on. Former Cincinnati teammate Cal McVey was one of the first to leave, replaced at catcher by future Hall of Famer Jim "Deacon" White. Another was Cincinnati alum and first baseman Charlie Gould; his spot was taken by a player who would eventually be enshrined in the Hall, Jim "Orator" O'Rourke. A few old Cincinnati teammates would be signed by the club, outfielder Andy Leonard and all-purpose ballplayer Charlie Sweasy when Fred Cone and Dave Birdsall departed. Some who left even returned to Boston after a few years away, as was the case with McVey. And so it went, rarely missing a beat as the clubhouse door revolved around the four elite fixtures of the team.

The fifth player who would stick with Boston through their years in the NA was third baseman Harry Schafer. Although his light hitting prevented him from ever being considered a star, Wright valued Schafer just as he was, a dependable fielder who consistently gave his all for the team. He noted in a letter to Chadwick, "Schafer plays his best at all times, has his mind on the game when the ball is in play. . . . His throwing to first from across the diamond is very accurate, and his handling of short hits and medium-paced grounders is first class as is his fly catching. . . . Hot ground hits or ugly bounding balls are not his forte, he don't like to face or shin them. But he will take the hottest kind of thrown or batted ball on the fly."[37]

As the initial season of the NA began in earnest with this team, Harry and Ivers Adams were confident they were embarking on a journey that would bring a title to the city of Boston. A month before the campaign began, Harry and family moved into a house on New Heath Street in the Boston Highland section of the city, joined by brother George and Charlie Gould; next door was a boarding house where the former Forest City players Spalding, Barnes, and Cone resided along with the other four members of the team.[38] As one big extended family, Harry was able to watch over his own brood as well as the boys on the club in their daily preparations for the upcoming season.

They worked out at the Tremont Gymnasium in town, intermixing two to four hours of indoor training with practice outside when the weather permitted.[39] As could be gathered from a letter Harry sent in response to an inquiring manager of the Hornell Base Ball Association in western New York a number of years later, efforts in the gym or in outdoor preparation were fairly regimented. Harry offered valuable advice on both the physical conditioning and expected behavior of his players, provided free-of-charge to the Hornell manager by the best leader in the sport as he brought his team into preseason form.

> Exercise . . . throwing, pitching, and catching, running & jumping, swinging light clubs and dumb bells, rowing, pulling light weights, and in fact doing a little bit of everything to keep [the players] going and assist in making them supple and active . . . then meet on the grounds for practice . . . indiscriminate throwing, batting & catching. . . . No loafing or shirking should be permitted. . . . To preserve harmony in a nine it is essential there should be no 'chafing' or fault-finding with or by the players.[40]

As the players were brought into shape through these intense workouts that spring, what better way to officially start the first season of the NA than to have Boston's first league game be against the Olympics of Washington, pitting the two factions of old Cincinnati Red Stockings against each other on May 5. However, the game failed to match expectations. For one thing, it was marred by overly strict umpiring, resulting in an unheard-of eighteen walks issued to Boston and ten to the Olympics. For another, sick or injured players took their toll on the Olympics' lineup, with former Cincinnati stalwarts Charlie Sweasy absent due to illness and catcher Doug Allison retiring during the match with an injured thumb.[41] The Red Stockings had no such issues, just poor play with more than their share of mishandled balls at key junctures. However, Boston managed to prevail in the ninth inning with a patented Red Stocking rally of yore to score five runs in winning the contest, 20–18. The season had begun.

Disaster struck the following week. George Wright, who had suffered a torn knee ligament in August of the previous year, had recovered nicely from the incident during the off-season. Newspaper reports even had him skating, indicative of his steady healing.[42] Then, in a game on May 9, on the home field of the Haymakers of Troy, Wright collided with his own teammate Fred Cone in the sixth inning while chasing a fly ball, George severely re-injuring his leg and needing to be carried off the field.[43]

Reportedly, prior to the impact George had yelled out that he would handle the ball, but the noise of a nearby passing train drowned out his voice enough for Cone to fail to hear his call.[44] Cone was in the process of making the catch when George ran into him at full tilt, slamming his leg between the knee and ankle into Cone's knee.[45] This caused damage to the same leg he had hurt playing against the same team, the Haymakers, when he suffered his mishap the prior summer. Boston held on to win the game, 9–5, but it was to be the beginning of a difficult, extended stretch of depressing results for both George and the team.

At first, it appeared that George would be sidelined for only a few weeks, at least one newspaper account indicating that his accident had resulted in his kneecap being dislocated.[46] The day after the injury, Harry confided in a letter to his friend Nick Young of the Olympics that "[George] is now confined to his room from the injury to his leg received in the 'Haymaker' game in Troy. We *must* have him in condition for our game with you."[47] Harry was hoping for a speedy recovery for his brother, at least in time to face the Olympics later in the month. It didn't happen, and the Red Stockings went down to defeat.

By mid-June, George still was out of the lineup. However, he must have been showing enough progress for Harry to feel comfortable inserting him into the game against the Mutuals on June 17. In a letter to Young earlier that day, Harry summed it up when discussing his team, several of whom had injuries. "One of our 'cripples,' George, will play first base, Gould going to right field. George is yet very lame, not being able to run at all."[48] Indeed, George did play that day at first base and even batted, with a substitute running for him, but to no avail, the Mutuals winning, 9–3.

Even worse, it seems George had rushed things, as sometimes happens with athletes wanting to get back into action without fully recovering from their injuries. Exhibiting the primitive state of nineteenth-century medicine, having no X-ray capabilities, it was noted that "On a recent examination of [George's] leg, the surgeon found the injury more serious than at first anticipated, one of the bones having been broken."[49] He would not play again for another five weeks, finally appearing in an exhibition game late in July. Overall, the injury had kept him from participating in sixteen games, more than half of Boston's league schedule that year. Most consider it the major factor in the team finishing in second place, the only time they did not capture the pennant in the five-year existence of the NA.

Earlier in the year, even before the season had begun, George had resurrected his sporting goods business, this time with friend and teammate Charlie Gould as a partner rather than with his brother. Perhaps Harry was too busy to participate in George's new venture. Certainly, his hands were full with the myriad activities of constructing and managing the new Boston club as well as his secretarial duties arranging the logistics for the forthcoming campaign. By early April 1871, Wright & Gould was advertising their business of "Base Ball Goods of All Kinds" at 18 Boylston Street, sharing this location with the headquarters of the Boston Base Ball Club.[50] Later that month, an article in a Boston paper about the excitement of base ball and the new team in Boston noted, "The fine new club-room in the rear of Wright & Gould's Base Ball Emporium, No. 18 Boylston street, was formally opened last Saturday evening" with a large crowd attending a welcoming supper.[51]

While playing in Boston, George was intent on keeping an iron in the fire with his sports equipment enterprise. After Gould left the team following the 1872 season, Wright continued alone in the venture. He advertised as "Geo. Wright, Dealer in Cigars, Tobacco, &c., and all kinds of Base Ball Goods" and moved to 591 Washington Street along with the Boston team headquarters.[52] Harry supported his brother by giving him the contract to supply the Boston team uniforms, which was a nice chunk of business. George continued to deal in cricket materials as well.

By 1876, Harry had developed what he titled "The New Pocket Score Book," supposedly an improved variation of a score card that he sold through George's operations, now promoted as selling "Base Ball, Cricket, and Gymnasium Goods," this time at 39 Eliot Street, where the club had relocated its headquarters.[53] His dedication to keeping his venture alive during its infancy in Boston by offering a widening variety of items that might catch the fancy of the sports public would serve him well for the remainder of his life.

Over the next four years, George would largely recover from his re-injury of 1871, but he would be intermittently plagued by recurring knee problems for the rest of his base ball career. During that time he married a Boston girl of Irish descent, Abbie Coleman, in November 1872.[54] Rejoining the Red Stockings' core of proven talent and augmented with a supporting cast eager to show their own skills, the club would claim the championship in 1872 and each year thereafter. Every season they won more games than the last, such that by 1875 they amassed an incredible record of seventy-one wins against only eight losses, not once losing on their home field.[55] In fact, Boston won with such regularity that the NA would increasingly be referred to by base ball fans, jokingly if not derisively, as "Harry Wright's League."[56]

Besides being the star player of the Red Stockings, George began to dabble in other means to promote base ball as well as his role in it. In 1874, his image appeared in a poster that became the first endorsement of a product or service by an American athlete.[57] A Boston cigar maker, Nichols & MacDonald, licensed the right to use a photo of George, taken in 1871 or 1872, as the basis for the poster.[58] In the advertisement, George proudly stands under the prominent banner of "Red Stockings Cigar," accompanied by a drawing of a leg encased in a crimson stocking positioned horizontally. He's in an erect hitting posture, bat in hand, casually resplendent in his Boston uniform as he prepares to swing at a pitched ball. The rendering of a base ball diamond is in the background, a few players sketched on the field as well as some teammates on the bench, all in support of the King of the Game. He doesn't need to be puffing on a cigar for the subliminal message to be clear: George Wright, best of ball players; Red Stockings Cigars, best smoke in town.

George went on to publish two short books concerning his Red Stockings, not much more than glorified journals. The first was titled *Record of the Boston Base Ball Club Since Its Organization*, published in 1874. As the detailed subtitle explained it, "With a Sketch of All Its Players, for 1871, '72, '73 and '74, and Other Items of Interest."[59]

In literal keeping with the subtitle's theme, the book's cover displayed a hand-drawn sketch of George as its centerpiece, a handsome rendering of Boston's base ball legend. The contents were a hodgepodge of base ball information and lore, centered on a paragraph or two covering each of the Boston players during this time period, ghost-written by an unknown author presumably fed details from George about his teammates. This was followed by a compilation of newspaper articles on some of Boston's key games and accompanying box scores through the early 1870s, NA league statistics of clubs and players culled from the papers, and some humorous anecdotes thrown in for good measure. All told, a concise fifty-two pages. Although brief, it did contain something unusual in its tidy reviews of each of the players who competed for the Boston club over the 1871–74 time period. It served what must have been its purpose, to have the name, image and "comments" of base ball superstar George Wright published in a book for the public to peruse, making some money in the process.

His follow-up volume in 1875 was appropriately titled *George Wright's Book for 1875*. It was even shorter, at only twenty-nine pages, patterned in the same manner as his previous volume, but without the ball player sketches. However, it included something else rather novel, what he termed "My Base Ball Attitudes."[60] These "attitudes" were contained in a photographic plate of twelve images, nine of him posing to demonstrate batting techniques along with proper form for catching fly balls and fielding grounders, along with three of teammate Ross Barnes doing the same. Explanations of each accompanied the photos, describing how playing as shown could assist in improving an individual's skill at the game. The superstar's intent with the displayed images: read my book and learn to play the game just like me. The pictures of George and Ross demonstrating how to play base ball must have been irresistible to many followers of the game, rare images of star ball players giving visual lessons on the sport.

The first printed journal on base ball had appeared a few years before the Civil War. *The Base Ball Player's Pocket Companion*, published in Boston, was a short-lived annual guide available from 1859 to 1861.[61] It was supplanted by a more detailed annual publication, *Beadle's Dime Base-Ball Player*, which made its debut in 1860. This was written by the leading authority on the fledgling game, its chief journalistic proponent, Henry Chadwick. Its purpose was plainly stated,

> We . . . introduce this book to our readers, feeling confident that it will be interesting to all, and beneficial to many, especially to those who have but a limited practical knowledge of the game . . . to promote the interests and popularity of our American Game of Ball.[62]

Since the formal organization of the game was relatively new, the initial rules of the sport were provided in the guide, followed by a brief history and description of the NABBP, its workings, and the rules and regulations for 1860. Of great importance was to review the positions, their location on the field, and provide Chadwick's guidelines as to how they should be played. As well, roles of the batsmen, umpires, and scorers were discussed. For completeness, The Massachusetts variation of the game was covered as well as the New York game that would eventually become the standard. Finally, suggested procedures in the formation of a base ball club were noted. In total, this was a forty-page compendium explaining what base ball was and how to play it, supplemented with some historical flavor and bureaucratic regulatory background. All that was left was for Chadwick to shout: "Play Ball!"

By 1871, box scores of games were a rich field of data regularly mined. *Beadle's Dime Base-Ball Reporter for 1873* provided detailed examples of box scores and the information contained within, as well as how to actually follow and score a game, inning by inning, batter by batter. A competitive journal, *DeWitt's Base Ball Guide*, began publication in 1868, and Chadwick took over editing responsibilities of DeWitt's the next year in addition to continuing to edit Beadle's guide as well as performing his daily journalistic reporting of the game itself. Henry was irrepressible when it came to writing about the sport, supporting both *Beadle's* and *DeWitt's* well into the 1880s, when both journals finally expired due to superior competition.

However, in the mid-1870s, neither guide offered what George Wright's short books had conveyed in 1874–75: a view of the game, how to play it, and brief backgrounds on the heroic players from the champion Boston club, all from the perspective of the greatest player of the era, George himself. Next would come the promotion of America's national game across the ocean to an English audience that had never witnessed it before. It would be an ambitious undertaking that, for a good portion of 1874, consumed both the Wrights and Albert Spalding.

7

Spalding Follows His Vision

As part of the inaugural edition of DeWitt's Base Ball Guide, published in 1868, an item was buried deep within its pages that was both intriguing as well as prescient. It came as part of the coverage of the annual meeting of the NABBP that had occurred the previous December. Appearing on page 79, it was a proposal to send a group of ball players to England to demonstrate the game of base ball.[1] A pilgrimage to the very heart of the sporting world, where games of bat and ball had developed in varying manners over the years, to be crowned by the playing of cricket as the national sport. As time went on it was mostly forgotten, overtaken by the whirlwind of events and passions concerning base ball from which sprung the phenomenon of the Red Stockings, first in Cincinnati, then again in Boston.

However, Harry Wright had been cogitating on this topic for some time. Born in England before his family emigrated to America while he was still a baby, Harry harbored a desire to return to his native land to exhibit with a triumphal flourish what he felt was an even more exciting sport than cricket. There were others in the base ball fraternity who shared a similar vision, but none had acted upon it. As 1874 began, with his Red Stockings settling into what was becoming an expected repetition of success that had brought championships for his team the previous two years, Harry's mind again picked up this theme of international exposure of the game. He was confident that a visit to England would elicit enough genuine interest among the sporting public there to generate revenues to at least cover expenses, if not turn a profit, as well as boost gate receipts at home upon a victorious return to the States.[2] It was time for an overseas expedition to show the cricket crowd of London that there was another worthy game in town.

On January 5, Harry sent two letters off in quick succession, one across the Atlantic, the other south to Philadelphia. The former was in response to a standing invitation from an English cricket acquaintance, R. A. Fitzgerald, secretary of the esteemed Marylebone Cricket Club. Harry suggested that it was time to accept this request for two base ball nines from America to visit England to demonstrate the game to the "Mother Country." This would best be accomplished by a trip in August, "giving exhibitions of our National Game, and, should you think we could make it sufficiently interesting or attractive, we would be pleased to play, or rather try to play a cricket match or two."[3] Although the Wrights were two strong practitioners of cricket, the Americans only had a few other professional ball players whom Harry thought would be suitable for a competitive contest with the English cricketers, so he wanted to limit the potential for those matches.

The other correspondence was to James Ferguson, president of the Athletics Base Ball Club of Philadelphia, the only other team that had been able to claim an NA title, back in the league's initial season of 1871. Harry laid out his plans and inquired into the interest of the Athletics in joining the Red Stockings to make the trip, indicating they were Harry's preferred partner in this adventure, "giving exhibition games . . . and also to play some cricket matches which I have no doubt would prove attractive there, the two clubs to divide the receipts equally."[4] Further, Wright noted that someone needed to travel to England immediately to make all the necessary arrangements if the expedition was to successfully take place that year. In this regard, he pointed to a young ball player with whom he had much faith, Albert Spalding.

> Mr. A. G. Spalding has volunteered to take the trip and make all arrangements in regard to games, receipts, Hotels. . . . Spalding as a man and a Gentleman would be likely to create a very favorable impression, not only as a representative of the two clubs, but as an American base ball player and a professional, and that he has the necessary business qualifications I can readily testify.[5]

Harry had developed a close relationship with Spalding, exchanging opinions and valuing his straightforward and honorable nature, not unlike his own.[6] Others may have entrusted this mission to someone more senior with greater administrative experience, but Harry felt comfortable that this imposing, self-confident young man would handle the negotiations as he himself might conduct them.

As usual, Spalding was to remember somewhat differently how he had arrived in England as the emissary of the American base ball venture. In his autobiography, he described promoters conceiving of a trip to England in 1874 as a reciprocal initiative by America in response to various visits that British cricketers had taken to the United States over the past decade to develop interest in their national game.[7] Although this was true, he failed to acknowledge that various thoughts about this journey had been expressed by many, some as early as 1867 as noted in the DeWitt Guide. He then implied that a dreamy vision of his own desire to take a trip across the ocean precipitated it all.

> While playing with the Boston team, in 1874, I became possessed with
> an intense yearning to cross the Atlantic. I wanted to go to England. . . .
> It occurred to me that since Base Ball had caught on so greatly in popular
> favor at home it might be worked for a special trip for me, to be followed
> by a second one, in which a couple of teams could be taken over to
> introduce the American game to European soil.[8]

No doubt Spalding felt his presence was vital to making the first-ever visit of organized professional base-ball to England a reality. He went to London and was joined by a Harvard student named Warren Briggs, to discuss the alternatives and agree to the schedule of exhibition games, locations, and expectations for the American party related to this tour.[9] For a twenty-three-year-old, Spalding handled it all quite well, mixing with the upper crust of the English cricket establishment. More pointedly, he cultivated a supportive relationship with British cricket expert C. W. Alcock, secretary of the Surrey Cricket Club, who was charged with making detailed arrangements in England while Spalding traveled home with the good news about the impending trip.

In his eagerness to have the English sporting world accept his proposed base ball tour, Spalding agreed that cricket would constitute a significant portion of the program. Seven matches between the two countries would be part of the competition, many more than thought prudent by Harry. This would now necessitate "emergency" cricket instruction to the ball players, even practicing onboard ship while crossing the ocean, if they were to give the British any type of competition.

Despite this somewhat naive overreach on Spalding's part, he returned home with what he thought was a splendid agreement. He fully expected that his efforts had seeded fertile ground for the expedition, noting in a newspaper editorial on the subject after his return,

> To be sure, our game is little known in England, but the novelty of the thing, together with our superior fielding, which base ball develops to a greater degree than cricket, will prove attractive and be appreciated, for it is a well-known fact that no people take more interest in out-door sports than the English.[10]

As it turned out, Spalding's reliance on Alcock, though well-connected within the cricket fraternity as well as the English journalistic world, would place the focus on the cricket arrangements rather than base ball, resulting in generally scant publicity for the latter. This often led to smaller crowds than anticipated, especially at the venues outside of London. In all, fourteen games of base ball were to be played between Boston and Philadelphia as they crisscrossed England and ended in Dublin. Added to the seven cricket matches, plus travel, it was an ambitious schedule. The Americans were excited to be displaying the sport of base ball to as many British spectators as possible in its initial organized debut across the Atlantic.

The day before the ocean voyage commenced, on July 15, the two clubs played a tight game before an estimated six thousand spectators at the Athletics home field, the local team emerging victorious, 6–4. It was the type of exhibition of play the soon-to-be adventurers hoped to offer the curious crowds in England, with superb fielding and timely hitting, all lasting less than two hours compared to a cricket match that typically consumed two days.[11]

Boarding the steamship *Ohio* the next day, the two teams had each brought along their starting nine plus a few substitutes. They were accompanied by journalists as well as numerous dedicated supporters eager to see for themselves what would unfold. For the Boston club, Harry and George decided to bring along their younger brother Sam Jr., an infielder who was added to the roster for his accomplished skills at cricket. Included in the contingent for the Athletics was star pitcher Dick

McBride, who also was a superb cricketer, and a young Adrian Anson playing right field for the club.

The crossing lasted less than two weeks, but it took some time to get used to the sea. The first day out both teams arrived for breakfast, but only four remained to finish their repast, the others fleeing topside to deposit their meals into the ocean.[12] The "tourists," as they were called, landed in Liverpool on July 27. In his 1875 book on base ball, George described the anxiousness of brother Harry to be the first of the group to set foot on English soil. It turned out to be a harrowing experience, Harry attempting to balance a satchel in each hand as he jumped ashore, slipped on the rain-slicked dock and fell, "landing in England solid" as George wryly noted.[13] Tragedy was averted; an injury to Harry, especially at the outset of the string of matches to be played, would have been a major calamity.

As it turned out, the Liverpool stop presented its own concern, simply because the lack of advanced publicity added up to crowds in the hundreds rather than the thousands that had been anticipated.[14] Nevertheless, the inaugural game of base ball was an exciting one, the two teams tied at nine apiece in the eighth inning and remaining so until the tenth, when the Athletics scored five runs and prevailed, 14–11. Though it proved an interesting initial display of the sport to the British, the local paper described it tritely as "an improvement on the old [game of] 'rounders,' and although it is scarcely likely to supersede the favorite games of our summer seasons in England, yet it is an undoubtedly splendid means of exercising the limbs and muscles."[15]

This would be the fate of base ball's first formal introduction as the tour proceeded through Great Britain. What was generally reported was a politely condescending comparison of the sport to the well-known English child's recreation of "rounders," supplemented with support for the game as a physical work-out, all of it damning with faint praise. After all, it just wasn't cricket, was it?

After another game in Liverpool, Boston winning 23–18, the visitors moved on to Manchester, where the crowds were somewhat larger due to better advance notice of the scheduled contest. The newspapers were more favorable here, giving praise for the pregame exhibition of throwing and catching by the players as they tossed the ball with great speed and accuracy. A lively contest, won 13–12 by Philadelphia, featured such strong fielding that "Veteran cricketers on the ground really asserted that they had never seen a ball handled so deftly, though occasionally might be heard the remark—'That wouldn't do in cricket.'"[16]

In fact, the Americans' fielding was the singular skill that was admired by the English as they compared base ball to their beloved cricket, the seemingly casual ability of the visitors to catch screaming line drives, field sharply hit grounders and to throw with accuracy to any base. By the time the teams had given their exhibition matches to crowds in London, where the first ball game drew five thousand intrigued onlookers, the sheer ability of the Americans handling the base ball was the wonder of the show. Subsequent games in Sheffield and Dublin elicited similar responses. A pleasing footnote to the tour for Harry came at his birthplace of Sheffield, where his Red Stockings won both base ball games against the Athletics.[17]

The scheduled cricket matches began in London. Since the Americans were mostly novices at this game, they were given an advantage of playing eighteen men versus eleven or twelve for the veteran English teams. This larger number of players was not as overwhelming as it sounded, since in cricket there is no designated out of bounds, the ball being able to be hit in front of as well as behind the batter, thus significantly diluting the advantage of having more fielders spread across a larger area. But having more players did bridge the gap of experience suffered by the Americans, and their superior fielding capabilities helped to even the competitions.

The first of the cricket matches was against the revered Marylebone Cricket Club, an institution within the sport. For the most part, the American's "swung for the fences," taking great hacks at the ball using the flat, wide cricket bat rather than their accustomed smaller, cylindrical base ball club. The result, though "bad form" in cricket, where the batter is expected to make more blocking swings to prevent the bowled ball from hitting the wicket, was tremendously successful against the English. Spalding and Anson were particularly adept at unleashing great fly balls, several of which exited the grounds entirely and scored many runs in the process. Spalding also noted that "George Wright put up the real thing, both as to form and achievement, and helped our score amazingly."[18] When the dust finally settled, the Americans had beaten the expert cricketers of Marylebone by a score of 107–105. Cricket, American style, propelled the New World to emerge undefeated versus the Old in the remaining six contests.

When the tour finished at the end of August, Boston had won eight base ball games to the Athletics' six. However, the expedition lost money due to the smaller-than-expected turnout. As Anson put it in his autobiography many years later, the visitors might be thought of as the Argonauts of base ball, "though they brought back with them but little of the golden fleece."[19] Specifically, the Red Stockings financials for 1874 note their portion of the gate receipts in Europe as $1660.69, while their traveling costs for the trip totaled $2,318.13, yielding a net loss of $657.44.[20] It was a similar situation for the Athletics.

Most English spectators were certainly not convinced of the sporting virtue of base ball versus their cherished cricket. Anson noted that it was near-impossible to convert them to the merits of the game due to "the deep-rooted prejudice of the English people against anything that savored of newness and Americanism."[21] This statement would later be seen as rather ironic given his own prejudiced views on race relations in base ball that he would vocally express over the coming years. Still, the Americans had acquitted themselves admirably, gaining grudging praise from the English for their rugged physicality as well as their splendid skills at the sport.

Spalding gave little concern to the financial losses of the tour. In his autobiography, he recounted his memory of what amounted to a combination of the first great business project of his life with his athletic accomplishments, giving it all a resoundingly positive review. He quoted from the *London Field*'s take on the sport: "It is a fast game, full of change and excitement. . . . To see the best players field, even, is a sight that ought to do a cricketer's heart good, the agility, dash, and accuracy of timing and catching by the Americans being wonderful."[22] They had sensed what he already knew: that base ball's virtue was in the joyful abandon of its playing rather than the correctness of its form. At the same time, he undoubtedly noted the negative effect the tour's paucity of advertising had on attendance, a lesson he would draw upon repeatedly in the future.

Once back in the States, the Red Stockings took care of their other main item of business by securing their third straight NA championship. Little did Harry Wright realize that Albert Spalding was already envisioning his next venture, something even more daring and certainly potentially more profitable. His newfound celebrity from the visit to England led Spalding to thoughts of being more than another ball player, perhaps graduating to managing his own club.[23] The methodical success of the Red Stockings as they won yet another pennant, steered by the incomparable player/ manager Harry Wright, showed how it could be done. Wright had looked east, to Boston, for his opportunity after the Cincinnati Red Stockings had disbanded. Now Spalding was to cast his gaze in the opposite direction, west to Chicago, in his quest to grow his future in base ball.

Back in 1871, the inaugural year of the NA, the Chicago White Stockings were one of the nine teams that had paid their ten-dollar entrance fee as a professional base ball club, the ninety dollars going to the purchase of a pennant to be awarded to the league champion for display. The year before, when the White Stocking had first formed, the city boasted a population of almost three hundred thousand, ten times its size only twenty years earlier.[24] It had now become the largest city in the west, and fifth largest in the country, home to both native-born and a growing immigrant contingent who supported a fast-industrializing community. Foodstuffs, animal as well as agricultural, were processed here and sent by rail to feed a growing eastern population. Industrial manufacturing was part of the growing city economy, transforming raw materials into goods shipped throughout the country. And base ball had become firmly entrenched, followed passionately by many in town, especially a multitude of immigrants who played and watched it with civic and national pride.

The Chicago White Stockings were certainly a powerhouse, in early fall leading the NA by a slim margin over both the Philadelphia Athletics and the Boston Red Stockings, setting up great interest in the remaining league games in October. Exhibiting the public's concern about gambling, as well as the locals' feeling of the game's control by forces back east, a newspaper article about one contest ended with a plea "that there will be no games 'thrown' for the sake of keeping the championship in the East."[25]

On the evening of October 8, all that became an afterthought. A fire started in a barn outside of town and soon spread into the heart of the city. It raged for over a day, destroying 17,500 buildings, claiming the lives of close to three hundred people, and leaving ninety thousand homeless.[26] The fire destroyed the White Stockings' Lake Park field, with only a few of the team spared loss of home and belongings due to their serendipitously living outside the city.[27] No White Stocking was injured, but most players had lost all their property and were financially ruined.

The team gamely completed its season on the road, suited up in borrowed uniforms and playing before small crowds. The players' attention divided, the team lost most of its remaining games and with them the pennant, folding shortly thereafter, not to be resurrected until 1874.

By 1875, the reconstituted team's administration included its secretary, William Hulbert. He was a self-made, prosperous businessman who had lived in Chicago from an early age and loved the opportunity it provided to those adventurous enough to grasp it. He often stated his feelings about his adopted hometown with a favorite expression, "I would rather be a lamp-post in Chicago than a millionaire in any other city."[28] Hulbert, like a number of businessmen in town who wanted to assist in its growth, eagerly invested in the White Stockings in 1871 when they became a charter member of the NA. After the Chicago Fire of 1871 and the subsequent collapse of the franchise shortly thereafter, he and others supported its revival in 1874. But the team was a collection of mediocre talent for the next few years, not a realistic challenger for the championship. Hulbert wanted to do something about it, and Albert Spalding provided that opportunity.

At the time, Spalding was at the height of the most successful professional pitching career in the sport, playing for the most dominant team in the NA, surrounded by superlative teammates and a managing genius who trusted him and supported his efforts. Perhaps he could have been more satisfied with all that he had achieved in his young life, surveying the base ball world from its pinnacle at twenty four years of age in 1874. Yet, he envisioned much more for himself.

In the background, disturbing trends in the sport were evolving into distressing habits by the end of the 1874 season. The Red Stockings were winning with such regularity by the end of that year, taking their third consecutive title that fall, that the public was losing interest in attending the games, resulting in lower gate receipts. Gambling on the contests' results, though discouraged at many ballparks, was just as prevalent in saloons and pool halls right around the corners from the stadiums. "Hippodroming," the practice of some ball players being paid to throw matches, continued to erode confidence in the legitimacy of the games themselves. And the number of those in the sport who were drinking heavily, called "lushing," was growing with every season, players as well as spectators becoming rowdier with each slug of liquor.[29]

Spalding was sick of it all. He yearned for a system of controls for the game, something that the NA, as an association of ball players, didn't appear capable of or interested in addressing.[30] The first step had already been taken, the professionalization of base ball, such that under-the-table payments no longer were needed to induce talented players to join a team. This had turned the sport from a game played for exercise and enjoyment into a business, with players demanding a market wage for their services, and ball clubs seeking uniform payment by spectators to support the entertainment being provided. However, it did not address the excesses of the sport that were so blatantly out of control.

Spalding knew one thing: he would not let events dictate his next moves. It was time to take control of his own destiny, to employ his own motto of success that would drive him throughout his adult life, "Everything is possible to him who dares."[31] In early 1875, he met a man who seemed to share this view, someone to whom he *and* the sport could hitch their stars. As Spalding saw things, this was William Hulbert.

> He seemed strong, forceful, self-reliant. I admired his business-like way of considering things. I was sure that he was a man of tremendous energy—and courage. He told me of the interest of Chicago in Base Ball . . . how she had been repeatedly robbed of her players, and, under Eastern control of the Professional Association, had no recourse. I told him that I was quite familiar with the entire situation; that it was the same all over the West—no city had any show under the present regime; that the spirit of gambling and graft held possession of the sport everywhere; that the public was disgusted and wouldn't patronize the pastime.[32]

As they discussed the situation, he knew that it would only be a matter of time until Hulbert became his boss as well as his next mentor. For his part, in Spalding, Hulbert suspected he had found the key to remaking his team into the club that had come so close to becoming league champions years before until a devastating fire had destroyed much of his city and with it his team's chance at greatness. He instinctively knew what to say next, appealing to Albert's western roots and promising, "If you'll come to Chicago, I'll accept the Presidency of this Club, and we'll give those fellows a fight for their lives."[33] All that remained to iron out were the details.

By mid-1875, Hulbert had traveled to Boston and signed Spalding to one of the most lucrative contracts yet for a base ball player, an agreement for the 1876 season comprising a salary of $2,000 plus 25 percent of net gate receipts as well as a covert side-deal for an additional 30 percent of the net profits of the club.[34] In exchange for this compensation, besides becoming the team's pitcher he would assume the captaincy and managerial duties for the squad. In 1876, the board made him secretary of the club, just as Wright was in Boston. As player, captain, manager, and secretary all rolled into one, he had effectively become the Harry Wright of the Chicago White Stockings. In what seemed like an instant, Spalding had taken a great leap in his grand ambition to expand his already large presence in the base ball world.

As much as he desired to take this next giant step in his career, Spalding also wanted to make sure he would be playing for a winner.[35] Star Boston teammates and fellow westerners Ross Barnes and Cal McVey needed little persuasion to accompany Spalding on this adventure, and catcher Jim "Deacon" White required just a little more convincing. Barnes was offered a salary of $2,000 plus 25 percent of the profits, but not the extra 30 percent kicker used to sweeten Spalding's deal; McVey a straight $2,000 annual compensation, and White a salary of $2,400 plus $100 if the club was a financial success.[36] Thanks to Spalding's groundwork, Hulbert signed them immediately to contracts for the following year.

Albert then recommended that Hulbert grab two more gems from the Athletics of Philadelphia, having already paved the way with infielders Adrian Anson and Ezra Sutton to join the White Stockings. Spalding accompanied Hulbert down to Philadelphia to ink the deals there, signing both for $2,000 each.[37] In one trip east, Hulbert had sewed up six of the best ball players in the game, the talent that would make the Chicago club league champions in 1876. Sutton never did come to Chicago, deciding to stay with the Athletics. Anson had similar thoughts due to his engagement to a woman from Philadelphia who did not want to leave her hometown. In the end he honored his commitment to Spalding and his contract with Hulbert, taking his bride to Chicago and becoming a star player there for over two decades.

Still, it was only July of 1875, and if league rules were to be followed, all of this needed to be kept under wraps for the balance of the season. The NA strictly forbade signing a ball player to a contract during one season for the next one; this could only take place after the season had ended. The feeling was that the ball player signing before the end of the season wouldn't give maximum effort during the balance of games with his exist-ing ball club, looking forward instead to playing for his new employer.[38] Now it would be up to these ball players to act as if nothing had occurred in their clandestine meetings with Hulbert, meanwhile giving their best for their current clubs. Ordinarily, this would be tough enough for one individual to accomplish; to have this group keep it all under wraps until the end of the season seemed impossible. In fact, the secret only lasted two weeks.

By July 21, the newspapers had gotten hold of the information concerning these ball players' plans to jump to other clubs the next year.[39] Much finger-pointing accompanied the news. Some papers claimed that Spalding, Barnes, McVey, and White, the "Big Four" from Boston, had a moral responsibility to inform Red Stockings' management about their offers from Chicago so that Boston would have a chance to meet these financial terms. Others plainly stated that they hadn't followed the league's rule not to contract with others until the season was complete, so they should be banished from base ball. A few opinions were less defensive, some noting that Harry Wright had enough firepower left on the team such that he could find replacements and perform well during 1876, going so far as to propose that "The friends of the Red Stockings are not 'scared' by any secession, present or prospective."[40]

Through all the commotion created by this situation, the season of 1875 ended much as it had started for Boston's expectations as a championship ball club. The Red Stockings again captured the NA title, victorious in seventy-one games against only eight losses, not losing once in their home park. If anyone had wagered that they would see lesser efforts expended by even one of the "Big Four" after the disclosure of their mid-season deals with Chicago for 1876, they would have decisively lost their bets. Spalding turned in his best year ever, winning fifty-four games and losing only five; Ross Barnes hit .364, twenty-four points above his batting average of the year before and topped the NA in hits with 143; Cal McVey batted .355 with a league-leading thirty-six doubles and eighty-seven runs batted in; and "Deacon" White won his first batting title with a .367 average.[41] Indeed, The "Big Four" had lived up to their stellar reputations, despite their future commitments to another team.

Still, at season's end there was talk that the much-publicized contract-signing violations that had occurred in mid-season would necessitate a stern reaction from the NA, probably to include expulsion of those players involved. As Spalding recalled it in his book, he was so concerned about being banned that Hulbert responded with a lightning bolt of inspiration, "Spalding, I have a new scheme. Let us anticipate the Eastern cusses and organize a new association before the March meeting [of the NA], and then see who will do the expelling."[42]

As was his tendency, decades later Spalding was to claim it was his own idea to make a clean break by forming a new base ball association, which was eagerly supported by Hulbert.[43] Either way, the two men agreed that a new league could get ahead of the potential problem they had created with the premature contract signings. The added benefit, which would be the real key to future control of base ball as a business, was that their plan for this new organization would separate the administration of the endeavor from the players themselves, a clear division of management and labor. This would be the path they would pursue in order to have each concentrate on what they logically did best. The team's organizational management would be focused on the details of running the operation. This would be separate and distinct from the players' and coaches' duties, who would concentrate on delivering improved performance on the field. If handled correctly, this division of responsibility would generate more money for everyone while providing an improved sporting experience for the public.

The National Association of Professional Base Ball *Players* was about to disappear, much as its predecessor had five years before, to be replaced by the National League of Professional Base Ball *Clubs*. The owners of these teams were hoping to increase their financial returns on what, to date, had been a marginal investment, barely covering costs in exchange for not much more than bragging rights as to who had the best team. More importantly, at least to the owners, this new direction would inevitably cede them almost complete control over the finances of the sport, a powerful position against which the players would eventually rebel.

By the spring of 1876, Hulbert, with Spalding's help, would unite the professional clubs with this approach. Hulbert accomplished his goals in a succession of closed-door meetings, first with the western clubs, followed a few weeks later with those of the east. The western teams were all for a new league that would provide more equality between clubs, distinctly lacking in the NA, where eastern teams continually raided the west for talent and often failed to honor their scheduled games with smaller western competitors that often generated meager gate receipts. As for the eastern contingent, Harry Wright was supportive of this direction, concerned about the future of base ball if it remained unreformed; his approval ensured Boston's cooperation, vital to bringing the other eastern teams on board.[44]

Under the banner of cleaning up the mess that the NA had become, with its loose organizational structure, haphazard enforcement of regulations, and inability to control the gambling and general rowdiness surrounding the game, everyone signed onto the plan. A club's entry fee was increased to $100 from its previous $10, hopefully creating more serious commitment to the venture versus previous casual involvement by mediocre teams. To boost attendance, teams would only be allowed in cities having a population of 75,000 or more, unless otherwise agreed by unanimous consent; to generate more revenue per team in any given city, only one club was allowed within that city or its general vicinity.[45] An agreement to forbid Sunday games was a hard sell, but it helped place the game on a moral high ground as well as limit the type of spectator who might use his day off to drink, carouse, and make mischief in the stands at a Sunday afternoon contest. Strict rules were installed to govern the conduct of players, especially related to gambling and contracts. This new system was quickly agreed to by the eight teams making up the league: Boston, Philadelphia, New York, and Hartford from the east joining Chicago, St. Louis, Cincinnati, and Louisville in the west. It would be a new start for a game that was badly in need of an overhaul.

Henry Chadwick referred to the situation as "a startling coup d'etat," concerned that the needed reforms for the game might have been agreed too hastily, without input from a wider group of affected participants, like himself.[46] But opening the discussion to a larger audience would have slowed down the process considerably, and Hulbert was not about to impede his immediate plans, either for Chicago's base ball glory or for the game in general. Morgan Bulkeley of the Hartford club was chosen as the first president of the new league, but everyone knew that William Hulbert was the power behind the throne; a year later, he would officially become league president, holding that office until his death in 1882.

While Hulbert was orchestrating his bloodless coup, Albert Spalding was preparing to launch the company that would cement his name forever in base ball history. "Spalding & Bro." was the title of the company that he and brother J. Walter Spalding were to unveil to the public in early 1876, a sporting goods business that would come to dominate an industry that it, in large part, created. Spalding had harbored this vision from almost a decade earlier while following the exploits of the Wright brothers in both base ball and their sports equipment business. Now, just as he had adroitly executed his change in base ball hosiery from red to white, to spectacular personal benefit, Spalding & Bro. would be an almost immediate success.

Founded in February 1876, by early April, even before the season began later that month, the brothers boldly advertised their "Western Baseball Emporium." The lead to the Sporting section of advertisements in the *New York Clipper* featured "Spalding's New League Ball" just above that of George Wright, "Dealer in Baseball & Cricket Goods."[47] Proudly noted was that the ball itself was made under the patent of "L. H. Mohn," a misspelling of L. H. Mahn of Boston, who years earlier had bought a patent on a base ball that he profitably made and sold under his own name as well as was now producing under license to Spalding.[48] Albert and Walter's company was indeed a larger family affair, partially capitalized with an $800 investment from their mother, Harriet, and bringing in Albert's brother-in-law in the coming years, eventually becoming known worldwide as "Spalding & Bros.," an iconic brand to the sporting public. That spring, friend and benefactor John Walsh, president of the Western News Company of Chicago, placed a generous purchase order for ten thousand base balls for his employees, priming the pump for a future of sales to the public as well as the professional marketplace.[49] Shortly afterward, Hulbert made sure Spalding was named the National League's exclusive supplier of base balls. As in most things he touched in the world of base ball, with a supportive network and careful planning to achieve his vision of the future, everything seemed possible for Albert Spalding.

George Wright, Boston Red Stockings, 1872. *Courtesy of Bruce Garland*

Albert Spalding, Boston Red Stockings, 1874. *Courtesy of New York Public Library, A. G. Spalding Baseball Collection*

1869 Forest Citys of Rockford, Illinois. Spalding, *third from right*, would turn nineteen in September. *Courtesy of Byron Museum of History, Byron, Illinois*

1869 Cincinnati Red Stockings taken at Washington, DC, studio of famed Civil War photographer Mathew Brady. *Standing, l to r:* Cal McVey, rf; Charlie Gould, 1b; Harry Wright, cf/mgr; George Wright, ss; Fred Waterman, 3b. *Seated, l to r:* Andy Leonard, lf; Doug Allison, c; Asa Brainard, p; Charlie Sweasy, 2b. *Courtesy of Cleveland Public Library/Photograph Collection*

PICTURES BY SMITH & BOUSLEY, OF SALEM, MASS.

"Base Ball Attitudes," showing how to play the game. From *George Wright's Book for 1875*. George is in nine images, Ross Barnes in three (*first row, third image from left; second row, first image on left; third row, second image from left*).*Courtesy of Historic New England*

1879 NL champion Providence Grays at hometown Messer Park. *Standing, second from left*, John Ward, p; *third from left*, Joe Start, 1b. *Kneeling:* George Wright, ss/mgr. *Standing, right of George*, Jim O'Rourke, rf; *far right*, Paul Hines, cf. *Courtesy of Providence Public Library/Rhode Island Collection*

A. G. Spalding, Spalding & Bros. sporting goods industry pioneer, circa 1880. *Courtesy of Chicago History Museum, ICHi-061811*

A. G. Spalding, retired business mogul, 1910. *Courtesy of Bain Collection, Library of Congress*

87 UNION SQR N. Y.

World Tour players visit the Sphinx while they play a game in the Egyptian desert, February 1889. *Courtesy of New York Public Library, A. G. Spalding Baseball Collection*

THE BASEBALL TOURISTS AT THE CLUB HOUSE, KENNINGTON OVAL, LONDON

1888–89 Spalding World Base Ball Tour, Chicago and All-America teams at the Kennington Cricket Oval, London, March 1889. Spalding and Wright in center, Albert on left, and George on right in long black coats. *Source: Harry Palmer's 1889 book* Athletic Sports in America, England and Australia, *p. 409*

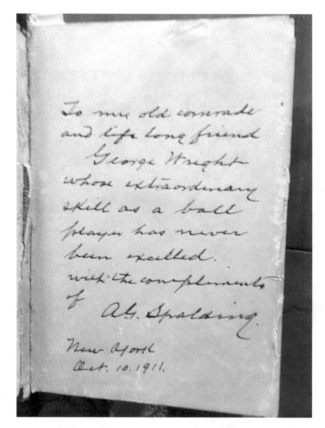

In 1911, Spalding published his highly successful book on the history of baseball, *America's National Game*, doubling as his autobiography. He sent a copy to George Wright with this inscribed tribute. *Courtesy of Bruce Garland*

8

Trouble with the Curve

There was something very fitting about George Wright being the first batter in the initial game of the newly formed National League of Professional Base Ball Clubs. As someone who had been the acknowledged superstar of the sport for the better part of a decade, George's place in the annals of base ball history was already assured. Positioned in the leadoff spot in his team's batting order, customary for him since his Cincinnati Red Stockings' days, George's appearance to begin a new chapter of the sport was a reassuring sign pointing toward the league's stability and the continuity of the game.

Spalding, Barnes, McVey, and White had departed Boston and gone to Chicago for the 1876 season. The Boston club had even given up its designation as the "Red Stockings." Harry Wright had graciously returned this nickname to the resurrected Cincinnati team, now a charter member of the NL, from whom he had taken it when they dissolved after the 1870 season. In the future, his club would mostly be referred to as just the "Bostons" until they donned red hats in 1884 and were sometimes called the "Red Caps."[1] No matter the team's designation, here was "Smiling George," taking his place at the plate as he had done with such regularity for so many years, ready to open another campaign on a club managed by his brother in a new version of the major league of professional base ball.

To begin the inaugural season of the NL, on April 22, 1876, the Bostons played the Athletics in Philadelphia before a crowd of three thousand. Although George did not get a hit in his first plate appearance, his solid batting and nimbleness on the basepaths in the fifth produced a run for his team. It was a close match, with every tally at a premium as Boston eked out a 6–5 win. The Athletics' attempt at a comeback fell one run short in the ninth inning when, with two on and two out, their final batter grounded weakly to the Boston pitcher who tossed to first for the final out. Of note during the game was the Boston catcher, Tim McGinley, still determinedly playing after being hit in the eye by a foul ball.[2] The participants in the sport were still fearlessly unprotected, ignoring what they deemed "manly" risks in plying their trade.

The question of who might win the league's inaugural championship was an open one in America's centennial year. Boston could no longer assume it would take yet another pennant, especially with Chicago's new wealth of talent. The base ball public was reinvigorated by the prospect of a real competition for the title. As the Declaration of Independence a century before had formally stated the intentions of the colonies to break away from England's dominance and become a rival entity, so too had the new National League announced its attempt at establishing parity between East and West teams. The *New York Clipper* noted, "The centennial campaign is looked forward to with more eager interest than that of any season in the history of the professional championship."[3]

Unfortunately for Boston, the loss of the "Big Four" was a double calamity. These players were exceptionally talented and replacing them in kind was extremely difficult. However, just as great an obstacle would be to replace them and blend the new teammates in with the others to form a unit that functioned as seamlessly as had the previous Boston teams. This simply could not be expected overnight, which would be shown during the 1876 season.

Adding to this situation was the beginning of the inevitable for George Wright. Over the year, his superlative hitting capabilities began to desert him. This was reflected in his batting average, which dipped below .300 for the first time in his professional base ball career. Although he did hit .299 during the year, over the next few seasons this figure continued its decline, to .276 in 1877 and then to .225 the following year.[4]

Much of Wright's decline appears to have been related to the growing number of pitchers who had added the curve ball to their arsenal of deliveries. Years before, when George first encountered a curve ball on June 18, 1870, he tangled with the generally acknowledged inventor of the pitch, Arthur "Candy" Cummings of the amateur champion Brooklyn Stars. As he led off the first inning for the Cincinnati Red Stockings, the crowd buzzed with anticipation as to how he would handle this initial experience, Cummings tossing "horizontally curved line balls." George took a few pitches to gauge their flight, then calmly sent a grounder bounding between shortstop and third base for a clean single.[5] However, as the curve ball was adopted by more pitchers, evidently George had a difficult time hitting this delivery effectively, helping to hasten his departure from the game.[6] A Boston club history years later mentions that "the introduction of the in-shoot and curve bothered him. He didn't care to get hit with a ball, and after 1875 became a little nervous when at the bat."[7] Since it took extra speed to deliver the spinning action of a curve ball, those who were attempting to master the pitch could just as easily become wild with it, sending an accelerating sphere a bit too close for comfort for the batters, hitting some in the process.

On the other hand, his fielding remained unassailable. George again won accolades for being the league's best shortstop in 1876, noted by some as "the champion short-stop of the League arena." George's ability to cover a large area made him especially adept at handling hard-to-reach fly balls while backing up his teammates at second or third base.[8] When fielding grounders, he often absorbed much of the force of these hits by defusing their energy with his feet, "meeting a ground ball with his heels, brought together as the ball came within handling distance, and meeting it well in front to deaden it by giving with it."[9] Throughout his playing career, these abilities rarely deserted him.

In November 1875, Albert Spalding had married a woman from Boston, Josie Keith, stealing away a final piece of the city before moving west. Ever the base ball man, even while on his first days of honeymooning in his old hometown of Rockford, Illinois, Spalding gave an interview with the *Chicago Tribune* about the coming season. In it, he reviewed the prospects for key clubs in both the east and west as well as giving a few hints of changes to come for the professional organization.

[Boston's] nine for next year will not be as good a one as in the past season, as many of its best players have left. . . . In sporting circles they are not looked upon as favorably as formerly. . . . The four best clubs are located in Louisville, Cincinnati, St. Louis and Chicago. . . . Chicago [has] eleven good men. . . . White is recognized as the best catcher in the country. . . . McVey and Barnes are acknowledged the best batters in the world. . . . [Anson] stands 6 feet 3 inches, and his pluck and endurance is

only equal to his strength and size. . . . It is the intention of the larger clubs
to make some rules about contesting for the championship, so that clubs
that have no earthly chance to win will not be allowed to play with first-
rate clubs.[10]

A follow-up article in the *Tribune* a few months later, after the formation
of the National League, provided further comments by Spalding about
these developments.

It is my opinion that this new departure of the leading clubs in the country
will have a wonderfully beneficial effect upon the whole business. It will
have a tendency to raise the game in the estimation of the public, and
base-ball will be looked upon in the right light: as an honest, manly [sport].
Championship matches will draw a better average attendance. . . . Both
clubs and players will have greater respect for the laws and regulations of
the new association than any one ever had for the old.[11]

The article closed by noting that Spalding and younger brother J. Walter, a bookkeeper at a Rockford bank, were leaving for Chicago, where
they were planning to open a store to sell "all kinds of base ball goods and
turn [their] place into the headquarters of the Western Base Ball Clubs."[12]
Spalding, not yet twenty-six, and his nineteen-year-old brother Walter,
were, indeed, seizing the moment that had been created by Albert's move
to the Windy City. They opened up their store at 118 Randolph Street,
a few doors down from the White Stockings office. Teaming with William Hulbert in running a reconstructed Chicago ball club, followed by
forming a new league in which that team would be the leading contender,
topped off by embarking on a new business venture in the world of base
ball—it all pointed to a fantastic way to launch the season of 1876 for
Albert Spalding.

The year itself was a significant one for the country, not short of
drama as the nation turned one hundred years old. On March 10, seven
weeks before Boston played its season opener in Philadelphia, a young
immigrant from Scotland working in a small laboratory in downtown
Boston shouted for his assistant in another room and changed the world.
When Alexander Graham Bell famously called out "Mr. Watson, come
here. I want to see you," Thomas Watson listened to these words over an
experimental device called the telephone, patented only three days prior
and destined to become ubiquitous around the world.[13] No one had seen

anything quite like it before; it represented American inventiveness at its finest.

On July 5, after wonderous celebrations of America's centennial had taken place beginning the eve of Independence Day, complete with fireworks and torchlit parades deep into the night throughout many of the country's cities, towns, and villages, the nation would begin to read of a ferocious battle at the end of June in Montana. General George Custer, along with two brothers, a brother-in-law, and a nephew, were among 315 US Army troops killed while clashing with thousands of Native Americans near the Little Horn River.[14] Both events were as unexpected as they were earth-shattering, displaying in stark relief the progress and the predicaments of an evolving, century-old country with a population of disparate segments, each determined to stake its claim in a fractious future.

Such was not the case as the base ball campaign began. Certainly, there was much anticipation surrounding the coming contests between the Bostons and the Chicago White Stockings, with their four ex-Boston players. However, those knowledgeable in the game were far from shocked with how the year would play out. The *New York World* viewed it this way: Chicago would have "the most effective pitcher and the best catcher in the professional fraternity, and the other players are up to the highest standard," while it gave a polite downgrading of the Boston team, noting it "is not a team to be trifled with or underrated, [but] it is not the nine to go through the Centennial year with the career of success which marked the team of 1875."[15]

Indeed, when the White Stockings came east in late May for their first games with Boston, Chicago summarily dismissed their rivals with a three-game sweep. Those wanting to view the initial contest overwhelmed the stadium, an estimated ten to twelve thousand spectators taking every seat, occupying every knothole in the fence, and spilling over onto the grounds themselves.[16] Though the game was close, Boston proved no match for Chicago, losing 5–1. The crowd significantly shrank to a more normal three thousand for each of the ensuing two contests, both White Stockings victories, 9–3 and 8–4. The headline in the *Boston Globe* after the first Boston loss accurately summed it all up: "We Have Met the Enemy, and We Are Theirs."[17]

After their third triumph, Chicago was on top of the standings by a healthy margin, having won fifteen games against only three losses, while Boston had slipped to fourth place with a 9–9 record.[18] By the end of the season, both clubs would be in identical positions, Chicago winning the first title of the National League. Boston's futility versus the White Stockings was nearly total, succumbing nine straight times to Chicago until winning a final match-up at the end of September. As White Stocking third baseman Adrian Anson remembered it, "Harry Wright was happier that day . . . than he would have been had somebody made him a present of a house and lot, so anxious was he to win at least one game from Chicago during the season."[19]

Albert Spalding had led Anson and the rest of the White Stockings to the championship with superlative pitching and able management. He topped the league by hurling forty-seven victories against only twelve losses, a .797 winning percentage, also contributing a .312 batting average.[20] His friend Ross Barnes had a tremendous year on offense with a .429 average, amassing 138 hits, including twenty-one doubles and fourteen triples, while scoring 126 runs, these performances all representing the best in the league.[21] It had been as complete a resurrection for the Chicago club as could have been imagined only a year prior when Spalding convinced his band of eastern stars that success lay in the west.

Over the past few years, ever so slowly, ball players were beginning to become more sensitized to the hazards of their physically unprotected situation. Of utmost concern was the catcher. Inching ever-closer to the batter to have a better chance at throwing out base runners and fielding bunts, he was subject to continual battering by pitched or foul-tipped balls. Game summaries in the newspapers were riddled with comments about catchers being hit by vicious foul tips, which often blackened eyes and occasionally broke noses and teeth. They usually played through the injuries, being termed "plucky" for their fortitude. But across all levels of the organized game, the punishment suffered by catchers was becoming intolerable, especially when eye damage was involved. Whereas Boston's catcher McGinley gamely carried on after being hit in the eye with a foul tip in the team's season opener, others were not as fortunate. Typical of a bad injury, one catcher in Pennsylvania was reported as being "disabled by a ball which struck him in the eye,"[22] usually meaning he was removed from the game to convalesce. In extremely rare instances, as in Eau Clare, Wisconsin, a "catcher was hit in the eye and fell dead."[23] Indeed, the mounting danger to players positioned behind the batter was obvious.

By the winter of 1876–77, Fred Thayer, an enterprising upperclassman and captain of the Harvard nine, was putting the finishing touches on a piece of equipment that would sweep the game over the next decade with its increasing usage. Others would claim to have had early involvement in its invention, including Howard Thatcher, the graduating Harvard catcher on the 1876 team, his successor James Tyng, and Warren Briggs, the Harvard graduate who had accompanied Spalding to England in 1874 and had become a Boston semipro player in the mid-1870s. Each had his own thoughts on how his ideas, and in some cases early attempts at making a mask, had preceded Thayer's efforts.[24] But none appeared to provide more than casual food for thought in Thayer's determination to perfect a workable mask for daily use. History generally accepts Thayer's version of this accomplishment, which found its way into a letter many years later to Albert Spalding.[25] The note describes his desire to help Harvard's best athlete, Tyng, overcome his fears in playing the position of catcher that had been vacated by Thatcher when he graduated.

> In one or two games in which [Tyng] had caught behind the bat he had been hit by foul tips and had become more or less timid. . . . It was up to me to find some way to bring back his confidence. The fencing mask naturally gave me the hint as to the protection for the face, and then it was up to me to devise some means of having the impact of the blow kept from driving the mask onto the face. The forehead and chin rest accomplished this and also made it possible for me to secure a patent, which I did in the winter of 1878.[26]

An item in the *Boston Globe* notes Tyng employing the mask at base ball practices in Harvard's gymnasium in January 1877, describing the device as "made of brass wires, and fully protects the face from foul tips and thus enables the catcher to stand behind the bat with greater confidence."[27] Thayer had worked with a local Cambridge tinsmith to make practical improvements on a fencer's mask. Tyng debuted the upgraded product in competitive play on April 12, 1877, when Harvard beat the semipro Live Oaks 11–3 in Lynn, Massachusetts, in the first game of their season. Some at the time felt that the use of the mask provided an unfair advantage.[28] Since Tyng made only two errors during the game, considerably lower than normal for a catcher at that time, this new device could have been seen as giving a competitive edge. Shortly afterward, on

April 20, Harvard's paper the *Crimson* gave an opinion about the new piece of base ball equipment.

> The new mask was proved a complete success, since it entirely protects the face and head and adds greatly to the confidence of the catcher, who need not feel that he is every moment in danger of a life-long injury. To the ingenious inventor of this mask we are largely indebted for the excellent playing of our new catcher.[29]

As promising as this invention seemed at that moment, there was much skepticism in the base ball public to overcome. One newspaper made light of the concept by imagining what other strange items of ball player protection were forthcoming, stating, "We shall probably soon behold the spectacle of a player sculling around the bases with stove-funnels on his legs and boiler-iron riveted across his stomach."[30] Another paper, although admitting the benefits of a mask, took the position that generally speaking it was safer "to hire another fellow to take your place, while you sit on the fence and watch the players get crippled up."[31] Some professional catchers just dismissed the mask with reactions similar to Albert Spalding's batterymate, "Deacon" White. When Spalding asked him to try out the device, White disgustedly tossed it aside after a few minutes, saying it interfered with his vision.[32]

Others were not as wary, but acceptance was sparse. As the season wore on, a few of those who might have first doubted its effectiveness gave it a try. The catcher for the minor league Syracuse Star club, Pete Hotaling, "wore the wire mask, or rat-trap, and evidently doesn't intend to have his teeth knocked out."[33] Previously his eye had been seriously injured with a foul tip, so he tried the "cage," being mocked with the nickname "monkey" because of it.[34] Charley Snyder of the Louisville Grays appears to have been the first catcher in the National League to wear a mask when he donned the gear for a game against Cincinnati on July 3, a month before another major leaguer, Mike Dorgan, tried it on August 8 against Snyder's Louisville club.[35] By the end of August, Scott Hastings of the NL's Cincinnati team was noted as being "the only League catcher who has adopted [the mask]."[36]

Someone who easily recognized the value of the catcher's mask was Geroge Wright. From the time he was a young ball player who had been painfully hit in the throat while catching, George had not only shifted to the infield to avoid this unpleasant experience but had created a simple rubber mouth guard to help provide some sort of protection for those playing this position. Now, as Thayer brought his invention to the fore, Wright saw a real opportunity for the game as well as his sporting goods business. By the fall of 1877, George asked Thayer to bring a mask to his store for examination; he and teammate Harry Schafer tested it and were so impressed that, as George remembered it, "I made arrangements at the time with Mr. Thayer to patent the mask, control the sale of it, and pay him a royalty. . . . The mask was patented in 1878."[37]

Early in the 1877 season, soon after the mask's introduction, the sporting goods firm of Peck & Snyder in New York City was advertising the "New Catcher's Mask, made of spring wire and padded with curled hair filling" for three dollars, along with Wright's "Catcher's Mouth Rubber" for fifty cents.[38] By August, their advertisements were much bolder, stating the mask was "Now used by all the prominent catchers when playing behind the bat."[39] Although far from true, with continual incidents of catchers being injured with the ball, it should have been. Rather, if catchers employed any protection at all, they usually preferred the hidden rubber mouth insert that Wright had introduced almost a decade before.

By the beginning of the 1878 base ball season, the mask had been patented by Thayer and Wright had secured his license. George displayed the device in a newspaper advertisement of a catcher with mask on, the normal erect pose of the player rotated horizontally to catch the viewer's eye, with the caption "Thayer's Pat. B. B. Mask. Every Catcher Ought to Use One. Sure Protection for the Face."[40] Soon, Spalding & Bro. as well as other sporting goods houses were promoting it, even though Wright had the exclusive license to sell the mask. In 1883, Thayer and Wright finally filed suit against Spalding over the "safety masks" for catchers.[41] After three years, the patent infringement lawsuit was settled quite profitably in Thayer and Wright's favor, Thayer having "used his law degree to defend his patent."[42]

While the White Stockings had become the champions of the National League in 1876, Spalding sensed his playing career was ending. He had again been the most successful pitcher in professional base ball, winning forty-seven games in the season just completed. Yet, as the curve ball became the dominant weapon for the pitchers of the league, Spalding knew he could not compete much longer at this position. He simply had never been able to master throwing a curve, although he had tried earlier in his career.

Much as "Candy" Cummings had introduced George Wright to the curve ball in 1870, Spalding had met Cummings the same year when the Brooklyn Stars had played Albert's Rockford club. Decades later, Spalding recalled his discussion with the master of the curve, noting,

> Cummings had a beautiful pitch. He secured his curve by a peculiar wrist motion. . . . I talked with him about it and tried to get the curve, but I couldn't do it. . . . People in Chicago were greatly worried back in 1876 because the old White Stockings had no "curve pitcher." We managed to win the pennant with my "straight arm," though, and that was the last pitching I did.[43]

Indeed, by early October 1876, there were hints that the star pitcher of St. Louis, George Bradley, would bring his highly effective curve ball pitching to Chicago for the coming year.[44] By 1877's season opener, Spalding, as manager of the club, had installed himself in the infield for the season, pitching very occasionally but mostly playing first and even second due to an extended illness of Ross Barnes. Besides his pitching and hitting talents, Spalding was more than competent as a fielder, winning praise in the press for his abilities at second as a fill-in for Barnes.[45] With the league outlawing the formerly accepted practice of fair-foul hitting for 1877, coupled with a chronic energy-depleting malady, Barnes was never again able to have his previous impact on the game, retiring soon thereafter.

George Wright had taken a lead role in popularizing the catcher's mask. Now Albert Spalding became a major proponent for the use of a base ball glove, especially for pitchers, catchers, and first basemen, all of whom were thrown the ball repeatedly during the game. Until this time, gloves were virtually unused by ball players. The esteemed catcher of the original Cincinnati Red Stockings, Doug Allison, had employed a pair of buckskin "mittens" in a mid-season contest in 1870 after a stretch of unusually severe battering of his hands while catching, becoming the first recorded instance of the use of gloves in a game.[46] Since then, this piece of protective equipment, often nothing more than a pair of bricklayer's or railroad brakeman's gloves with the fingers cut off, possibly stuffed inside with a bit of sponge or even hay for cushioning, was what passed for the first gloves in the sport.[47]

Spalding had seen a player wear a glove a few years earlier, flesh colored so as not to draw too much attention and ridicule.[48] By 1877, after years of severe bruising of his left hand, he admitted to himself that protecting the hand outweighed his anxiety that wearing a glove was a sign of weakness. He selected a black one for his use and added padding for further protection, generating public sympathy rather than jocularity for this "unmanly" compensation to the raw physicality of playing base ball.[49]

Now Spalding's use of an impossible-to-miss black glove in 1877 not only proceeded to legitimize this item to the public, but it also provided a living advertisement of a celebrated ball player's use of a glove. It cleverly fused Spalding's heroic aura with a very saleable product, over the course of time generating huge revenues. The base ball mitt would eventually become the one essential piece of equipment to own for anyone, young or old, professional or novice, who wanted to play the game. Someone always had a base ball and a few could bring bats to a game, but soon everyone wanted to have his very own glove.

The next year, Spalding retired as player/manager of the White Stockings, turning his attention to the administrative side of running the club as well as devoting more time to his thriving sporting goods business. Through his close connection with Hulbert, Spalding pressed to have the National League award his company the exclusive rights to publish an "official League Book," which they did for the 1876 season, to be published in early 1877, and likewise for ensuing years.[50] At the end of February 1878, Spalding published this *League Book* covering the 1877 season, along with a new journal, what he termed *Spalding's Official Base Ball Guide*.[51] This was a similar publication meant to appear league-approved, though it was not officially sanctioned. It contained information and statistics about the league from the previous year but also incorporated tutorials on pitching and hitting, training tips, and numerous advertisements for a variety of base ball goods. Both the official and unofficial publications were significant revenue generators, mostly from advertisements placed in the guide by others wanting to sell their base ball goods and services. At a price of only ten cents per copy, each was readily affordable to a wide variety of readers.

The 1878 edition of the unofficial *Spalding's Official Base Ball Guide* even had an advertisement placed by George Wright's Boston sporting goods business. The ad primarily focused on "Thayer's Patent Harvard Catcher's Mask," noting Wright had "purchased the sole right from the inventor, to manufacture and sell the above Mask."[52] This clearly inferred that no one else, including Spalding, could sell the masks legally. Yet, in the next portion of the ad, it stated that George's store carried "Spalding's Base Balls, Bats, and Scorebooks," implying that George was acting as an authorized agent for Spalding's goods.[53] Oddly, only four pages beyond was an ad devoted to Spalding's sales of catchers' equipment, with a drawing and text about the exact same catcher's mask that Wright said was exclusively his to sell.[54] Spalding would eventually have to pay for this major overstep of legal rights on his part related to his company's mask sales.

The guides would become a key marketing tool in the company's promotion of Spalding's sporting goods venture. With the National League's stamp of approval on the *League Book*, and Spalding's intentional misleading use of this to provide "official" status for his own base ball guide, Beadle's and DeWitt's competing base ball publications became afterthoughts to the public, disappearing by the mid-1880s. Spalding's journals became the gold standard in promotional literature on base ball, then other sports as he diversified his line. A few others would follow this model, most successfully the sporting goods business of old Philadelphia Athletics' second baseman Al Reach with his competing guides for base ball's American Association and other sports. George Wright would also make periodic forays into publishing sports guides. But no one did it better than Spalding or was more influential in his attempts to use this vehicle to reach the American public to sell them on the benefits of sports and the equipment that he sold to play them.

By 1879, Spalding had taken his banker brother-in-law William Brown into the business, prompting a slight adjustment to the name of the company, from "Bro." to "Bros." The addition of this family member brought with it much more—an injection of capital to purchase a facility in Hastings, Michigan, that would manufacture bats from wood obtained from the ample forests prevalent in the region.[55] Spalding's business was expanding quickly, from a retail and wholesale operation to adding means to make some of the products they sold, helping to reduce costs and increase margins. It would be the beginning of a pattern over the years to back-integrate to manufacture other sports equipment that would significantly increase profits for the company.

During this time, Harry Wright had steered the Bostons to regain the league championship in both 1877 and 1878. He constructed a team that brought back "Deacon" White from Chicago to augment the powerful play of Jim O'Rourke and Andy Leonard in support of the first pitching triple crown winner, Tommy Bond, who in 1877 won forty games and collected 170 strikeouts on his way to a 2.11 earned run average.[56] George Wright was now playing second base more regularly as he gradually decelerated from his days as "king of the shortstops." At the same time, his sporting goods entrepreneurship had been rejuvenated thanks to the newly invented catcher's mask. However, he was also balancing other responsibilities besides base ball. He and wife, Abbie, were the proud parents of two little girls, Elizabeth and Georgiana, the family living on Sagamore Street in Dorchester, a section of Boston with a picturesque view of the harbor.

It was at this house, on December 19, 1877, that family patriarch Sam Sr. passed away. Three of his four sons, Harry, George, and Sam Jr. had kept vigil with their beloved father, who had instructed them in the game of cricket decades before and now was unconscious, dying of paralysis.[57] Sam had been retired for eight years from cricket, following his sons to Boston. In a letter to the *New York Clipper*, George wrote, "He died very quietly. For the last week, he has not known any of us. Harry, Sam, and myself, have been continually at his bedside, doing all we could to make him comfortable. . . . I must say, with tears in my eyes, he was a proud father of us all." The paper eulogized, "After an innings [*sic*] in the game of life of sixty-six years duration . . . the veteran was bowled out by old Time."[58] Sam Sr. was a respected athlete, father, and mentor to his sons, who never forgot their formative days with him, inspired by his love of cricket to learn the game, play it expertly, and while doing so becoming acquainted with the sport of base ball as well.

Certainly, the early love of cricket instilled in Harry and George by their father provided an initial sports education as they made their mark in both games of ball and bat. But this was not to be for Sam Jr. The youngest of the brothers, Sam was a solid cricketer, brought along on the 1874 trip to England by Harry as one of the few ball players who could credibly play cricket in the matches scheduled there, but he was only a marginal talent at base ball. Harry often talked of Sam being a better shortstop than George when they were both children learning the game, "more earnest and persevering, and time and again, I have seen him take balls that George would shirk."[59]

As he grew into adulthood, Sam never developed the ability to consistently hit the ball as his brothers could, resulting in a short-lived professional career. A profile of Sam published in the *New York Clipper* noted his fine play at shortstop with the New Haven professional team in 1875 and 1876 followed by a stint with the semi-professional Lowell club in 1877–78, again complimenting him on his skill at short but noting politely that "he does not rank very high as a batsman."[60] By 1879, his lackluster performances finished with a poor showing on the Cincinnati team. As George's sporting goods business grew, he periodically employed Sam in its cricket department for his keen knowledge of the game, but he would never be more than a footnote in the family history of the sporting greatness of the Wright brothers.

The initial year of the NL had been a success for Hulbert, Spalding, and their Chicago White Stockings. The league took pains to enforce its regulations, sending a strong message to the base ball world that business would not be conducted in the lax manner of the old NA. At the end of 1876, the league expelled the Philadelphia Athletics and New York Mutuals for a number of years because of their decisions not to follow through with games scheduled late in the season against western opponents, where their share of the gate receipts was not expected to cover travel expenses.[61] This was exactly the type of behavior that the NL had been established to eliminate, and Hulbert made sure that the two teams would suffer the dire consequences of their blatant reversion to old habits.

Even more significantly, at the end of the following year, four players of the Louisville team were banned for life by the club, firmly supported by the league. The quartet was found to be working with gamblers to throw games late in the season, resulting in Louisville's loss of the championship.[62] Spalding recalled the situation as "the most sensational event" of the early NL, "the first great victory won over gambling and the gamblers."[63] The league sent this swift, severe message to other players and the public alike of its complete intolerance of gambling. Shock waves rippled through the sport, which had not seen such blatant exposure of this type of activity since the Mutuals scandal of 1865. The punished players from that scandal were accepted back into the organized game a few years later, muting the severity of the sentence they had been given.

Now, the precedent of banning ballplayers from the game for life would hold fast over the entirety of the players' careers, a punishment that would not occur with such magnitude again until the Black Sox gambling transgression of the 1919 World Series.

Through it all, George Wright's career in the sport was beginning to decelerate. He had been termed the best ballplayer in the country on so many occasions that he must have been somewhat surprised when his skills began to falter. Now, being shifted to second base by Harry to accommodate his lessening range and with his hitting proficiency starting on a downward slide, he decided it was time to take on a final challenge, managing a team of his own. When the Providence Grays, a promising club that had finished third in the league in 1878, offered him the opportunity to play as well as manage, he jumped at the chance. He convinced his teammate, star outfielder Jim O'Rourke, to join him, together leaving Boston to bolster the already strong fortunes of the Grays for the 1879 season. It would be a memorable year for both base ball and for George Wright, ending with dramatic success and another test for the fledgling National League.

9

Providence and Prejudice

It was late in the game, in the eighth inning, but the Bostons still had hopes of rallying to beat the Providence Grays. With none out, Boston's Jack Manning was at third, Ezra Sutton on second, and Jack Burdock at the plate. Burdock swung at the pitcher's delivery, and both base runners saw the ball headed for a gap in shallow left centerfield. No one was going to catch this sinking line drive, and they took off as fast as they could, barreling around the diamond toward home to score the runs that would tie up the game.

Seemingly out of nowhere came the streaking form of the Gray's Paul Hines, swiftly charging from his position in center, straining with every stride to get to the hit before it would land behind second and shortstop. Just as the ball was about to touch ground, he managed to lunge and snag the liner, inches above the turf, his hands cradling the ball awkwardly while his legs were churning in this desperate sprint, almost causing him to lose his balance.[1] Hines's momentum drove him on toward the infield and eventually third base, which he quickly touched. He next sent the ball to Charley Sweasy, the Providence second baseman, who was signaling Hines to throw it his way, stepping on the bag with ball in hand. A triple play!

George Wright had watched the scene play out from his vantage point that spring day of May 8, 1878, coaching the Boston runners from behind third base. As he remembered it many years later, it was even more thrilling. It was an *unassisted* triple play, the first such feat in base ball history. According to George's narration of the event, "The man who had been on third had already crossed the home plate and the other runner was

125

halfway beyond third base. So by touching the bag Hines completed the triple play."[2] Hines's throw to second baseman Sweasy was unnecessary in this accounting, done "for good measure." It was to become one of the most debated plays in the history of the sport, discussed even now as being either assisted with Hines's toss to Sweasy or, by 1878 rules, unassisted by virtue of Hines touching third base after both runners had supposedly bolted past that bag in their race to score.

Newspapers of the day each had their opinion, some calling it assisted while others claimed Hines had recorded three outs himself. The *New York Clipper* took the former position, "Burdock's fly back of short was captured by Hines after a sharp run, he putting out Manning at third, and throwing to second in time to put out Sutton."[3] The *Boston Globe* felt otherwise, stating, "[Burdock] hit a high fly, which was a twister, but Hines ran for it, took it on the fly at the short stop's position, putting out Burdock. Without stopping in his run Hines kept on to third, which both Manning and Sutton had passed running home on the fly, and there stopping, **Made a Triple Play** with no assistance."[4] The play had caused a momentary sensation within the game, but the excitement soon faded.

A decade later, the event was resurrected by the former Boston and Providence ballplayer-turned-journalist Tim Murnane. He had played first base for the Grays during the game and insisted in a newspaper column he had written that Hines had completed an unassisted triple play, which Hines supported with his own recollections. Others lined up with their view of the story. William Rankin, a *New York Clipper* reporter, Providence second baseman Charlie Sweasy, and Ezra Sutton, the Boston baserunner who had started out on second, all claimed it was an assisted play due to their contention that Sutton had not gone past third base before Hines touched it. The catchers of the two clubs, Doug Allison and Charlie Snyder, as well as umpire Charley Daniels, said Sutton had already crossed third when Hines touched the base.[5] It was rather amazing, so many actual participants in the game itself with such contradictory opinions. And so the arguments continued back and forth, dissecting the details of this most unique of plays, even now rarer in base ball than pitching a perfect game.

A report in a St. Louis paper the day after the event seemed to resolve the issue by indicating that Hines had touched second, then third, after catching the ball. "Hines got the ball, however, ran across second to third and touched the bag, making a triple play"[6] In fact, this was the version that journalist and *Sporting News* founder Alfred Spink recalled in his 1910 book on base ball, "Hines caught the ball on a hard run and, being quick witted, saw his opportunity, and keeping up his stride, ran over and touched second base, and going to third base, did likewise, completing a most remarkable play."[7] However, with no definitive answer to the question of assisted or unassisted, it's one of the enduring disputes of the sport. The debate only added to the wonder of the play itself, and George Wright was there to see it unfold.

George and the Bostons had competed against a formidable base ball nine. Though just in their first year of major league existence, the Grays had secured Hines from the White Stockings, where he had been an outfielder on the 1876 championship team along with Spalding, Ross Barnes, and Adrian Anson. In 1878 at Providence he would go on to win what later was termed the league's first-ever batting "triple crown," leading the NL by hitting .358 to go along with collecting the top honors of four home runs and fifty runs batted in.[8] Two original Cincinnati Red Stockings, Charlie Sweasy and Doug Allison, played second base and catcher. Murnane was the first baseman, having already played this position with success in Boston. And a young rookie pitcher would make his league debut with the Grays in mid-season, eighteen-year-old John Montgomery Ward, a future Hall of Famer who won twenty-two games, pitched eight shutouts and recorded an ERA of 1.51 that year.[9]

Providence was certainly making the most of its opportunity to field a team in the NL. Located only fifty miles southwest of Boston, it was a city of close to one hundred thousand people in the late 1870s, growing significantly with industrial opportunities from the textile industry, machine shops, and jewelry-making operations, many within an easy trolley ride to the new ballpark, the expansive Messer Field.[10] Providence, as well as the state itself, stood in the long shadow cast by neighboring Boston, both from a base ball perspective as well as in national prominence. The region had its own thriving interest in the sport of base ball, fielding successful amateur teams and company-sponsored nines rich in spirited rivalries, from Woonsocket in the north to Narragansett on the state's southern shoreline, including Providence's own Brown University squad founded in the 1860s.[11] When the league's Hartford team in next-door Connecticut folded after the 1877 season, it was an opportune time for Providence to host a major league ball club.

City fathers were anxious to increase business revenues and foster community spirit with this new entry. After the encouraging 1878 season, they decided to build on their modest success by adding greater talent to the roster. This moment coincided nicely with George Wright's desire to manage a team of his own after his eight years playing in Boston. Both he and teammate Jim O'Rourke were outstanding ball players, yet both felt their value was not being properly recognized by the Bostons' owners, especially their miserly president, Arthur Soden, who wanted to cut costs, from George's salary to making the players pay for cleaning their uniforms while on the road.[12] By mid-1878, Wright's discontent was evident; it was rumored that he would be moving on to Brooklyn to manage a team the next year.[13] Wright and O'Rourke were ripe for the picking, and a few key Providence backers traveled to Boston to harvest this windfall crop, signing them both to contracts with the Grays, George becoming manager as well as captain and shortstop.

"Old Reliable" Joe Start, star first baseman for the White Stockings, was brought in to replace Murnane. At thirty-seven years old, Joe was still an excellent fielder and dependable batter. Fleet-footed Mike McGeary took over for Charlie Sweasy at second, while heavy-hitting catcher Lew Brown displaced Doug Allison. "Monte" Ward was re-signed as the main pitcher, a young talent whose delivery confounded many a hitter. "He turned his back on the batter, faced second base and, turning quickly, cut the ball loose for the plate."[14] It sounded eerily like the idiosyncratic pitching style of another New England hurler of almost a century later, Boston legend Luis Tiant. The multi-talented Paul Hines was at the prime of his base ball career as a swift outfielder and strong hitter, remaining with the Grays through 1885 and their eight-year existence.

As the finishing touches were put on assembling the 1879 team, George Wright was also deciding how to handle his growing sporting goods enterprise in Boston. While he was away managing and playing for the Grays he decided to add a few clerks to his store in Boston, one of whom was a young businessman with previous retail experience named Henry Ditson. Amiable and capable, he would soon fill a much more prominent role in the operation.[15]

In addition to enlarging his Boston store's staff and assuming his new roles with the Providence club, he was setting up a new sporting goods facility in that city. In early March, George was seen "superintending the arrangements of his Baseball Emporium in the Infantry Building, on Dorrance Street."[16] He went right to work obtaining new business, the following week securing the adoption of his "league ball" by the Rhode Island State Baseball Association.[17] An advertisement in the April 1 edition of a local Providence paper noted that season tickets for the Providence team could be purchased at George Wright's Base Ball Emporium at 49 Dorrance Street.[18] It was an auspicious beginning for the new manager of the Providence Grays.

The year before, the team had installed a special trolley line spur that brought spectators right up to Messer Field, where weekday afternoon games started at 3:30 p.m. to give downtown merchants time to close at three and get to the ballpark.[19] The Providence organization was anxious to prepare their stadium to make it convenient for the players to work out and stay in shape before and during the season. To this end, they set up a special arrangement for the ball players at the park: "The Providence Club will have a room arranged under the grand stand on their ground . . . intended for baseball practice on rainy and cold days. The blackboard therein bears the following: 'The Providence nine have a good Start and will end all Wright.'"[20]

On May 1, the league season began on a high note for Providence with a lopsided win at Cleveland, 15–4. The Grays collected twenty hits, with Start, Wright, and Ward garnering three apiece.[21] Heavy batting would be a trademark of the club, providing Ward with significant run support on his way to forty-seven wins during the year. Beyond this, Wright was able to meld the team into a cohesive unit, much as he had experienced with his brother's teams in Cincinnati and Boston. When injuries came along, he found able substitutes to fill in for incapacitated players, keeping the winning momentum going. One such situation would stand out in this regard, not only for the substitute utilized, but for that player's unknown significance at the time, as he was destined to eventually become a landmark in the only major league game in which he played.

It was an injury to Joe Start that precipitated the situation. During a game on June 19 against Cleveland at Messer Field, Joe's second finger on his left hand was broken while trying to field a low throw from third base.[22] O'Rourke finished the game at first for Joe, the Grays emerging victorious, 8–1, but this was a momentary fix. By Saturday's June 21 game against Cleveland, Wright had installed Brown University's first baseman William Edward White in Start's place with encouraging results in the Gray's 5–3 win.

> No matter how wild the ball was thrown [White] completed the play in every instance but one, and that when McGeary gave him a ball that struck the ground before it got to the bag. The [Brown] 'Varsity boys lustily cheered their favorite at times, and howled with delight when he got a safe hit in the ninth inning, as they also did his magnificent steals of second in that and the fifth inning.[23]

The Grays had already played several games against the Brown University squad in April as they warmed up for the major league season. A contest on April 12 was won by Providence, 9–3, a local paper commenting about "White excelling" in his play of first base for Brown.[24] Later in the month, White played in another of these matches, on Saturday, April 26, and was again impressive, fielding first base well and stroking a triple off Ward in the Gray's 13–3 victory.[25] So Wright knew him and was impressed, not hesitating to employ White in Start's place, a common practice for big league clubs like Providence or Boston that had nearby college talent at Brown or Harvard to tap into when needed. It was assumed that White would play in more games while Start recovered, but it turned out that the game versus Cleveland was the only one in which White would ever play for Providence or in the major leagues.

The whole incident was nothing more than a forgotten sidelight until the early 2000s, when baseball researchers stumbled onto the fact that William Edward White was a light-skinned African American, fathered by a white slaveowner and his mulatto former slave and housekeeper in Georgia at the beginning of the Civil War. Being one-quarter black made him legally black in most states. As such, it made him the first African American to play in the major leagues, well before Jackie Robinson's notoriety in breaking this barrier in 1947 or even prior to Moses Fleetwood Walker and his brother Weldy playing in the major leagues in 1884. Born in 1860 in Milner, Georgia, White's "well-to-do merchant father and railroad president," A. J. White, had sent him north for higher education, where he passed as white and even registered as such in the 1880 US census in Providence.[26]

Since this discovery, the question has been why did White play in only one game for the broken-fingered Joe Start after such an auspicious beginning? Was it because the Grays discovered his racial background? Although no one has definitively answered this query, an item in a Providence paper the day after White's successful substitution for Start provided pertinent information. "White, who played with the Greys [*sic*], Saturday, has concluded to go home, and it is stated that O'Rourke will play first base."[27] Further investigation of William Edward White found him not to be a Brown University student at all when he took Joe Start's place for Providence against Cleveland, but actually a graduating senior from the Friends' School in Providence prior to his attending Brown later that fall.[28]

Brown University had made use of his excellent base ball skills when playing Providence that spring, White exhibiting such capabilities that George Wright was happy to have him fill in for Start when needed a few months later. White's commencement exercises took place a few days after his appearance in a Grays uniform and, like others at school, he was headed home for the summer.[29] It appears the experiment with White and the Providence Grays had been short-lived but satisfactory for all concerned. Almost 150 years later, George Wright's great-grandson Denny could only laugh at the idea that George would have had a racial motivation to decide not to use White in future games for his team, stating that "what George wanted above all else was to field a winning team, regardless of color."[30]

After the Cleveland series ended, the Grays left to play a six-game set over the next week, alternating between the two cities of Boston and Providence, less than a two-hour train ride apart. The Providence newspapers trumpeted this much-anticipated first confrontation of the season between the teams managed by the Wright brothers, two league heavyweights along with Chicago. Advertisements for the games were everywhere, "AND NOW THE SPORT COMMENCES! . . . GEORGE vs. HARRY!—OR— Providence vs. Boston!"[31] At the time, the two New England neighbors trailed the White Stockings, who occupied first place while the Grays and Bostons were nipping at their heels in second and third. Providence prevailed in the series, winning four of the six games with consistent heavy hitting up and down the lineup. In the fourth contest, won in Providence by the home team, 15–3, the Grays smashed two home runs in the sixth inning, one by catcher Lew Brown and the other by right fielder Bobby Mathews, while George collected two triples and a double in the game.[32]

As the year progressed, the tension mounted between the title contenders. Chicago, which had bolted out of the gate by winning fourteen of fifteen contests in the first month of the season, slowly slipped from atop the standings. Conversely, Providence and Boston steadily ascended in lockstep. Both teams won sixteen league contests during the month of August while only losing three each. They remained red-hot through the first three weeks of September, Providence going 10–2 and Boston 9–3, while Chicago stumbled to a dreadful record of 1–8 in that period.[33]

The Wright brothers had not faced each other since their six games three months prior. In that interval, George had made only one significant change in the lineup, of which Harry would have heartily approved. In August, exasperated by catcher Lew Brown's continued drinking, Wright replaced Brown with impressive rookie catcher Emil Gross, a powerful hitter who blended in easily with the other Grays and bolstered their already strong performance. Now, another six contests between Boston and Providence would decide the winner of the 1879 season, with the Grays only needing two wins to clinch the title. Again, the half dozen matches would be played in alternate fashion between the two cities, providing each the chance to cheer on their hometown heroes as they battled for the pennant.

The first game, played in Boston, was a convincing win for the home team, 7–3. This, although their normal pitcher, Tommy Bond, who had been so effective for the Bostons during the past few seasons, was unable to play. Manager Harry Wright was caught in a huge predicament, which he creatively solved by employing the former Harvard base ball star and catcher's mask proponent, James Tyng, who had graduated from Harvard earlier in the year and had been pitching with a local amateur club.[34] Tyng rewarded Harry's judgment by performing brilliantly under pressure, delivering a rousing victory for the locals in his first game as a major leaguer by shutting down the powerful bats of the Grays.

The next day's tussle started out as a tight affair, Tyng again pitching superbly, when the heavens opened and washed out the contest after only a few innings with the teams tied at 1–1. The Grays hitters could only be kept in check for so long, and in the subsequent match they scored four runs in the first inning and never looked back, winning 15–4. Tyng's spell had been broken, his "Tyng-Twisters," as one paper called his pitches, had been solved.[35] One victory remained for Providence to claim the championship, the game to be played in the friendly confines of Messer Field.

The score stood at six apiece in the ninth inning. George Wright was at the plate with a two-strike count and two already out. He was just one pitch away from a strikeout and the Grays having to play on against the unpredictable Tyng and the always-dangerous Bostons, who had just scored three runs in the eighth to tie the contest. Then, the improbable happened. Years later George would comment that it was an "unwritten law that the hitter should do his utmost to connect with the ball" rather than reach first base by being "given a base on balls."[36] Yet, Tyng suddenly lost his control and George took nine straight wayward pitches in a row and was awarded first base, nine called pitches out of the strike zone still being the rule for a base on balls. A double by Joe Start pushed him to third. The applause was deafening when Paul Hines drove a single past shortstop Ezra Sutton, the crowd rising as one as if to accompany Wright across home plate. The moment would be etched into the memories of the Messer Field faithful for the rest of their lives. "The excitement was intense, and the Providence nine received a perfect ovation."[37] The Grays were the champions of base ball for 1879.

The *New York Clipper* summed it up beautifully, stating that a Bostonian, upon hearing the news of his city's defeat, exclaimed, "By George, Harry, you're whipped, old boy!"[38] The brothers had battled to the end during this magical season, both employing similar styles of team management to extract the last ounce of effort from their charges. George, in his first attempt, was able to lead by deeds as well as words, fielding brilliantly and providing timely hitting. To this was added confidence borne from a decade of experience under Harry's winning guidance in both Cincinnati and Boston.

The *Clipper* article noted that both clubs "have been run on the 'Boston plan' of selecting their players on account of their reliability for honest play and for harmonious working together as a team."[39] Harry may have lost the battle, but his leadership methodology was credited with winning the war. The paper went so far as to speculate that Chicago's failure to win the league championship each year since their inaugural title in 1876 under Spalding was due to a lack of unity, a quality sorely missing since Albert first managed the team.[40]

By late October, the Grays even took on the celebrated visiting English cricket team of Daft's Eleven at the Union Grounds in Brooklyn, losing to them in a spirited game of cricket but thoroughly enjoying the challenge of playing the best.[41] George could not resist playing the Britishers again, this time with a group of American cricketers in the Philadelphia area. Unfortunately, he suffered several broken bones in his hand from a swiftly bowled ball, which bothered him well into the new year.[42] At age thirty-two, George realized his injuries were becoming more frequent and taking longer to heal.

Wright's sporting goods business in Boston continued to grow during the year. By early November, he felt it was time to bring on a partner, elevating Henry Ditson to this role. Putting an exclamation point on this decision, they opened a "new and centrally located baseball headquarters at No. 580 Washington Street."[43] Although it focused on base ball equipment, it carried a widening array of all kinds of sporting goods. One such item featured in Wright & Ditson advertisements in the Boston papers during November and December was the "Eureka rowing machine," noted in an accompanying short article to be the best type of exercise for the muscles, a must-have for clerks "confined to a close room during the day."[44] Perhaps Ditson, the former clerk, had made a special point of including this in the store's offerings.

Before the year was over, on December 19, George's wife Abbie gave birth to their first son. They named the child Beals, an odd first name but readily recognizable if one remembered that Tommy Beals was a good friend and teammate of George's on the Boston clubs of the mid-1870s, and George indicated as much when asked.[45] People speculated on the potential for Beals to be trained by his father to become the next generation of Wright family ballplayers. As time would reveal, Beals indeed would excel with a ball and club, but of a completely different sort.

Much had transpired with Wright as the old year gave way to the new. His sporting goods business was picking up in Boston, a new baby boy had joined Wright's growing brood, and George wanted to focus on family as well as rest to heal his broken hand. George sensed it was time to settle back down in Boston and begin to phase out of playing base ball. He decided to approach the Providence club with the idea of leaving the Grays to return home to play for his brother's squad.

While George was contemplating this shift in teams, the NL had already decided on a heretofore unheard-of change to address a major issue of club finances that perpetually faced each team. The early years of the league were marginally profitable at best. The clubs were attempting to establish the price of a ticket at fifty cents, which was a struggle for some spectators to pay as a leisure-time activity, especially against the backdrop of a nagging national recession. On moral grounds, Sundays were declared off limits as game days, which restricted the available attendance for workers who only had this day off. The result was that some teams, mainly those in the largest cities, made money while most did not. Player salaries, being in the aggregate the largest single expense of each club, were at the center of this economic equation.

Every year after players' contracts had expired, they were free to open negotiations with any team that was willing to pay for their services in the following year's campaign. This created a time of financial limbo for the club owners, fraught with anticipation about how much a ball player might demand for the next year or if he might take his skills elsewhere. It pitted the teams against each other in a fight to obtain the best talent available, while the players scrambled for a slice of the clubs' relatively finite funds.[46] It was a true test of a free market, where a club's management and labor competed against each other as well as other teams in establishing the value of each ball player's services in the major league marketplace.

At the end of September, league representatives met in Buffalo, New York, to address this vexing issue. They established what they called the reserve system. Owners developed a list of five players for whom they could "reserve" the rights for salary negotiations for the coming season. All the other clubs agreed not to employ these five players for the next year, essentially colluding to prevent fair marketplace competition for those on each team's reserve list.[47] This forced the five players so designated to either come to terms with the club who had reserved their rights or not play major league baseball for the coming year. If a reserved player decided not to participate in this system, that player could either search for an opportunity in a minor or semipro league, which paid significantly less, or cease playing ball professionally altogether. "[The league's] explicit intent was to hold down labor costs and thereby insure [*sic*] franchise stability."[48] The concept was simple, if not fair, giving huge financial leverage to management, the system eventually expanded to include all major league players contracted on a team's roster.

The reserve agreement was made public in the fall, and although it was not part of the players' contracts for 1879, Wright understood this was the new playing field for his discussions with the Providence club for 1880. The Grays had not made a profit in 1879, despite winning the championship. Under the new system, George, along with Paul Hines, Monte Ward, Joe Start, and Mike McGeary were placed on Providence's reserve list. There were conflicting reports concerning whether or not the Grays directors offered Wright a reduced contract for 1880 but, in the end, George told them he was leaving base ball to devote his time to his growing business.[49] He had requested his release from the Buffalo agreement, which the directors of the club rejected, stating that under the agreement they would retain his services for 1880 unless he decided to sit out the upcoming major league season, which he did.[50]

After winning the major league championship in his debut, George was never to manage again, becoming the first and only individual to win a major league base ball title in his only season as manager. Simultaneously, he had become the first casualty of the new reserve system, abruptly retiring from the league. He ended his career by playing a small number of games for the Bostons and Providence during the 1881–82 seasons.

Anxious to fill the void left by a Providence team bereft of its capable manager and shortstop were the powerful White Stockings club that had slid precipitously from contention during the 1879 season. They were led by Spalding protégé and friend Adrian Anson, known as "Cap" as he captained, played for, and managed the team. Anson had grown to become the dominant force on the field. At several inches over six feet, he was a comparative giant for this era, a big target at first base, the best hitter in the league, and a leader who desired to win at almost any cost.

Anson was sometimes known as "Baby" at the beginning of his career at nineteen because of his innocent, youthful looks. But as he aged, the nickname had stuck due to his penchant for "crying" to the umpire when things did not go his team's way, wailing his displeasure so that everyone in the stands could hear. This, in stark contrast to George Wright's philosophy on potential disputes with the umpire. He harkened back to his brother Harry who, "always would insist that we say nothing. Let the other fellows kick was our rule, and I have always found a successful team does the same thing."[51] Anson knew base ball inside and out, and he took the opposite approach. He attempted to intimidate the umpire by whining or screaming his viewpoints, employing his sheer size to bully anybody who opposed him, anything to get a competitive edge.

At the same time, he trained his teammates in the basics of the game, creating new wrinkles as he went along. He had his players signal each other on offense and defense to coordinate their efforts. They expertly employed the newly emerging technique of the hook slide to elude being tagged out when stealing. Later, Anson would experiment with a pitching "rotation" to rest the tired arms of his hurlers. Driven by his drill sergeant's intensity, Chicago won three titles in a row, from 1880 to 1882.

It was during these years that the clubs in the NL began to become more profitable. As in every industry, financial success invariably attracts competition. So it was that first the American Association (AA) appeared in 1882 followed by the Union Association (UA) in 1884. These interlopers sought to capitalize on the growing fortunes of base ball as public entertainment, adding major league teams in cities such as Baltimore and Pittsburgh as well as smaller towns like Columbus, Ohio, and Troy, New York. They slashed game prices from fifty cents to a quarter, played on Sundays, and offered alcohol in the stands, all geared to appeal to the working class. Many of these clubs were backed by the growing revenues of alcoholic beverage purveyors, from brewers to saloon proprietors, who were more than happy to have the spectators buy a drink while watching the game. And each of these new major leagues ignored the reserve system that had been firmly established by the NL.

In early 1884, the NL moved determinedly to make peace with the AA, along with a large minor league known as the Northwestern League. They developed a means to agreeably coexist by signing a pact known as the National Agreement. This accord confirmed and expanded the reserve system from five to eleven players on each team, guaranteed minimum salaries for all roster players, acknowledged and respected each other's suspensions and expulsions by refusing to contract with such players, and set finite rules for contract duration and negotiating periods.[52] When the UA appeared as a less substantial rival in 1884, the organizations bound by the National Agreement took a different tack. They refused to acknowledge the UA's very existence, threatening to blacklist players who joined it and forcing many UA clubs to bring onto the field over-the-hill talent, some of whom had not played in years.[53] Through these tactics and others, the UA was crushed before it had the chance to establish itself and grow.

George Wright chose to vigorously engage in the formation of the UA, as a business opportunity as well as to participate versus a league that had spurned him by invoking the reserve system in 1880. He invested in partial ownership of Boston's entry into the upstart league, bringing back retired Boston teammates first baseman Tim Murnane and pitcher Tommy Bonds. The UA was happy to have the legendary George Wright in its camp. His support was not only as an owner; George's financial investment had earned him the league's approval to supply the official baseball and guidebook for the league, as well as an inside track to sell the clubs their uniforms and other gear.[54] It was a promising incursion for Wright & Ditson into the growing base ball equipment dominance of Spalding & Bros., but this profitable business bonanza only lasted a year until the UA collapsed.

As these leagues formed, they created opportunities for more ball players to become major leaguers. By 1884, three major leagues existed where only one had stood at the close of the 1881 season. To fill these opportunities the major leagues looked to the many minor league teams that had sprung up across the country over the past decade, spread to the four corners of the country and populated with a variety of talent. And those in minority populations were as eager to be included in the mix as anyone else. Some would be grudgingly allowed admission to the fraternity while others would continue to be excluded, the dividing line mainly being the color of their skin rather than their playing abilities.

A prime example was the case of Moses Fleetwood Walker, an accomplished black catcher who had played for a few minor league ball clubs in Pennsylvania and Ohio in the early 1880s. He was plying his trade in the Northwestern League for the Toledo Blue Stockings when Cap Anson's team came to town to play them in an exhibition game in August 1883. Toledo was in the midst of a pennant race for the league's crown, with Walker's talent well-established and his skin color largely a non-issue as they fought for the title, when Anson announced his club would not play a game "with no nigger."[55] When the Toledo club management threatened to withhold the White Stockings' share of the already-collected gate receipts, they called Anson's bluff and the game proceeded as scheduled, Walker stationed in right field. The game itself was a true test for both clubs, Chicago getting "their big feet on the necks of the little future greats," as one newspaper described the tussle, emerging victorious by the tightest of margins in ten innings, 7–6.[56]

The minor league Blue Stockings had previously played other major league clubs in exhibition games without incident, primarily against AA teams, which the local newspaper took pains to point out as it excoriated the racial prejudice espoused by Anson.[57] As the Baseball Hall of Fame notes in Anson's biography, "[His] racism may have been common by the day's standards, but his influence and stature gave his actions additional impact and supported the segregationist attitudes that impeded the game for another six decades."[58] Nine years earlier, a young Anson had bemoaned the unacceptable prejudice that the British had shown during base ball's tour of England in their narrow-minded rejection of base ball as being an inferior American game compared to their cherished cricket. Now, the irony in his outrage was writ large as he applied this same biased approach to those with differing skin tone who desired to play his beloved game.

The following year, Toledo's success in the minors propelled them into the AA, with Walker still catching for them. As such, he was the first recorded African American player in the majors, well before Jackie Robinson in 1947 and notwithstanding the recently discovered one game appearance of William Edward White in 1879. To add emphasis to this landmark accomplishment, Walker's brother Weldy also played with Toledo for a few games that season. However, both turned in less than adequate performances in 1884, especially Moses. Racial animosity followed them whenever they played teams in the South like the Louisville club. It was even evidenced by a teammate, pitcher Tony Mullane, who ignored Walker's signals when catching and contributed to his poor performance.[59] Finally, due to injury, Walker was released by the Blue Stockings in September, having played in only 42 of the team's 104 games, only 6 after mid-July due to his various ailments.[60] With his departure from the major leagues, the door was slammed shut to African American participation at the major league level until Robinson's debut with the Dodgers.

Walker was to encounter Anson one final time a few years later. Moses played for various minor league clubs over the next three seasons. In 1887 he became the batterymate for rising African American pitching star George Stovey on the Newark club in the International League. Anson's White Stockings came to town for an exhibition match in July and he once again screamed his racial epithets, this time cowing Newark into keeping both Stovey and Walker off the field with the threat of lost revenues if Chicago canceled their appearance. As Michael Lomax noted in his book on black baseball in the nineteenth century, "The loss of gate receipts that the White Stockings could generate outweighed any stance for social justice."[61] Anson's opinionated excesses, bellowed for all to hear, had regrettably become accepted as just another part of the business of base ball.

Other minorities managed to surmount prejudice toward their presence, claiming positions on the diamond because of their skill, their minority status being deemed "more acceptable" than dark skin. Of note was the emergence of deaf mutes in the major leagues in the 1880s. The deaf and mute players, termed deaf and "dumb" in the vernacular of the time, initially came from a special school in Columbus, Ohio, the Ohio School for the Deaf, that focused on helping them learn to cope with their disabilities while being the first residential school for this minority that included instruction in base ball.[62] As historian and professor Rebecca Edwards described it in her in-depth examination of deaf players in major league base ball, "Deaf people did not want charity from hearing people. They wanted inclusion in American civic, social, and economic life. . . . As it would be for so many other minority groups, baseball was a vehicle for demanding inclusion in American life, by displaying passion for America's national pastime."[63] Because being deaf invariably included being mute, or "dumb," they were usually each nicknamed "Dummy" by the speaking world, now a term of derision but then simply a matter-of-fact descriptor of their condition.

The first ever deaf-mute player in the majors was Ed "Dummy" Dundon in 1883–84 with the Columbus team of the AA. He had been the star pitcher for the Ohio School team but was only marginal at best as a professional. In large part, this was due to his ever-increasing consumption of alcohol. Tom Lynch was the second deaf and mute player in the major leagues, pitching one game for the White Stockings in August 1884, before injuring himself and never playing in the majors again.

The third deaf-mute to play major league base ball, and the one who made the biggest impact, was William "Dummy" Hoy, like Dundon a graduate of the Ohio School but a decidedly better player. He would go on to perform admirably in the majors, a lightning-quick centerfielder who stole close to six hundred bases during a fourteen-year career from 1888 to 1902 in which he smacked over two thousand hits and batted .288.[64] Although largely credited with introducing umpires' hand signals into the game with his need to know the ball and strike count while batting, his teammates in the outfield distinctly remembered his own signal to them when he was going after a fly ball. Hall of Famer Sam Crawford described it as "a kind of throaty noise, kind of a little squawk," whereas Louisville outfielder Tommy Leach called it "a little squeaky sound," indicating Hoy would take the ball.[65] There was no need to be loud and brash to get his point across to his teammates. All that was required was to give a tiny, barely audible sign to indicate he would take capable control of the situation. With all of "Baby" Anson's base ball bellicosity, he could have learned a thing or two from "Dummy" Hoy.

10

Global Base Ball

Albert Goodwill Spalding was nothing if not an enthusiastic proponent of base ball. His adult life was centered around the game, playing it or managing those who did, administering organizations solely structured to further its existence, and providing equipment essential to its competition. The base ball trademark for his company was the family name stretched across the picture of a ball, Spalding covering the globe, a concept both appealing and prophetic for Albert.

Spalding was inherently formal in nature, an outward paragon of self-control and rectitude. However, when he allowed himself the pleasure of describing the virtues of base ball, he could become impassioned to the point of equating the game to the very spirit of America itself. One such instance resulted in the alliterative assertions found in the introduction of his autobiography.

> I claim that Base Ball owes its prestige as our National Game to the fact that as no other form of sport it is the exponent of American Courage, Confidence, Combativeness; American Dash, Discipline, Determination; American Energy, Eagerness, Enthusiasm; American Pluck, Persistency, Performance; American Spirit, Sagacity, Success; American Vim, Vigor, Virility.[1]

These were characteristics that both America and Spalding had in ample supply as they each strove to achieve their goals in the world. Spalding himself was already applying these qualities to forge a successful future in the realm of sports.

In early April 1882, William Hulbert passed away from heart disease at the relatively young age of forty-nine. He had crammed a whirlwind of business accomplishment into that time, including living to see the realization of his own sporting dreams for his beloved city of Chicago. He had become president of the White Stockings in the winter of 1875–76, being at the helm of the organization when in 1876 they won the first championship of the league he largely created himself. The next year, Hulbert added the title of National League president to accompany his command of the White Stockings, leading both organizations until his death. His obituary in the *Chicago Tribune* described him in these roles as having "great force of character, strong will, marked executive ability, unerring judgement of men and measures, and strict integrity and fairness. . . . He was rightly considered to be the brains and backbone of [the National League]."[2] Spalding would wholeheartedly agree with this commentary, perhaps with a stipulation that all that had been said about Hulbert applied to himself as well. He had been Hulbert's right-hand man in the White Stockings' organization as well as in constructing the National League, helping to devise policy to guide their paths forward.

By the end of April, the Chicago Club stockholders recognized as much by unanimously elevating Spalding from secretary to president and director. Simultaneously, he became the principal owner of the team, buying in with funds accumulated from the prosperity of his sports equipment business.[3] The stockholders felt that "a better man for the position could not have been elected," acknowledging that though he already was devoting much of his effort to making his sporting goods venture a success, he could be counted on to do the same for the base ball club.[4] His former teammate and good friend Cap Anson was the manager of a squad poised to bring home a third straight pennant in 1882. Albert at thirty-one knew he was ready to ascend to the highest rung of the organization's leadership.

The year before, with his sports equipment business expanding briskly, Spalding had moved the company from Randolph Street to larger quarters at 108 Madison Street.[5] Within the next twelve months, the store was exhibiting goods well beyond the range of balls and bats for base ball and cricket, including items for boxing, skating, lawn-tennis, gymnasium exercising, archery, and croquet, as well as playing cards, backgammon sets, and chessmen and boards for indoor amusement. Not to be overlooked in the realm of sporting goods, outdoor activities of hunting and fishing also had a prominent place in the offerings of the company. Rifles, revolvers, knives, rods, reels, and nets were popular gear required in these pursuits. And, like base ball uniforms, hunting and fishing apparel was sold to complete these sports offerings. Dealing in weaponry led to handling associated items such as pocket-knives, razors, scissors, and even table cutlery, all prominently advertised for sale by Spalding & Bros.[6]

In April, one Chicago paper touted Spalding & Bros. as sole western agents for a wide variety of bicycles of "American Design—English Manufacture." The ad pointed out that "to superintend [the] Bicycle Department we have engaged the services of a practical Bicyclist in the person of Mr. L. W. Conkling, the celebrated amateur rider, who is thoroughly 'up' on bicycles in all their details."[7] With the bicycle industry in its infancy, the initial awkward, high-wheeled "boneshakers" were slowly being supplanted by machines designed to be easier for the average individual to ride and control. Having a skilled bicyclist on hand in the store to demonstrate just how simple the use of these vehicles could be was a marketing tool that enabled the purchasing public to become more confident in the use, mastery, and enjoyment of this new form of exercise and transportation. As the popularity of bicycling began to soar in the country over the next decade, the company would begin to produce its own bicycles, manufactured in Chicopee Falls, Massachusetts. This was part of Spalding & Bros.' efforts to back-integrate into manufacturing its own brand of most items they sold.

Spalding's guides used "trusted experts" to explain how to play various sports and accomplish a host of physical exercises and activities. Spalding's "Official Base Ball Guides" contained special articles in which well-known players shared with curious readers their secrets of success in hitting, pitching, fielding and base running. The earliest guide, published in 1878, was edited by Spalding and *Chicago Tribune* sports journalist Lewis Meacham. When Meacham passed away a short time later, in 1882 Spalding hired the dean of base ball journalists and historians, Henry Chadwick, to edit the annual guides, providing them with an added stamp of authority. When Spalding began to branch out into publishing annual guides on other sports, he took the same tack; for his Official Intercollegiate Football Guide, beginning in 1883, he retained the celebrated Yale player and coach Walter Camp as editor.

The base ball guides included advertisements for Spalding's equipment that displayed sports celebrity endorsements to attest to the highest quality and suitability of his products to be used in playing winning base ball. The 1878 publication had a full page of such endorsements for Spalding balls and bats with famous players such as Cal McVey, James White, and Joe Start extolling the virtues of these products. George Wright was prominently included in this group, stating,

> I have frequently played with the "Spalding League Ball," and have always found it to be an A No. 1 ball in every respect. I will have it on sale at my store during 1878. . . . I have used the "Spalding Bat" and have sold the same in my store, and they have become the favorite bat in Boston and vicinity. They are thoroughly seasoned, finely finished.[8]

As early as 1879, Spalding recognized that publishing rule books and instructionals on a variety of sports, exercises, and amusements beyond base ball was a profitable venture that appealed to the public and expanded their interest in these leisure time activities. His base ball guide for 1879 touted the appearance of a new publication, *"Spalding's Journal of American Sports,"* which included articles on a host of outdoor games along with price lists for implements required for their play. Underneath this notice was a list of journals, pamphlets, and guides for all sorts of activities, from the "Science of Self Defence" to "Jig, Clog, and Breakdown Dancing."[9]

Typical of this ongoing promotional effort was a treatise published in 1882 entitled "Spalding's Complete Manual of Boxing, Club Swinging and Dumbbell Exercise." It was promoted as "edited by Geo. H. Benedict, the champion Club-swinger of America" and being "the most complete book of instruction on these arts."[10] Club swinging was a muscle-strengthening and mobility exercise popular at the time, consisting of juggling and swinging elongated, bowling pin–shaped wooden items called Indian clubs. Of course, the guide clearly pointed out that boxing gloves, Indian clubs, and dumbbells could be conveniently purchased by mail-order or in person at Spalding's establishment, along with all other forms of sports equipment. Spalding even formed a venture, the American Sports Publishing Company, which produced this and the other manuals and journals that were all part of what was termed the Spalding Athletic Library.

On October 26, 1884, Spalding's emporium on Madison Street in Chicago experienced a devastating fire. The items cataloged in the damage were varied and numerous. The guns and revolvers on hand were valued at $40,000, the stocks of bicycles and fishing tackle were each worth $20,000, while inventory of base-ball items, Indian clubs, cutlery, and other miscellaneous goods added another $50,000–$60,000, totaling $130,000–$140,000 for the whole lot, worth $4–$5 million in 2023 dollars. The portion of goods lost to the fire was estimated at $80,000 ($2.5 million in 2023). By the time the fire was put out that evening, Spalding had determined that his insurance was more than adequate to cover the loss, had signed a lease for space in a building a few doors away, and contacted his manufacturing partners to replenish his damaged stocks in full, not wanting to miss a beat in the steadily climbing success of his enterprise.[11]

On April 1, 1885, the brothers opened a large store at 241 Broadway in New York City, the company's first expansion outside of Chicago.[12] What better place to open an operation than in the largest sporting goods market in the country, in the backyard of the largest competitor in the business, Peck & Snyder? May the best man win! J. Walter's son Albert, a famed violinist named after his uncle, noted in his autobiography that his recently wed parents moved from Chicago to New York City so that Walter could personally oversee this venture.[13] A year later, the company had opened over a dozen "supply depots" with other retail stores across the country, from Portland, Maine to Denver, Colorado, as agents for Spalding & Bros. products.[14] This growing distribution arm of the company would flex its muscles by quickly and cost-effectively putting Spalding equipment into the hands of those who wanted it.

In less than ten years, Spalding's plunge into the relatively new sporting goods market had turned into a major force within an industry exploding with opportunity. They advertised their goods as much through their Official Base Ball Guide and individual sports publications as through newspapers. Albert initially used his professional ball playing notoriety as a promotional vehicle, which was stipulated in the founding agreement with his brother Walter, whose duty was to manage the partnership.[15] As Walter's son pointed out, "The brothers complemented each other admirably. A. G. [Albert] was resourceful and imaginative. J. W. [Walter] was sober and balanced. A. G. inspired enthusiasm. J. W. won confidence."[16]

When Spalding's days as player and manager of the White Stockings ended, he focused more energy on working within his National League network, headed by William Hulbert, to base-load his business with contracts from the league to supply balls, bats, uniforms, and official league compendiums, all of which announced his position as the leading supplier for professional base ball. The major league's demand for base balls was consistently growing, which Spalding would satisfy in an imaginative manner. Anticipating that some producers of balls would give away their product to the NL to obtain this supply contract, which would bring inherently attractive publicity to their product, Spalding decided to *pay* the league to take his base balls. Paying the NL a dollar per dozen balls was a relatively inexpensive investment in securing this plum supplier position and its associated prestige. It generated dramatically greater sales of Spalding base balls to other base ball organizations as well as the public, who wanted to use the ball that was the standard for the major league.[17]

At the same time, Spalding was immersed in the running of the Chicago White Stockings as president and director of the club. He was a staunch supporter of the team's field leader, Cap Anson, admiring his playing ability while managing the club to championships in 1880–82 and 1885–86. The White Stockings represented the first dynasty of the NL, consistently leading the league in attendance. With the six-foot two-inch Cap Anson supported by another handful of six-footers when the average stature of a professional ballplayer was several inches below that mark, the imposing presence of the White Stockings taking the field was enough to send a shiver of inferiority down the spines of the competition.[18]

According to Anson, the team of 1885–86 was his strongest, with an infield known as the "Chicago stone wall" due to the fielding skills and cohesiveness of Ned Williamson at third, second baseman Fred Pfeffer, and Tommy Burns playing shortstop. As first baseman Anson described their coordinated efforts, "so long had we played together and so steadily had we practiced that there was scarcely a play made that we were not in readiness to meet."[19] This resulted in batters often attempting to hit over them rather than trying to pierce their defense with grounders or line drives. And when those hitters lofted fly balls beyond the infield, more often than not they were tracked down and caught by the fleet-footed, sure-handed Chicago outfielders, especially the wonderfully talented young speedster Billy Sunday, a utility player supporting the powerful hitting duo of center fielder George Gore and left fielder Abner Dalrymple. These teammates all skillfully backed the tremendous pitching tandem of Jim McCormick and future Hall of Famer John Clarkson.

Besides Anson, the Chicago player who dominated the sport during those years of the White Stockings' supremacy was future Hall of Fame right fielder and catcher Mike "King" Kelly, a handsome, debonair Irishman who was a crowd favorite. He won batting titles in 1884 and 1886 while leading the league in scoring.[20] Kelly employed his agility, timing, and fearlessness to steal scores of bases every year, even inspiring a popular song, "Slide, Kelly, Slide," emblematic of the public's infatuation with him as much as their delight in his ability to swipe a bag once on base.[21]

Kelly combined his all-around base ball talent and charisma to intoxicate the crowds. He thought of himself as an entertainer as much as a ball player. In his autobiography he claimed that "People go to see games because they love excitement and love to be worked up."[22] With his superior performance and crowd-pleasing antics, that's exactly what he provided, often stretching the rules to the breaking point in his desire to please the spectators as well as win.

An example came in a game early in the 1881 season in Chicago versus the Bostons when Kelly pulled a trick for everyone to see except the lone umpire, who had his eyes trained on a close play at first. Kelly was on second base when Cap Anson's hot grounder forced a low throw to Boston's first baseman. As the newspaper described it the next day,

> It was strongly suspected that Kelly, in his eagerness to reach the plate from second, somehow forgot to go by way of third, but slighted that bag entirely by some ten or fifteen feet, thereby saving much valuable time and distance. The umpire of necessity was fixing his attention upon the play at first base . . . and hence could not possibly know whether Kelly touched the bag or not. The umpire was doing his duty, and, since he did not with his own eyes see Kelly skip the base, he could not under the rules give him out.[23]

This was one of four runs that Chicago scored in the inning, going on to defeat Boston by a single tally, 5–4. In effect, Kelly's blatant "cutting" of the bag at third on his way to score had cost Boston the game, and the crowd roared its approval. Here was the essence of Mike Kelly, scoring a much-needed run by performing one of his many outrageous feats for his legion of admirers.

However, as with many classic heroes, Mike had an Achilles heel, and his was a shot of whiskey with a beer chaser. As Anson described Mike in his autobiography, "He was a whole-souled, genial fellow, with a host of friends, and but one enemy, that one being himself."[24] His carousing was legendary as well as pervasive among his teammates, leading to an untenable situation for the club. Spalding noted, "Kelly's habits were not conducive to the best interests of the club or his team-mates. He was of a highly convivial nature, extremely fascinating and witty, and his example was demoralizing to discipline."[25] Spalding firmly believed that rules were made to be followed, not broken. Kelly couldn't wait to disregard a few along the way if it meant winning a ball game or just having a good time. He was truly an original, known to his devoted followers as "our Kelly," or even "the Only Kel," a celebrity distinct above all the thousands of Kellys in the Irish communities spread across the country.[26]

Now, a titanic struggle was brewing under the surface of the winningest team in professional base ball. Proud as they were of their White Stockings who delivered such sterling results during these pennant-winning years, Spalding and Anson were continually grappling with their expressed commitment to eliminate the drinking that had become a menace to base ball in the eyes of many a paying spectator. There was simply no room for lushing as a vice among its players if they were to reach the highest levels of performance.[27] Unfortunately, many on the team thought otherwise.

Anson would lecture his players on the evils of the bottle, especially pointing toward Kelly and his wayward behavior, but to no avail. Spalding, from an organizational management perspective, even went as far as to hire Pinkerton detectives to track individual players' nighttime activities and file reports on their partying, then fine the heavy drinkers. Kelly, when famously confronted on one occasion with the results of this surveillance, noted that the detectives had got things wrong when they claimed they spotted him gallivanting at three in the morning, drinking a lemonade. He quipped, "It was straight whiskey; I never drank a lemonade at that hour in my life."[28]

In the end, with Anson's blessing, Spalding simply sold Kelly to Boston for the outrageously record-breaking sum of $10,000. Boston had landed the most popular player in the league, an irrepressible son of the Emerald Isle in a town full of Irish base ball lovers, and Kelly signed a contract for a salary of $5,000, more than double what he was earning in Chicago. It appeared to be a win all around. As it turned out, it was much less than what met the eye.

With the sale of Kelly, Spalding claimed that, for his patrons' sake, it was time to break up the monotony of his ball club's continual winning. A dozen years ago he had experienced something similar when he played for the Red Stockings team that won four pennants in five years. Attendance had steadily dropped due to the public's tiring of Boston's dominance of "Harry Wright's League."[29] This may have been part of Spalding's reasoning in unloading Kelly, but one result was that the White Stockings would not win the championship again for twenty years. Boston had hoped that adding Kelly as a box office draw would propel them to the pennant, but instead they drifted downward rather than rising to a title. And Kelly, for all the money he was paid, saw it slip through his fingers with more boozing, performing well in Boston for a few years but eventually exiting the sport somewhat prematurely, well on his way to digging an early grave a month shy of his thirty-seventh birthday.

Understandably, White Stockings supporters were not happy to see Kelly go, and many Chicago newspapers took Spalding to task for this high-handed maneuver, as he noted in his autobiography. But he felt it contained a silver-lining that wasn't obvious at first glance. "Being at the time President of the Chicago Club, and having been instrumental in promoting the sale of Kelly, I came in for much notoriety. While these daily 'roasts' [in the newspapers] were being served out to me I noticed that the attendance kept increasing." As the season progressed, the condemnations of Spalding lost traction and dropped off, but with a curious loss of attendance at the games. Paying patronage recovered, however, and the club ended the year with record-setting revenues when Spalding addressed this situation by covertly supplying further "ammunition" on other White Stockings' organizational "mismanagement" to the papers that had crucified him earlier so that they could resume their tirades against him and the club.[30]

Spalding had stumbled upon the axiom attributed to P. T. Barnum, "All publicity is good publicity." Having the public actively speaking about him and the team, whether positively or negatively, had boosted attendance at the games. Barnum was a master at stirring up controversy that resulted in curiosity about his ventures, a born self-promoter. His earliest operation in the mid-1800s was the exhibition of the exotic and strange at his American Museum in New York City, where unusual people of different sizes, weights and talents along with various creatures of frightening or surprising nature were showcased. Later, his Barnum & Bailey Circus, audaciously titled "The Greatest Show on Earth," staged productions that attracted the public with fierce and unusual animals and daredevil, captivating performers from around the world. All this generated interest and ultimately income.

Barnum made bold statements about his activities, sometimes outrageous but always intriguing. As Peter Levine described in his Spalding biography, "The Spaldings understood that late-nineteenth-century Americans were attracted to displays of extravagance and to bold claims of greatness, power and wealth."[31] Kelly's sale for the fantastic price of $10,000, though creating a stir among the public and the press, was a display of the White Stockings commanding position in the world of base ball. Spalding claimed he could extract this extravagant sum of money for Kelly because Chicago's players were the best in the game, and they had more of that caliber on their roster. Just come to the ball park and see! In fact, a year after selling Kelly, Spalding duplicated this feat with star pitcher John Clarkson, once again shipping a premier player to Boston for another ten grand.

The advertising and self-promotion of Barnum and Spalding catapulted them into the public eye, not so much for their fortunes as for their ability to interest people in their activities. Such was the way with the development of entertainment in a country that had a growing portion of the urban population with increasing time and disposable income to spend. Weren't the strange and wonderous new exhibits that Barnum revealed to the world well worth the price of admission? Didn't Spalding's involvement with America's national game produce a superior team that spectators needed to see as well as high-quality equipment that every player needed to buy? Newspaper articles on Barnum and Spalding fairly screamed their affirmation on these questions, making it all headline news.

In 1888, Spalding was to again exhibit his penchant for grand publicity in the announcement of a unique venture for base ball. The March 25 edition of the Chicago papers carried the news of his proposal to bring the sport to Australia. Spalding himself had been the advance man for Harry Wright's "crossing the pond" to England by American players fourteen years before, meeting with dignitaries and arranging details of the journey and games to be played there. Now Spalding had dispatched Leigh Lynch to Australia, a theatrical talent and stage manager familiar with the country, to determine the probability of success of a visit "down under." Spalding had been considering a plan to bring two clubs of American ball players to Australia for several years before sending Lynch to make appropriate inquires in that country and, if meeting a favorable response, make the necessary arrangements.[32] The idea wasn't new; it had already occurred to Harry Wright back in 1880 when he had reportedly discussed it with veteran base ball manager, businessman, and promoter Frank Bancroft, but the journey never materialized.[33]

The *Chicago Tribune* commented on the proposed trip with a review of Spalding's maturing organizational talents as well as his aggressive promotion of the game. They noted that from his time as a player in 1876 when he helped the "Big Four" bring a championship to Chicago to his current leadership of the White Stockings club, "As base-ball grew, so Spalding grew." His surveillance of opportunities for the business of base ball had resulted in the scheduling of this unrivalled trip to Pacific shores, stopping at Hawaii, then known as the Sandwich Islands, before moving on to Australia and New Zealand.[34] Publicizing base ball to this portion of the world, the sport itself demonstrating the fast-moving nature of America's very way of life, fit Spalding's inherently superior feelings about the United States. He "recognized that it was good business to promote sport in terms of its social promise," that sport "built character, encouraged order and discipline, and produced the type of citizen necessary for continued American greatness."[35] This would all be on display to the geographies they would traverse. Ever the businessman, the major goal of Spalding's venture was to expand base ball's popularity to new markets, in so doing developing opportunities to sell more equipment.

Recalling the effects that limited advertising had at many stops on the American ballplayers' tour of England in 1874, resulting in unexpectedly low revenues from poor gate receipts, Spalding arranged well in advance for several publicity details. Special, full-color posters to precede the arrival of the Americans were printed for distribution. "Spalding's Australian Base Ball Tour" was splashed across the top of these, accompanied by drawn images of the individuals expected to be on the tour and the vessel carrying them across the Pacific, the steamship S. S. *Alameda*.[36] The two teams of players participating would be the Chicago White Stockings and a team of all-stars composed of players from other major league clubs, dubbed the "All-Americas."

The group would cross the continent by rail, leaving Chicago at the end of the base ball season on October 20. En route, they would play a score of exhibition ball games at locations like St. Paul, Minneapolis, Omaha, Des Moines, Denver, Colorado Springs, Salt Lake City, Los Angeles, and San Francisco before leaving on the ocean voyage west.[37] The posters were distributed liberally prior to arriving at these various locations, as well as internationally, to stimulate interest and gate receipts.

As the base ball season was ending, Spalding had arranged the equivalent of a "photo op" for the White Stockings with President Grover Cleveland in Washington, DC, on October 8. Cap Anson and the team were escorted to meet the president by Congressman Frank Lawler of Illinois, of whom Spalding had requested the arrangement of this meeting.[38] Upon being introduced to the players, Cleveland, a Democrat, said he had heard of their planned trip to Australia; Anson noted that "the majority of the players of his club were Democrats, whereupon the President replied, 'Then they cannot be beaten.'"[39] An artist, Mr. George Coffin, was present and sketched a rendering of Cleveland's meeting with the team in the East Room; Spalding made thousands of copies to distribute on the trip.[40]

In addition to publicity generated from these images, Spalding even engaged a balloonist to travel to Australia with his entourage. Performing under the title "Professor," Coryell Batholomew was a daredevil in his late thirties who was enthralled with hot air balloons and acrobatics. He combined the two in developing an act that involved ascending thousands of feet in a hot air balloon, then jumping from it with a parachute that, once opened, would allow him to extend from a trapeze and hang in various poses, invariably arriving on the ground to great excitement and applause.[41] It was a sure-fire attraction to entice curious crowds to attend the tour's international stops. Those viewing his performances were fascinated but, unfortunately, in one of his early demonstrations in Australia, Bartholomew landed on the rooftop of a building near the playing field, injured his legs and needed the balance of the journey to recover.[42]

Meanwhile, arranging for all the players to make the trip had been tricky. Spalding had secured most of the White Stockings; Anson and hitting sensation outfielder Jimmy Ryan were especially eager to make the journey, as were the infielders of the vaunted "Chicago stone wall." Nailing down the team that would face the Chicagoans proved more difficult. Chief among the holdouts were luminaries Mike Kelly and New York Giants right fielder Mike Tiernan, who both backed out after initially committing to the tour, claiming health concerns or general disinterest in the journey. The project's planned expenses for travel, hotels, and meals were quickly adding up, so Spalding's monetary inducements of fifty to one hundred dollars per man were modest, counting on the vacation-like atmosphere and the players' anticipated status as heroes both at home and abroad to make up for the meager pay.[43] In the end, National League star John Montgomery Ward agreed to captain the All-Americas, and a more than competitive squad signed on for what promised to be the adventure of a lifetime.

George Wright was not to be left behind. Spalding had approached him in late August in Boston, asking that he lead the preparation and training of the players for upcoming cricket matches that were to take place in Australia.[44] He had accepted the invitation, excited by the challenge of playing cricket against the Aussies while he took a break from his hectic work schedule. He noted in an interview, "I was a cricket-player before I played base-ball, and while I gave up the latter I stuck to the former. I am now going to the antipodes to compete with the Australians in their favorite game."[45] George was accompanied on the cross-country journey to San Francisco to meet the other participants by his brother Sam Jr. as well as fellow sporting goods businessman and friend W. Irving Snyder of Peck & Snyder of New York City, who was also invited on the tour by Spalding. Spalding had not asked Sam Jr. to come on the tour, but he traveled west with George to spend the winter with older brother Dan near San Jose.[46]

Although he had retired from playing base ball in the early 1880s, George was only forty-one at the beginning of Spalding's tour, fit, active, and ready to represent his country on the international playing field. In a newspaper article John Ward wrote just before the tour departed from America, he extolled the virtues of having Wright join the others. "Our cricketing prospects took a boom [*sic*] last week by the arrival of George

Wright, the veteran ball-player and cricketer. Mr. Wright leads all New England in batting [for cricket] and as an all-around cricketer and coach is unquestionably the best man in America."[47]

Simultaneously, an even more intriguing development occurred. Ward had just learned that Spalding was in negotiations to expand the tour beyond Australia, planning to return to America by continuing on around the world. He described the notion to the press as "a scheme which for boldness and scope tops anything ever before attempted in the field of sports." Spalding engaged a European transportation expert to explore boat transportation to India, then through the Red Sea to Cairo and the Suez Canal, finally on to various stops in Italy, France, and the United Kingdom before returning to New York City.[48] His already ambitious Australian Tour was morphing into something even more spectacular, the playing of base ball around the world.

With plans to circumnavigate the globe spinning in Spalding's head, a party of thirty-six intrepid travelers were passengers onboard the S.S. *Alameda* as it passed through the Golden Gate Strait and out to sea on November 18. In addition to George Wright, Irving Snyder, the balloonist Professor Bartholomew, Spalding, and the ballplayers, there were Leigh Lynch and others who were handling all the detailed logistics and publicity of the tour along with several newspapermen dutifully chronicling this adventure's progress for a curious world. Anson's wife accompanied him, as did Ned Williamson's, while Spalding had brought his mother Harriet, described by one reporter as "a queenly-looking, white-haired woman of 68 years, nearly six feet tall . . . [with] an exceedingly sweet and kindly face and manners."[49]

A party member who surely stood out was Clarence Duval, the White Stockings "mascot," brought along for general good luck and to entertain the anticipated crowds. Mascots were relatively commonplace within the major leagues during this period, sometimes dogs or cats, even diminutive young men who often had a minor disability or other distinguishing physical impairment. Perhaps this characteristic was to emphasize the good luck of others, ball players included. The importance of the mascot was to instill a winning aura for the team. In the case of Clarence, journalist Harry Palmer described him in his book about the world tour as "a little, slenderly built, impish-faced negro, with a remarkable talent for plantation dancing, 'hoe-downs' and 'walk-arounds,' and the gift of baton twirling. . . . On shipboard he danced for the party . . . the little beggar . . . afforded his fellow-tourists no end of diversion."[50]

Being called a "little beggar" was just the tip of the iceberg of casual slurs employed when many on the trip referred to Duval. In his autobiography, Anson described Clarence as "little darkey," "little coon," and "no account nigger."[51] This fit with Anson's racial bigotry that was routinely on display as he strove to eradicate African Americans from the major leagues. The same could be expected while on this tour, opening the way for other players and journalists of similar persuasion to do the same.[52] It was a difficult path that Duval had to walk as he endured continual indignities, forfeiting his own self-respect to play the fool for his pay, entertaining those who placed little if any value in his worth as an individual.

The first days on the ocean, as always, were the hardest for those unused to the bounding main. Most passengers were seasick, including George Wright. He had been planning to begin training the players in the basics of cricket but was forced by illness to postpone this instruction until after the travelers had left their first stop in Hawaii and were on their way to Australia. At that time, George arranged with the ship's captain to isolate a small section of the quarterdeck with canvas roofing and sidewalls to prevent pitched cricket balls that were struck in practice from leaving the vessel. In this manner, a protected alleyway useful for bowling and batting was established that could allow the players to be instructed in the game under George's tutelage.[53]

The troupe landed in Honolulu a day later than planned, on Sunday November 25. An old regulation from missionary times in the islands prohibited amusements on Sundays, causing the teams to miss their chance to play a ball game in paradise. The anticipated gate receipts in Honolulu would have been significant because many were familiar with the game due to numerous residents having played it on the mainland before emigrating to Hawaii. Spalding himself was not disagreeable to Sunday base ball, but he chose to abide by the rules of the island, forgoing a fine payday in the process.[54]

Instead, many took the afternoon to explore the wonderous sights of extinct volcanic mountainsides and lush forests leading to sandy beaches. An evening's feast followed at the invitation of Hawaii's leader, King Kalakaua, a grand "luau" introduced with flowered "leis" placed around the necks of the tourists by the native women. The meal included bountiful platters of baked and roasted meats, fish, tropical fruits, a variety of greens and the local delicacy of taro-root "poi," each prepared according to ancient custom. It was all accompanied by glasses of wine and punch for seemingly endless toasts to the visitors and the local luminaries. The evening was capped off by Clarence Duval performing plantation dances for the attendees. Palmer reported that the King, who "after laughing heartily at the little darkie's 'pigeon-wings' and 'walk-arounds,' had rewarded him with a ten-dollar gold piece."[55]

So it proceeded in every locale visited by the base ball entourage. Lynch had made plans well in advance at each location, providing time for the locals to arrange grand welcomes and comfortable lodging. The characteristic sights of each stop were of great interest to this traveling band, most of whom had seen no more than a bit of America and certainly nothing of the rest of the world. Banquets of the finest cuisine typical of the area were graciously offered by proud dignitaries at each stop on the tour in exchange for the chance to watch the players demonstrate base ball.

After an initial stop in New Zealand for a quick game in Auckland attended by over four thousand, a heavy hitting affair won by the Chicago team, 22–13, the scene shifted to Australia. Three contests each were played in Sydney and Adelaide, six in Melbourne, and one in Bellarat. Originally, intentions were to play in more cities on this portion of the tour, but the decision to extend the trip to a worldwide affair necessitated shortening the stay in Australia. Chicago bested the All-Americas while in Australia, but just barely, seven games to six. All along the way, the crowds were large, ranging from two thousand to as many as ten thousand per game, even with the Australian summer temperatures hovering around 100 degrees Fahrenheit. The spectators exhibited a hearty appreciation of the sport and those who played it. Chicago centerfielder Jimmy Ryan's diary noted that the crowds were impressed with the expertise shown in the fielding, base running, sliding, and batting demonstrated in playing the sport.[56]

An Australian newspaper article covered the first such game in Sydney on December 15, a close contest won by the All-Americas, 5–4. Attending were approximately five thousand five hundred curious spectators. A bit tongue-in-cheek, the journalist noted the sport's improvement on the English game of rounders, concluding, "With all its complications, however, baseball is a fine game, and we wish we had learnt it from our American cousins in place of euchre, Yankee grab, and poker."[57] These last three amusements were of a gambling nature, perhaps unpleasant reminders of losing money to Americans while playing these games. Three days later, the Sydney Eleven took on eighteen Americans in an abbreviated cricket contest decisively won by the Australians 115 to 81. As in the tour to England in 1874, when the British routinely allowed the Americans to use eighteen players to their eleven because of English cricket superiority, so too had the Aussies. But cricket against the Americans proved a poor draw for the Australian public, and the decision was made to forgo cricket matches in Australia for the duration of the tour.[58]

The *Melbourne Sportsman* reported on the first exhibition played there by noting such interest in the game by the crowd of almost ten thousand that they stayed through twelve innings of a Chicago 5–3 victory followed by a four-inning game of the Chicago team versus a nine mostly composed of Australian cricket players.[59] In Adelaide a few days after Christmas, over two thousand saw a game in which the umpire, Chicago pitcher Tener, declared in the fifth inning that All-America substitute hurler Ward's pitching style was illegal. Ward's delivery, in which he turned his back to the batter before coming around to release the ball, was well-known in the majors. Tener's decision flabbergasted Ward, who walked several batters while complaining vehemently as Chicago prevailed, 12–9.[60] Those in attendance, novices to the game, were undoubtedly mystified by this argument between the teams.

On January 8, the party boarded the German ship *Salier* for the beginning of the return to America by way of points further west. They were at sea for two weeks before landing at Columbo, Ceylon, playing to a tie game at 3–3 before a small crowd with little knowledge of, and less interest in, base ball. Then, on to the Red Sea and the Suez Canal.

A game was arranged outside of Cairo to combine sight-seeing with base ball, played before the Great Pyramid of Cheops and the Sphinx as well as a non-paying audience of several hundred wandering Bedouins and a few scattered visitors in the area. The spectators watched a five-inning affair in non-comprehending silence, but the boys had a great time of it on the dusty plain, the All-Americas winning 10–6. Ward noted for newspaper coverage of the game that at one point baserunner Anson was picked off first base, slipping in the desert sands, "ingloriously crawling back on his hands and knees. It was so very funny that even the Sphinx relaxed her stern features in an effort to smile."[61]

At the same time, George Wright sent a letter to the *New York Clipper* providing commentary on the trip, including the ballgame in the desert.

> The Australians seemed to be well pleased with baseball, and were more liberal in their views concerning it than the English people were with the two baseball teams (the Bostons and Athletics) that visited in 1874. They saw more in our national game than the old game of rounders, and thought that the game would be taken up in Australia as one of their sports. . . . The baseball games in Columbo and Cairo, Egypt were played without any admission fee being charged, Spalding playing the games merely to amuse the natives, who sat around the field with open mouths and eyes.[62]

Once through the canal and into the Mediterranean Sea, the party stopped at Italy and France. These countries provided paying crowds as well as additional, wonderous historic backgrounds against which the spinning and hitting of the sphere could take place. A game was played before over three thousand in Naples, Mount Vesuvius in the distance, while the All-Americas erupted for seven runs in the fifth inning on the way to a victory, 8–2. In Rome, a glade within the park of the Villa Borghese, the former home of an Italian prince, was the picturesque setting for a match won by Chicago, 3–2, viewed by the Italian King Umberto along with thirty-five hundred others.[63] Spalding had wanted to stage the game at the Coliseum, but the idea was rebuffed by the locals though he had offered five thousand dollars plus half the gate receipts going to charity.[64] In Florence, several thousand saw the game, the All-America's winning 7–4. From there the group moved on to Paris, organizing a contest on a makeshift field at the foot of the unfinished Eiffel Tower, a tight contest won by the All-Americas, 7–6. America had made its base ball introduction to the continent.[65]

The last portion of the tour was spent in the United Kingdom, ten games played in England, two in Ireland, and one in Scotland. The last time Spalding and Wright had brought two clubs here in 1874, they encountered a decidedly ethnocentric view of base ball by the English public, who politely dismissed it as the child's game of rounders in disguise. Now, Spalding's approach was more subtle, not attempting to present base ball as an alternative to their beloved cricket but offering it as a "supplement" to it in English sporting life.[66] With the copious advanced publicity for the matches, coupled with the other tour successes noted in newspapers around the world, these exhibitions had garnered significant public interest.

Literally the crown jewel of the sessions, the shimmering highlight of the tour itself, was the appearance of the Prince of Wales to observe the proceedings. On March 12, the future King Edward VII attended the opening match in London on a typically foggy day at the Surrey Cricket Club's Kennington Oval. About eight thousand spectators ringed the oval for the contest, the excitement swelling as the prince arrived in the early innings to cheers from the crowd. Cap Anson remembered that at that moment, "We assembled at the home plate and gave three hearty cheers for His Highness, this action on our parts bringing out a storm of applause from the stand."[67]

Spalding recalled that he was requested to join the prince in the royal box, from which they sat watching the game and discussing its finer points, at separate times each giving the other a hearty slap on the back or knee in reaction to a fine play on the field. Sitting in the presence of royalty, let alone touching the future King of England, was looked upon by some as grossly violating court etiquette. Spalding defended himself later by saying, "I must plead that I was not at court, but at an American ball game. If I sat in the presence of Royalty, it is certain that Royalty sat in mine. If I tapped the future King of Great Britain on the shoulder, it was nothing more offensive than a game of tag, for he had first slapped me on the leg."[68] Spalding considered himself American sports nobility, just as worthy to be casually friendly with the prince as with any other aristocrat.

As the ball game ended, a Chicago victory, 7–4, the London publication of the *New York Herald* had asked numerous attendees to scribble down their thoughts about base ball on small cards handed out at the beginning of the contest. Some comments were complementary, especially related to the fielding of the players, while others brought up the same old comparison to rounders. The prince asked for a card and penciled on it, "The Prince of Wales has witnessed the game of Base Ball with great interest & though he considers it an excellent game he considers cricket as superior."[69] A more diplomatic answer could not have been written, satisfying to his subjects as well as to the American tourists. The entourage would spend the next few weeks crisscrossing Great Britain, playing exhibition base ball in Bristol and Birmingham, Glascow and Manchester, Liverpool and Dublin, with interest and excitement generated at most every stop. But on that day in the royal box in London, Spalding had gone head-to-head with English royalty on competing sports of bat and ball, coming away from the encounter feeling he and his wandering troupe of ballplayers had shown the prince and, indeed, the whole world, the worthiness of America's national game.

11

Beyond Base Ball

By August 1888, the base ball pennant races appeared to be almost decided in both the National League and the American Association. The New York Giants were outclassing the Chicago White Stockings in the NL, while in the AA the St. Louis Browns continued to lead a steadily advancing but still distant squad of Philadelphia Athletics. None of this prevented those who fervently followed the sport from continuing to passionately express their support for the clubs and players they had chosen to embrace as their own, for better or worse.

Up until the mid-1880s, those who followed the game were generally called spectators or the audience. Occasionally in the early 1880s, journalistic references were beginning to be made of base ball spectators as "cranks." Official MLB Historian John Thorn traces this term to "the German word for sick [kronk] as well as the British dialect meaning of 'cranky,' which is feeble-minded."[1] This last label certainly gave a negative connotation, being affixed to those who had lost their mental balance. Typical was an Arizona newspaper in 1881 reporting that "[the state's] 'cranks' and 'imbeciles' are kept at a private asylum."[2] Hence, it was easy to refer to someone "crazy" about base ball as being a "crank."

The reporting on an incident at a home game for the Providence Grays on June 27, 1883, demonstrated the blending of the two meanings of the word. Before the contest, an obsessed follower of the team was sprayed with water from a hose by Gray's outfielder Cliff Carroll in a harmless practical joke. After the game, the victim returned to the stadium with a pistol and fired a shot at Carroll as he was leaving, narrowly missing him and grazing a nearby teammate. The assailant, Jimmy Murphy, was noted

as being "a base ball crank," said to be "mentally off," lending substance
to the dual nature of the term being affixed to him in newspaper reports
of the incident.[3]

In 1888, a slender volume was published in Boston, titled *The Krank*. Its
author, Thomas W. Lawson, was a local who would become tremendously
wealthy through fraudulent manipulation of stock investments in the late
1890s. Along with becoming fabulously rich, he was a fervent follower
of Boston base ball.[4] His book on kranks was a glossary of base ball
terminology, describing the focus of the text as follows,

> The Krank is a heterogenous compound of flesh, bone, and base-ball,
> mostly base-ball. . . . The Krank has a shell, into which he crawls in the
> month of November. He does not emerge from it until April. . . . Their first
> characteristic is, 'knowing it all;' the second, 'telling it all.'"[5]

The "krank" had become a staple in the written portrayal of the game.
He was a die-hard supporter of his team, overly knowledgeable to the
point of supercilious, boorish behavior on the subject. Even women could
be kranks; however, Lawson termed them "kranklets," a patronizing
designation that lost the brashness of the characterization.[6] By the end of
the decade, crank was starting to be replaced by "fanatic," or "fan" for
short, credit historically given to base ball player, manager, scout, and
promoter Ted Sullivan for coining the description in the late 1880s.[7] It
appears the game wanted to designate their faithful followers in a less
disparaging fashion.

While the cranks were spouting their wisdom at the ball parks that
summer, Albert Spalding was making significant progress on his plans
for his journey to Australia, including securing the participation of George
Wright as director of cricket for the tour. In joining the group on the West
Coast just before their sailing in mid-November, George would be away
from his business for over five months, confident that his partner, Henry
Ditson, would keep it all afloat. Ditson, known as "Harry" or "Dit" to his
friends, who partnered with George in his company after years of sole
ownership, was another "Harry" in whom George had total faith.

Although he was nine years George's junior, over the last decade
Ditson had proven to be a stalwart in the operations of the business,
detail-oriented and profit-driven. As Denny Wright described it, great
grandfather George was the salesman of the duo, with a confident flair

about sports in general and base ball in particular, "an ideas person rather than one who ran the numbers."[8] Harry was the perfect foil, more focused on the operations of the business. The company was now growing even faster than they had hoped, but not without good reason. Both George and Harry were active in building its success, seizing opportunities both inside and outside base ball to offer their assistance in organizational development of new sports associations and fostering emerging games and activities as well as selling the equipment needed to play them. They wanted to expand the spectator base of these games, hopefully to develop the followers into "fans" who would play as well as watch.

Due to George's stature in base ball, this sport would always be a focal point of the venture. But with more leisure time slowly becoming part of life for many Americans, different athletic pursuits were offering opportunities for equipment sales. Before George committed to participate in Albert's Pacific adventure, he joined his partner Harry at one of these new athletic activities. It was an event of great importance to them, hosting the Wright & Ditson Open tournament of lawn tennis. This was a championship that they had sponsored dating back seven years to 1882, the past four being played at the opulent Wentworth Hotel, a New England seaside resort. It was an easy train commute from Boston, fifty miles northeast on the island of New Castle belonging to the city of Portsmouth, New Hampshire, a desirable destination for summertime vacationers wanting to leave the sweltering heat and congestion of the urban eastern cities for a breath of fresh air on the coastline. George and Harry felt it provided the perfect environment for their event.

Lawn tennis was a relatively new sport in America, invented in England in the mid-1870s. It had crossed the Atlantic by the late 1870s, gaining in popularity since then. It was more commonly referred to as just "tennis," especially after playing surfaces expanded from grass to include clay and asphalt. From Wright & Ditson's initial sponsorship of a tournament in late July 1882, this meeting routinely garnered the top tennis players nationwide, who appreciated the convivial atmosphere of the gathering as much as the competition itself. Many of them viewed it as a tune-up for the United States Championships a month later, which in 1881 had begun to take place down the coast in Newport, Rhode Island.[9] Wright & Ditson had first set up their tournament in Cottage City on Martha's Vineyard, Massachusetts, but after a few years arranged with the Wentworth to sponsor the event in its more sumptuous surroundings, attracting an even larger group of entrants as well as spectators.[10]

The matches of 1888 were not a disappointment. A leading American lawn tennis doubles player, Valentine Hall, in his book on the sport published the next year, made special note of the proceedings.

> Wright and Ditson's annual tournament has become a feature of the tennis season, and all the players look forward to it for months before the time arrives. For the last five years all the best players of the country have contested, and last season [1888] was no exception to this rule. The success of the tournament is entirely due to the energy and skillful management of Mr. H. A. Ditson, who has, during the past few seasons, devoted much of his time in pushing forward and assisting the progress of this rapidly growing game . . . After the tournament a large ball was given, which made everyone happy, and all left with the impression that the Wentworth tournament was the jolliest tourney of the season.[11]

George and Harry certainly knew how to throw a lawn tennis gala, enticing top-notch players and entertaining them and their guests in style. George had quickly taken an interest in the game, historically derived from a related, rather convoluted contest played by European nobility mostly indoors with racquet and ball.[12] When Harry joined the business, besides shouldering more of the organizational load, he became a staunch supporter of tennis as a business opportunity, predicting it would become a major recreational activity across the nation. With this foresight as his guide, by the time he passed away one obituary would note that "from the very start of tennis he was in the forefront, doing everything in his power to push the game to national prominence. . . . [He was] the best informed authority on the subject of tennis in the country."[13]

For both partners, tennis would become a center of attention along with base ball. In May 1881, on the front page of one of the first installments of *Journal of American Pastimes*, a short-lived, newspaper-like semiannual publication of Wright & Ditson's, was a detailed illustration of a spirited match of lawn tennis, complete with a promotional blurb on the subject, which read in part,

> There is no doubt but it is a healthy and vigorous game, and not too violent, though it will give all the needed exercise; can be enjoyed without calling for too much exertion and consequently inducing exhaustion and

prostration. . . . A person does not need to become an expert to enjoy it. . . . Another grand point is its continuousness. You begin the game and are fully employed until it is finished, and have not to wait for your innings or your turn, as you have in most other games.[14]

The sport was becoming more fashionable in the Boston area and throughout New England. George's contacts with local private cricket clubs that were setting up tennis courts for use by their members, as well as his base ball connections with colleges and universities that were sponsoring tennis competitions, gave his business the opportunity to supply the equipment necessary for the game's enjoyment.

Most items were imported from England, but some, like tennis balls, began to be produced in America. The balls were made of vulcanized rubber with a cemented and stitched cloth covering for better wear, eventually making the core hollow and injecting it with air to provide more consistent playing properties.[15] The various products needed to play the game were packaged and sold in a set containing "bats" or racquets, tennis balls, and the net itself, along with ropes, mallets, and pegs for assembly, and a book of rules and instructions.[16]

By the early 1880s, the sport established a regulatory body, the United States National Lawn Tennis Association (USNLTA), to set rules and regulations, schedule events and promote the game across the country. Wright and Ditson, especially Harry, religiously attended USNLTA meetings, offering the company's superior quality wares for the sport. By 1883, in conjunction with Peck & Snyder, they developed a tennis ball manufactured in the United States that the association adopted for use as the official tennis ball throughout its member clubs, sold by the joint manufacturers at five dollars per dozen balls.[17] This, while Spalding & Bros. was renewing their contract to *pay* the NL one dollar per dozen balls for the privilege of being the league's official base ball supplier.

In 1887, Wright & Ditson secured sole USNLTA supply with their own model ball, made in this country, beating out competition from F. H. Ayers, the leading English maker of tennis balls for such prestigious tournaments as the Wimbledon Championship.[18] After a few more years of competition with Ayers for this supply position, the Wright & Ditson tennis ball effectively monopolized the USNLTA business until the early 1900s.[19] In 1888, they were awarded the contract to print the official rule book of US lawn tennis, an arrangement that also lasted for many years.[20] This journal was a much sought-after guide for experienced and novice players alike, crammed with information on playing the game and tips on winning strategies as well as reviews of the previous year's tennis tournaments across the country. In less than a decade, Wright & Ditson had become to the USNLTA what Spalding & Bros. was to the National League of base ball, sole supplier of the official ball and guide-book of the sport of lawn tennis, with accompanying lucrative sales.

Wright & Ditson quickly became the leading supplier of lawn tennis equipment nationwide, known for quality goods and a staunch commitment to the game. In support of the sport's growth, in addition to tournament sponsorship the company donated prizes for contest winners, including its most popular racquets. By the late 1890s, George would lead a group of the East Coast's tennis champions to promote the game on a groundbreaking tour to the newly developing tennis market in California.[21]

The ultimate marketing effort for Wright & Ditson in the sport of tennis was yet to come. By the turn of the century, the game's appeal had spread from the expertly manicured grass courts of private clubs and university campuses to more public venues. It was then that George's sons, Beals and his brother Irving, three years his junior, would begin to come into their own as tennis champions. Their energetic approach and winning ways furthered the sport in the eyes of the public as well as brought honor to the Wright family athletic tradition. Much as Wright and Albert Spalding had done in their successful days on the diamond, the Wright boys' tennis exploits attracted attention to the game itself.

Beals was a National Singles champion in 1905, the year before having won gold medals at the Olympics in both singles and doubles while winning national doubles titles from 1904 through 1906.[22] Irving, a tough competitor though not as strong as Beals, became a national champion in mixed doubles in 1917 and 1918.[23] For his accomplishments within the sport, Beals would eventually be enshrined in the International Tennis Hall of Fame in Newport, Rhode Island, completing the unique feat of having a father and son both inducted into separate sports' Halls of Fame.

Built in George's mold, both young men were of medium height, quick-reflexed, and skillful in the manipulation of the ball in battling their opponents into submission. Irving's grandson Denny remembers his father talking about the two brothers, "Irving being the more serious and organized of the two while Beals was fun-loving, a great guy to be around."[24] In a way, it sounded like Harry Wright and brother George.

Beals was especially adept at a technique both brothers used as a dangerous weapon in their tennis arsenal, the chop stroke. They were known throughout the tennis circuit for this maneuver, taking what had formerly been a little-used tactic and making it an effective counter-punch for their game strategy. It harkened back to the fair-foul hitting of George's early base ball days, the skillful application of spin to the ball to make it difficult to play. This shot was not employed by many, requiring great timing and a delicate touch to execute properly. It was meant to catch an adversary off guard by putting severe backspin on the ball, chopping down on it to make it come to a screeching halt when it cleared the net and hit the ground, rather than bouncing forward toward the opponent.[25]

Champion tennis player, author, and peer of the brothers, J. Parmly Paret, recalled Beals's use of the shot in this manner, "Beals Wright, who became so famous for his clever play in many international matches, developed the chop stroke to its highest possibilities, and it was truly remarkable the accuracy and attacking power he secured with it. . . . He drove the adversaries back from the net by lobbing and then chopped at their feet."[26] The London sporting journal *Field* favorably appraised this tactic in an appreciative analysis of Beals's aggressive volleying approach to the game, especially commending Beals on his use of this weapon in developing strategies of attack against his opponents.[27]

Although Wright & Ditson's devotion to the marketing of tennis was extensive, it did not divert their attention from base ball. The year 1884 was especially good for company sales for the sport. George had secured the supply of Union Association base balls and their official guidebook that year. His longtime association with the college game, through continual contact and support of teams at Harvard, Brown, and Yale universities, among others, resulted in the Wright & Ditson base ball being designated the official ball for use in the American College Association, along with the company being authorized to print the organization's official rule book.[28] George's connection with the Providence Grays may have been frayed by their use of the reserve system in forcing George to decide on an early retirement from the game, but the relationship was still strong enough for Wright & Ditson to be awarded the contract to design and supply the Grays' new uniform for their championship season in 1884, "Steel-gray shirts and pants, blue belts and stockings and blue caps."[29]

Wright & Ditson routinely was the choice as uniform supplier to various base ball teams in the majors, as well as minor league clubs, collegiate squads and amateur associations such as company-sponsored teams across the Northeast. An 1881 notice by Wright & Ditson in their *Journal of American Pastimes* proudly proclaimed their uniform-making expertise, including their rapid order response. "We have every facility for making *Base-Ball, Cricket, Lawn Tennis, Archery, Yachting, and Beach Uniforms.* . . . Please allow as much time as possible in getting up a full outfit; it takes from six to eight days to make them with care."[30] The *New York Clipper* even gave a forceful endorsement of the company's football uniform by claiming that Harvard's outfits made by Wright & Ditson, "are probably the finest ever manufactured. . . . Jackets are made of extra canvas, double-stitched . . . [with an] elastic insertion . . . which enables the players to bend more easily.[31] George took special interest in this facet of the business. Although he certainly did not play all the sports for which his company supplied uniforms, he still knew firsthand the general needs of players for comfort and durability in their athletic wear.

The company continually encouraged the formation of city and state-wide athletic associations, especially related to base ball. They often offered the hospitality of a room in their store as a meeting place for such endeavors. As 1883 unfolded, one such effort was touted in the Boston papers in this manner:

> Wright & Ditson, with their usual liberality, have come to the fore with a proposition to stimulate athletics, and especially base ball, among Boston amateurs, by offering a fine prize to the champion trade nine for 1883. The number of commercial nines playing in the city last year was very large, and almost every prominent house had its nine. All nines intending to enter can signify their intention to the above firm before February 1. A meeting will be held after that date and an organization perfected.[32]

For this trade association, when they met in February at Wright & Ditson's store to organize, Harry Ditson was elected vice president, enabling him to steer the group to choose his company's base ball paraphernalia.[33]

By the mid-1880s, another new game, played during the winter months, had caught the fancy of much of the sporting public in the Northeast and Midwest. It was called roller polo, an activity that today would be described as indoor hockey on roller skates. The sport featured two squads of six teammates skating back and forth on an indoor roller rink trying to score goals by using short, curved field hockey–type sticks to advance a base-ball-sized rubber sphere along the floor into a net at either end of the rink. Invented in the mid-1870s in England, it came to America and developed a following by the early 1880s, engendered by the roller-skating craze that was sweeping the country.[34]

The action was frantic, rough and tumble, with injuries abounding as the players often crashed into each other in pursuit of the ball or were whacked by an opponent's stick while swinging at the orb. The participants found it exhilarating and the public flocked to watch the action, if not the mayhem, on the nights when the games took place. As history and kinesiology professor Stephan Hardy put it in an article on the development of roller polo, "For workers, the sport rehearsed their everyday harsh, physical experience, where the tough hand ruled. For bourgeois fans, the game was a titillating window into that same world."[35]

The games were a bonus to business for roller rinks as well as skate manufacturers, who both embraced it. Beyond a rink's offer of a pleasant public skating venue, it could now showcase a pulse-pounding match of roller polo with its associated demonstration of skating skill along with the visceral excitement of a potential brawl or two. As with any fledgling sport, an organizational structure was needed to assure stability and growth. In 1882, the National Roller Polo League was founded in Dayton, Ohio, an association of teams in the Ohio Valley region, and other leagues across the Midwest and Northeast quickly followed.[36]

Micajah C. Henley was a major supporter of the sport. He was the dominant American manufacturer of roller skates in the 1880s, with a capacity to produce twenty-five hundred pairs of skates per day from his factory in Richmond, Indiana.[37] By the 1885–86 season, his company was publishing what was termed the "Official Polo Guide," with playing rules for the Western League and those of New York, Massachusetts, and New England. It contained tips on how to play the sport and included diagrams of how to lay out a playing surface in a rink. The basics of roller skating were detailed for those who had never tried the activity. Pages of advertisements followed describing equipment required to play roller polo, including regulation sticks, balls, cage goals, and, of course, roller skates, of which the superiority of the Henley models were extolled.[38]

Wright & Ditson wholeheartedly backed the game as well, with its opportunity to support a swelling market for sporting goods sales. In 1883, the New England Association of Polo Clubs was founded, including Ditson among its directors as well as Frank E. Winslow, a Bostonian who produced roller skates and was owner-manager of a large skating rink in town.[39] By 1885, Winslow had become president of the association, while Harry was now president of the Central Division of the organization, representing eight teams in the Boston area.[40] The Massachusetts League had ten clubs competing, the Maine State League had six. All these clubs needed equipment for the games and to outfit their players, a Wright & Ditson specialty. George and Harry were eager to oblige.

In late 1884, the company introduced its own team to publicize the sport across the Northeast, composed of base ball players from various clubs and led by Boston team captain John Morrill. This group would give an exhibition of base ball skills before the roller polo match, pitching, catching, and base running, which the crowd thoroughly enjoyed.[41] By January 1885, the *New York Clipper* reported that, "The Wright & Ditson [polo] team of ball-players is the first one formed on a purely professional basis. . . . The club has been the attraction of the season."[42]

George and Harry published their own guide, officially sanctioned by the New England Polo Association.[43] It contained league rules and regulations, constitutions and by-laws, game schedules, "hints" for playing competitively, and equipment advertisements. Additionally, there were a few wrinkles that George applied from his past base ball guide experience to make these journals more relevant to the results on the rink. Included were summaries of league standings for the 1884–85 season as well as brief histories of some of the key clubs and their players to provide some depth of coverage to develop a connection between the sport and its fans. The publication even provided thumbnail sketches of two leading players, a throwback to George's own book on Boston base ball of a decade prior, where he did the same for his teammates. Artistic illustrations of the two featured players in uniform accompanied the short biographies, showing off their handlebar mustaches as well as the fine-looking uniforms designed by Wright & Ditson.[44]

The sport of roller polo reached its zenith by the early 1890s, hanging on well into the first few decades of the next century in pockets of the Midwest. Along this arc, Wright & Ditson provided valued organizational support as well as quality sports equipment for the game. The company had become involved almost from roller polo's inception, lending a special promotional élan by forming its own professional team to travel throughout New England and beyond, drawing throngs of fans to the rink. As the sport's popularity shifted from roller rink to ice in the 1890s, George was there to monitor the evolution of interest in the game to the speedier ice polo, then finally to ice hockey, with its longer, broad-bladed sticks for better control of a flat puck that could glide along the ice rather than bouncing as did a rubber ball. He sponsored a trip to Canada for matches of ice polo and ice hockey in the winter of 1894–95, bringing to Montreal a group of tennis players from Harvard, Brown, and Columbia who could skate and had played ice polo. There Wright observed firsthand the superiority of ice hockey to polo on ice, returning to Boston with plans on the promotion of ice hockey as well as the implements to play it.[45]

By the fall of 1890, Wright had even become intrigued with the Scottish sport of golf. The story goes that he had received a set of clubs and balls mixed in with an order of cricket equipment from England. Being unfamiliar with the game, and not knowing what else to do with these implements, he displayed them in his shop, hoping by chance to see if anyone else knew what to make of them. As it happened, a Scotsman visiting Boston took notice and explained the sport to George.[46] The game was afoot!

The helpful Scot subsequently sent George a book on the sport's rules. Since there were no golf courses in the area, Wright needed to obtain a permit from the city to lay out a golf course on a portion of one of the public grounds, Franklin Park.[47] This wasn't an easy task, as no one on the Parks Commission knew anything about the game and feared that the park might be damaged. George used his connections with a few of the members, alleviated their concerns and obtained the permit.[48]

On December 10, 1890, armed with golf equipment and accompanied by three other willing companions, this foursome comprised the first golfers to play the sport on public property in New England, if not the country. Fred Mansfield, an expert tennis and cricket player, along with former lacrosse player Sam Macdonald and George's brother-in-law Temple Craig, were the three intrepid souls who braved the near-freezing temperatures and biting wind with George as Wright & Ditson clerk J. B. Smith laid out the course, including digging the holes himself and scoring the match.[49] Two sets of ten holes each were played by the group, Wright recording the lowest total score for each ten-hole round, a sixty-eight followed by a fifty-nine.[50] George wrote of the group's experience, "All decided they enjoyed the outing and the game of golf was a grand success, and all wished to try it again at some future day."[51] A second session did indeed take place in March 1891, Wright joining Mansfield and a few others by the seaside at Crescent Beach, in southern Massachusetts. He again scored the low total for the combined two rounds, 118.[52]

Now another game of ball and stick had been brought to the public's attention by George Wright, this one taking its time for momentum to build from a private club experience to a public activity. By the early 1900s, with Wright & Ditson's sales of top-quality golf clubs and balls, along with its steady promotion of events and supporting the design and building of public golf courses, George would be thought of by many as the Father of American Golf.

Even with all his success in bringing new games to the enjoyment of the public, George Wright never forgot his participation in Spalding's World Tour, regaling his family with tales about the "eye-opening" adventures in which he had participated. Great grandson Denny had heard from his father that the trip was one of the highlights of George's life, his great grandfather alluding to the excitement and riskiness of the global ocean voyage. Every so often George would show his family a commemorative volume, "the book with the Pyramids" as George's grandson called it, a keepsake of the tour that Albert Spalding had personally presented to each of the journey's participants containing some wonderful photographs of their various ports of call.[53]

During the 1880s, Spalding's well-established connections to base ball's National League had resulted in supply contracts with a steady stream of orders, both for NL requirements and for much of the public, making it the dominant supplier of base ball goods throughout the country. Wright & Ditson in Boston and Al Reach's Philadelphia-based sporting goods company were left with supplying the Union Association and the American Association with base ball goods as these two upstart major leagues attempted to establish themselves in the game during the mid-1880s. Reach had secured the AA supply contract for balls and guidebooks, a steadily increasing demand that he was happy to fill. Wright had done the same with the UA, however short-lived, supplementing this with collegiate base ball needs wherever possible.

Spalding had become recognized as the major supplier to the base ball equipment market, but as George and Harry were discovering during the decade of the 1880s, there was more than enough sporting goods business to go around if one was clever, resourceful, and dedicated to furthering the American public's seemingly insatiable appetite for sports in all its varieties. Wright & Ditson was masterful in its ability to scout out these trends. Then, through organizational support and the supply of quality products at reasonable prices, they helped to popularize those sports that seemed to possess longer-term viability.

As Professor Hardy noted, "Wright and his partner Henry Ditson had a nose for emerging sports. . . . They had quickly jumped into the young roller polo market in 1883. . . . Wright was also introducing Boston to the exotic game of golf."[54] Add in their strong push for growth of the nascent sport of lawn tennis and, in effect, they could be viewed as a new business development company. It was one that thrived on pursuing the introduction and nurturing of new sports to the American public as the best path to expand in the marketplace while not running head-on into the sporting goods behemoth that was Spalding & Bros. George and Harry, through their innovative approach, had brought their company to the pinnacle of the sporting goods market in New England, in doing so helping set the stage for the phenomenal growth of tennis, golf, and ice hockey across America at the dawn of the twentieth century.

12

Triumph and Transition

During the middle of 1887, Samuel Clemens, or as he was better known, Mark Twain, had returned to his summer place in Elmira, New York. A resident of Hartford, Connecticut, he always enjoyed coming back to the Finger Lakes region of the Empire State, seeking a more relaxed environment from which to continue writing his wonderful tales of American life. By then, whether it be in Elmira, Hartford, or practically anywhere else across the country, what had become engrained as part of the cultural rhythm of summer was a good game of base ball. Professionals battled for the pennant while local nines took to the ballfields, challenging each other to lay claim to the title of champion of their locales.

On Saturday, July 2, Twain and his good friend and neighbor, the Reverend Dr. Thomas Beecher, strolled down to the Maple Avenue Park in Elmira, invited there to umpire a twentieth-anniversary ballgame between the two old rival clubs of the town, the Alerts and the Unions. For this game, the teams would be mostly filled by middle-aged merchants and politicians of the area, once fine ballplayers but now gone to seed. Twain was such good copy for the newspapers of the day that when some got advanced notice that he and Beecher had been invited to umpire the contest, the *New York Sun* couldn't resist reporting on the match, in their Sunday edition featuring a front page article covering the previous day's antics.[1] Much of the commentary was purely tongue in cheek, but a game did indeed take place, the Unions beating the Alerts, 23–10.

The *Sun* journalist covering the contest was beseeched by the two honorary umps to sit with them while the game unfolded. As such, the reporter wrote that, "*The Sun*'s readers have got to suffer for this, for of all the utterly incompetent, shiftless, and ignorant umpires that ever tangled up the proceedings of a pair of ballclubs those two were the worst." Twain initially sat in a covered section of the stands while Dr. Beecher was closer to the diamond in the blazing sun. As it was noted by Twain of Beecher, "He ought to be here with me. But fortunately it doesn't matter. We will not agree on anything anyway, and the clubs have appointed Lawyer John R. Joslyn as referee. He is certain to agree with either the Doctor or me, and so everything will run smoothly."[2]

As if it wasn't enough that the witty Twain was on hand to comment on the action, the *Boston Globe* had asked another humorist of the era, Henry Guy Carleton, to weigh in on the proceedings. The result was a farcical sketch that proceeded to make its way across the country in various versions during the month, poking fun at the base ball fan Twain and joking about the frequent rule changes of the sport and the mannerisms of its practitioners.[3] One such account, from a Montana newspaper published two weeks after the contest, distilled Carleton's observations of the game down to unprecedented decision-making criteria proposed by Twain and Beecher for the match.

First—Ball is a strike that passes within eight feet of the plate, on either side of it.

Second—To wait for good balls causes delay and public dissatisfaction, and is not going to be allowed on this occasion. The batsman will strike at everything that comes, whether he can reach it or not.

Third—In waiting intervals pecking at the plate with the bat to see if it is there will not be allowed.

[Fourth] The pitcher must not wipe the ball on his pants, neither must he keep on inspecting it and squirming it and twisting and trying to rub the skin off with his hands.[4]

It was all good fun, the out-of-shape players trying to recreate their youth through a rusty exhibition of ball-playing skills, everyone enjoying themselves. The only consternation that seemed to arise at one point in the contest was when Twain and Dr. Beecher quarreled about a player being safe or out. The *Sun* reported that Beecher "lost his usual self-control, and referred to Mr. Clemens as a crank from Hartford."[5] In reality, this supposed criticism bestowed upon Clemens by Beecher was the unvarnished truth, for Mark Twain had been besotted by the game of base ball for over a dozen years.

Twain and his family had moved to Hartford, Connecticut, in 1874. As an author, he was attracted to the city to be closer to his publisher, the American Publishing Company, which was based there. The Twains lived in an erudite enclave, their next-door neighbor being Harriet Beecher Stowe, author of the abolitionist classic *Uncle Tom's Cabin*.[6] In Hartford, Twain became a certified base ball crank.

That year, the city organized the Hartford Dark Blues as a professional club in the National Association, the team owned by a wealthy banker, Morgan Bulkeley. Twain often attended games at the cozy two-thousand-seat stadium at the Hartford Base Ball Grounds, losing an umbrella at one match in May 1875 and famously posting a waggish advertisement in the local paper offering five dollars for the umbrella's return along with a reward for the boy who took it. "I do not want the boy (in an active state) but will pay two hundred dollars for his remains."[7]

By 1876, the Dark Blues became a charter member of the National League, finishing second to the powerful Chicago White Stockings. They boasted such elite players as fireballer Tommy Bond and curveball artist Candy Cummings. Bulkeley, with the support of NL founder William Hulbert, had become the first league president. Things appeared promising for the club, but the recession sweeping the country was particularly hard on the team's attendance, resulting in depressed revenues and causing them to drop out of the league after 1877, replaced by the Providence Grays. A decade later, Bulkeley and Twain were among local investors in a stock company, the Hartford Amusement Association, that funded Hartford's continuing participation in the organized game through its Eastern league entry.[8]

Twain's infatuation with base ball sometimes even extended into his novels. His book, *A Connecticut Yankee in King Arthur's Court*, published in 1889 about a Hartford resident from the 1880s who is transported back to medieval England, devoted a few pages to the game. Among other adventures, the time-traveler teaches the knights of the realm how to play base ball, with absurdities along the way. The protagonist noted of the players,

> I couldn't get these people to leave off their armor; they wouldn't do that when they bathed. . . . One of the teams wore chain-mail ulsters, and the other wore plate-armor made of my new Bessemer steel. . . . When a Bessemer was at the bat and a ball hit him, it would bound a hundred and fifty yards, sometimes. And when a man was running, and threw himself

on his stomach to slide to his base, it was like an iron-clad coming into port. . . . The umpire's first decision was usually his last; they broke him in two with a bat, and his friends carried him home on a shutter.[9]

This description of an umpire's fate seemed to offer some indication of Twain's feelings about the lone arbiter of a game's proceedings. Perhaps it influenced his decision to position himself well back in the stands when offered the opportunity to umpire the Elmira contest of the Alerts and Unions.

When Albert Spalding and his companions landed in New York City in early April 1889 to complete their World Tour, Twain and numerous other luminaries feted them a few days later at a grand banquet at Delmonico's on April 8. Twain's well-known love of the game, coupled with his national fame as a humorist and lecturer, made it almost mandatory that he be part of the festivities. The nearly two hundred fifty attendees included politicians, financiers, entertainers, businessmen, and sports enthusiasts, all gathered to toast the triumphant heroes upon their return.

At the speaker's table in the front of the room sat Spalding with former National League president A. G. Mills to his right and popular orator Chauncey Depew another seat over. Mark Twain was half a dozen places to Spalding's left, numerous politicians separating the two. Six other tables were each set at a ninety-degree angle to Spalding's and held another thirty-five to forty guests apiece.[10]

These long tables contained many lively pairings. Directly across from Spalding, given places of honor at the head of their table in the middle of the gathering, were George Wright and Irving Snyder, old friends and sporting goods rivals of Spalding & Bros. who had participated in the journey; their business partners Henry Ditson and Andrew Peck were at the left-most table of the six. At the other end of Wright's table were grouped Cap Anson, his father, and Spalding's brother Walter. At the next table was John Ward, captain of the All-Americas on the trip, providing his views on the journey to venerable sports journalist Henry Chadwick, sitting across from Ward. Situated another table over were thirty-year-old Theodore Roosevelt with his younger brother Elliott, father of future "First Lady of the World," Eleanor Roosevelt.[11]

Teddy had already served in New York state politics and was about to be appointed a federal civil service commissioner, followed by becoming New York City police commissioner. On the other hand, Elliott was a wealthy socialite who feigned working for a living at a brokerage firm. They had not accepted their invitations because of their knowledge of, or passion for, base ball, of which they had little. Rather, both were intimately acquainted with much of New York society attending the festivities, and this party was all about being seen as part of the city's self-congratulatory celebration of American exceptionalism.

According to the menu, an impressive dinner was served "in Nine Innings," leading off the first with an oyster appetizer and capping the ninth with fruits, cakes, coffee, cheese, and liquors, with a gastronomic delight of delicacies in between. Afterward, Mills welcomed the throng to the occasion. Spalding, Anson, and Ward each offered short responses to the toasts being given to the world travelers, grateful for the privilege of being part of such a unique and delightful adventure.[12] Then, to the immense enjoyment of the crowd, Twain delivered one of his patented speeches, part autobiography, part travelogue, punctuated with patriotism and all in good humor. He was at his best when he extolled the game itself as well as those who exhibited it to the world.

> Base ball, which is the very symbol, the outward and visible expression of the drive and push and rush and struggle of the raging, tearing, booming nineteenth century! . . . I would envy [the ballplayers] somewhat of the glories they have achieved in their illustrious march about the mighty circumference of the earth. . . . They have carried the American name to the uttermost parts of the earth, and covered it with glory every time. . . . I drink long life to the boys who ploughed a new equator round the globe, stealing bases on their bellies![13]

After Twain's effort, Chauncey Depew proceeded with a fine keynote speech, hitting all the right notes and accompanied by rousing cheers. Other speakers followed, but the evening wouldn't have been complete without actor, comedian and base ball fanatic DeWolf Hopper performing his rendition of "Casey at the Bat." It had been penned the previous year by journalist Ernest Lawrence Thayer for a San Francisco newspaper and was already becoming Hopper's enduring ode to base ball.[14] Its recitation was one of the high points of this spectacular evening.

From years-later audio and movie recordings of subsequent Hopper performances of the classic, his well-rehearsed vocal range of expression would have been almost musical in its delivery, accompanied by well-timed theatrical gestures. High notes shrilly accompanied the home crowd's desperate yearning for victory, while bass tones emphasized Casey's futile effort as he struck out, sending the Mudville fanatics home crestfallen with disappointment.[15] The nature of the poem invariably struck a powerful chord with the audience, for most every village, town, or city had a Casey, and Mudville might be almost anywhere across the base-ball-mad American landscape.

It was a hard act to follow, to be sure, but Hopper's fellow base ball enthusiast, good friend and thespian Dibgy Bell was up to the task with a specially composed lyric poem entitled *Spalding's Ride*. It described the mixture of pride and excitement of those who had greeted Spalding's indominable party dockside when they had arrived home after their months away. The eighth stanza, the poem's last, encompassed the journey.

Hurrah, Hurrah for our Spalding bold;
Hurrah, Hurrah for his well-won gold;
And when New York has its baseball ground,
May his statue of bronze on the field be found.
And upon it inscribed: "From the baseball cranks,
Who in manner befitting express their thanks,
To Spalding, who, freighted with ardor sublime
Played our national game in every clime
From 'Frisco, globe-circling, to New York Bay,
In lands ten thousand miles away."[16]

Spalding and his band had indeed traveled far over the past five months, but the trip was not over quite yet. His group proceeded to Baltimore, Philadelphia, and Boston, playing exhibitions and attending welcoming banquets thrown by adoring city fathers. They traveled to Washington, DC, for a match before going west to Pittsburgh, Cleveland, and Indianapolis for more base ball, finally arriving in Chicago where the trip had begun months before. It was the perfect ending for the globe-trotting tourists.

However, much like the Americans' 1874 journey through England, it didn't quite cover expenses when all was said and done, garnering no "gold" mentioned in Bell's recitation. Spalding, ever the optimist when it came to base ball, still felt it was worth the effort, if only to let the rest of the world know that America had its very own national sport that was a credit to the country and those who played it, in the process creating a budding demand for base ball goods in Australia and even in parts of England.

Outwardly, with the triumphant return of the World Tour, the game of base ball appeared to have reached a high point in its existence. Yet, underneath this gleaming façade stirred the perturbed souls of the players themselves, many of whom knew the business of the sport had just taken steps that signaled a rift between management and the players that would be difficult if not impossible to repair.

As Spalding's entourage spent its first few days on the ocean back in November 1888, the National League had held its annual meeting. One of the topics discussed was a proposal on player salaries, which was a significant departure from existing procedures, to the detriment of the players. It called for the classification of teammates into categories from A to E, based on measurable performance criteria such as batting, fielding, and base running but also including intangibles such as teamwork and conduct. These assignments would be made by the League Secretary and his staff, with resulting maximum annual compensations of A-rated players at $2,500; B, $2,250; C, $2,000; D, $1,750; and E, $1,500.[17] On top of the restrictive reserve clause that had been instituted in 1880 with five players for each club and quickly expanded to cover everyone on the team, this latest move by management was viewed as a step too far by many of those whose pay would be arbitrarily restricted. Chief among the individuals who were indignant upon learning of these plans was on the high seas with Albert Spalding, John Montgomery Ward, head of the Brotherhood of Professional Base Ball Players.

The Brotherhood had been founded by Ward in 1885, ostensibly as a benevolent association to further the interests of base ball and support players who had fallen on financial hard times.[18] During the 1880s, union activity across the country was increasing dramatically, with the largest of these organizations, the Knights of Labor, boasting close to one million members by 1886–1887.[19] Strikes at coal mines and railroads were becoming more frequent as workers demanded to be part of negotiations with management to determine fair pay and acceptable working conditions. On the night of May 4, 1886, a bomb exploded at the end of a union rally near Haymarket Square in Chicago, killing and wounding policemen, who fired back into the crowd of protesters.[20] Violence had reared its ugly head, now adding a horrific dimension to the labor struggles being experienced across the country.

With this as a backdrop, the Brotherhood was the first union ever established in sports, founded in large part as a reaction to the owners' institution of the reserve system for the 1880 season. In the intervening years, Ward had received a law degree from Columbia, and now was putting that education to good use. He had founded the Brotherhood largely hoping to improve relations between base ball's management and its employees, the players. At the same time, Ward had written a provocative article for a nationally popular magazine, *Lippincott's*, on what he felt was the impropriety taken by National League management when it came to the reserve clause, likening it to "slavery" for the ball player. He wrote, "Like a fugitive-slave law, the reserve-rule denies [the player] a harbor or a livelihood, and carries him back, bound and shackled, to the club from which he attempted to escape. We have, then, the curious result of a contract which on its face is for seven months being binding for life."[21]

Newspapers in the latter half of the decade periodically reported that National League president Nicholas Young would stubbornly refuse to meet with Ward about more equitable contract rules, especially related to the reserve system. At the same time, more players were signing up as members of the Brotherhood, and discussions with financial backers eager to support these players in a breakaway league of some sort were not infrequent.[22]

By the time Spalding's group had returned to the United States, Ward and other players on the journey had already heard about the league's classification plan and were shaken. It was reported that Ward was "outspoken in his denunciation of the classification rule, and says that it 'is in spirit a nullification of every benefit derived by the player, and, in its practical application, the National League has directly violated its promise not to reserve at a less salary.'"[23] Potentially the Brotherhood's answer to this clandestine action on the owners' part could have been to stage a strike, walking out on the lucrative games scheduled around the July 4 holiday, but many were fearful of making such a move and jeopardizing their contracts for the year.[24] Despite this, members of the Brotherhood were not finished with this matter.

In his autobiography, Spalding would term the whole situation a "battle royal for the control of professional Base Ball. . . . It was to be a fight to the death. . . . In place of powder and shell, printers' ink and bluff formed the ammunition used by both parties."[25] Each side would employ friendly journalists to make their case for why their group was winning the war, and why the other side deserved to lose. Both had their points, and both could have possibly survived if compromise were viewed as part of the landscape. Unfortunately, management, as represented by the league's "War Committee" of owners Spalding, John Day of the New York Giants club, and John Rogers of Philadelphia, did not have this word in their vocabulary. In fact, when Ward and Spalding finally met in person at the end of June to discuss the possibility of the War Committee meeting with the Brotherhood leadership, it was reported that Spalding was "inclined to belittle the importance of the conference. . . . If [Spalding] continues his present shilly-shallying tactics with Ward, immediate retaliation will be indulged in by the Brotherhood."[26] Would the league refuse to meet with the players? If so, would the ball players go on strike? The question now was who was bluffing whom? The answer, it turned out, was a bit of both.

The summer came and went with no strike activity. By October, Spalding contacted Ward about setting up a possible date at the season's end to discuss player grievances, but Ward responded by saying, in effect, that the time had passed for these delayed conferences to take place. Meanwhile, rumors were spreading about a potential new league to be formed by the Brotherhood.[27] Threats of lawsuits were starting to be bandied about by Spalding, determined to enforce the reserve clause in the contracts of the players on his club. By the end of the month, Chicago shortstop Ned Williamson seemed to give credence to some sort of impending action by the Brotherhood when he told a reporter, "With all of Spalding's bluffing, he will find the League players putting up a game of ball that will fill him with rage."[28] The finger-pointing was everywhere, everybody was to blame, and there seemed to be no solution in sight.

The dam finally broke on Monday, November 4, 1889. The Brotherhood met that afternoon, and a proclamation was issued by evening, printed in newspapers across the country the next day. Its basic premise was that those players supporting the Brotherhood had formed their own league, supported by independent financial backers. The announcement stated the issues on the players' minds as well as their proposed remedy, effectively their Declaration of Independence from NL tyranny.

> Measures originally intended for the good of the game have been perverted into instruments for wrong. The reserve rule and the provisions of the national agreement gave the managers unlimited power, and they have not hesitated to use this in the most arbitrary and mercenary way. . . . If the

League would not concede what was fair we would adopt other means to protect ourselves. . . . We believe that it is possible to conduct our national game upon lines which will not infringe upon individual and natural rights.[29]

A large majority of players in the National League were members of the Brotherhood, including many of the stars of the game such as Ward, "King" Kelly, and Buck Ewing. Two thirds of NL players signed with the Players' League, along with another thirty from the AA.[30] Financial support was readily available for this renegade organization, the NL having recently made good money over the past few years, which had escalated interest from new investors. Now, besides the NL and AA, a third league would be playing base ball in 1890, The Players' League. This association would be free of the reserve system, as well as devoted to profit sharing for management and players, hewing to the egalitarian path they espoused.

Reminiscent of 1884, when the NL, AA, and UA were fighting each other for a spectator's hard-earned cash, supply of ballgames overwhelmed demand. Most of the Players' League teams were located in National League cities, and the NL decided to go head-to-head with the PL, scheduling the vast majority of their games on the same day as PL matches. The result was a nightmare for the sport, dividing the fans and diluting attendance at any given NL or PL game. The public was tiring of the constant feuding between the leagues, including the legal and political battles being fought over the matter that were splashed across the daily papers.[31]

By the end of the season, the PL was reporting sales losses of $125,000, while the NL was swimming in red ink to the tune of $231,000. Adding to PL financial woes were the sunk costs of $215,000 for equipment and the building of new stadiums to showcase the Brotherhood's brand of base ball, all wasted if the PL could not stay in business.[32] The AA lost money too, but to a lesser extent than the other combatants, simply because most of their teams were located in cities outside the direct competition of the others.

Spalding knew what to do next. As he put it in his autobiography, "I knew that they were on their last legs, and I was equally aware that we had troubles of our own. We had been playing two games all through— Base Ball and bluff."[33] Behind closed doors, he met with PL management and delivered an ultimatum, feigning that the NL had deeper pockets and demanding "unconditional surrender" from the weary Players' League. To his surprise, capitulation came easily from a foe who had expected quick riches. As base ball historian David Voight noted, "Magnanimous in victory, Spalding imposed no reprisals on PL players, but he gave no ground on the key issues."[34] Spalding now trained his sights on eliminating AA competition. As the 1890s unfolded, Spalding was flush from his victory over the Players' League and would successfully overcome the American Association through negotiations to absorb half of it, four clubs, within the National League for the upcoming 1892 season.

By the end of that year, both the PL and AA had been erased from the future of base ball as major leagues. The sport had returned to a one league system, the surviving owners hoping that this monopoly would lead to untold riches for them all, much as they had observed with the business "trusts" that had sprung up all around them in most industries, including oil, steel, meat-packing, even sugar. But this idea was easier to envision than to implement, especially with the deep economic collapse called the Panic of 1893 that plunged the country into depression until 1897. Not since 1873, twenty years prior, had a financial downturn been national in scope. This generated a lost economic decade producing unemployment of over 20 percent and throwing tens of thousands out of their homes.[35] The steadily profitable days in base ball of the late 1880s would not return until the turn of the century.

Even as he was involved in this base ball consolidation, Spalding found time to do substantially the same in the sporting goods world, creating a monopolistic structure that would propel Spalding & Bros. to the heights of the industry for the next few generations. One of the crown jewels of this effort involved the purchase of Wright & Ditson.

Spalding had already begun to buy out major competitors in the sporting goods business as early as 1889. As the summer ended that year, while verbally jousting with John Ward and the Brotherhood, Spalding was simultaneously making the first of many significant moves to reduce competition in the sporting goods industry. The front page of *The Sporting Life* on September 4 contained an article announcing that "with one bold stroke, Spalding Bros. had absorbed their great rival, the A. J. Reach Company, lock stock and barrel." Al Reach had decided to sell his retail business, including his flagship Philadelphia store and its contents, as well as patents and machinery to make his gymnasium equipment, which was a virtual monopoly for Reach in that segment of the business, a tremendously valuable coup for Spalding & Bros.[36]

Al was a friend and ball playing peer of Spalding's from twenty years before, one of the players on the Philadelphia Athletics accompanying the Boston Red Stockings along with Spalding and the Wright brothers on the famous base ball tour of England in 1874. He had started selling base ball equipment and other sporting goods in the mid-1860s along with cigars and tobacco at a shop in Philadelphia while playing ball there. After over two decades, Reach was now cashing out and, according to terms of the contract, restricting his future activities in sporting goods mainly to the manufacture of base balls. It had cost Spalding over $100,000 to procure Reach's retail business, but he knew it was well worth the investment. As the article described it, Spalding & Bros. was "now in position to easily maintain its supremacy [in the sporting goods business] indefinitely."[37]

This type of monopolistic business practice was soon to be made illegal by the implementation of the Sherman Anti-Trust Act of 1890.[38] In July of that year, Congress enacted this statute as an attempt to bolster competition across industrial America, which up until then left businesses relatively unregulated as they fought for market share. Trusts, monopolistic business combinations that dominated markets such as oil and railroads, were destroying competition. The Act was intended to break up these activities, but initially it was rarely enforced. Still, Spalding was now aware that this type of buy-out of a competitor could be scrutinized under the new statute. He would have to proceed more cautiously in the future.

On November 16, 1891, Henry Ditson dropped dead at his home in Boston. He was only thirty-five, having suffered from heart disease for many years.[39] Needless to say, it was a shock to all who knew him, especially George, who had come to value "Dit" as a trusted partner and a friend. With his dedicated operational colleague now absent from the company, it took George only a few months to decide that he could not handle both roles alone, and he had no one on the bench to whom he could hand the reins.

Shortly after Henry Ditson's passing, George determined he was ready to sell his business, and Albert was keen to buy it. Wright & Ditson had developed lucrative positions in supplying equipment and publishing journals for the sports of lawn tennis and roller polo to go along with established sales in base ball and cricket goods and leading the promotion of golf in America. It all made for an attractive target for Spalding & Bros. to add to their business portfolio. By February 1892, Spalding purchased virtually all Wright & Ditson's company stock, 9,997 of the outstanding 9,999 shares, in a covert transaction undisclosed to the public.[40] Wright & Ditson was left as the company name, still run by George Wright as president, with Spalding & Bros. as a silent partner and the company operationally directed by recently retired Boston player/manager John Morrill as appointed by Spalding. In this manner, Wright & Ditson continued to appear to both the public and the government as a competitor of Spalding & Bros. This arrangement would be maintained through the first several decades of the 1900s.

Even though the Sherman Anti-Trust Act was now in place, monopolistic industrial activity would rarely be actively prosecuted by the government until after Teddy Roosevelt became president in 1901. In the spring of 1894, the famed sporting goods establishment of Peck & Snyder, perhaps the first and at one time the largest sports equipment company in the country, was swallowed up by Spalding & Bros. Seemingly unconcerned with potential government reprisals, in a March 10 advertisement in the *Sporting Life*, A. G. Spalding & Brothers publicly mentioned their acquisition, detailing their move into Peck & Snyders' vacated headquarters, "Removal—Having purchased the retail business of Messrs. Peck & Snyder at 126, 128, and 130 Nassau Street, and secured in addition thereto the large wholesale store in the rear, no. 15 and 17 Beckman, where both our wholesale and retail business will hereafter be conducted."[41]

Base ball as a sport had yet to profit appreciably from the monopolistic activities of the National League. That would come with a rebounding economy in the new century. But the same could not be said for Spalding's accelerating expansion of his company's sporting goods equipment empire, which was steadily adding to his wealth with the company's increasingly dominant industry position.

Through the mid-1890s, witnessing much of this activity in the intertwined industries of base ball and its equipment supply was Harry Wright. Following his years as Boston's highly successful manager in the 1870s, he led the Providence Grays in 1882–83 after his brother George had won a title at their helm in 1879. He had kept a hand in the sporting goods business with limited success, lending his name to a partnership for a few years in the late 1870s and early 1880s with Boston ball maker L. H. Mahn.[42] By the mid-1880s, he had gone on to Philadelphia, where he was to manage their club in steady, if unspectacular, performance, never again winning a pennant in the sport he loved so dearly. Health issues slowed him down considerably by the 1890s; he was simply not up to managing a ball club anymore. His final position in base ball was an appointment as chief of umpires for the National League in 1893, an honorary position created for him to observe and report on umpires' activities.[43]

By the fall of 1895, Harry was sick with bronchitis, then catarrhal pneumonia, affecting his eyes. His illnesses proved too much, and he passed away on October 3 at only sixty years of age.[44] The base ball world mourned his death, numerous newspaper accounts of his life's work in the game proudly noting his meaning to the sport as it grew from leisure-time activity into the full-fledged business he had fostered. As Henry Chadwick put it, "To Harry Wright belongs the honor of being the founder of the sport in its strongest, most distinguished and most permanent aspect, namely the professional side. He was the first to perceive the full possibilities of the sport; the first to conceive the national importance of it; the first to give it color, life, and symmetry."[45] Indeed, Chadwick, like many others, would refer to Harry as the "Father of Professional Baseball."

In the spring of 1896, the National League decreed April 13 as "Harry Wright Day," with any preseason games scheduled on that day to be played in his honor, the proceeds going toward a graveside monument. Albert Spalding and George Wright came together in his honor at Rockford, Illinois, taking the field in their old Forest City and Cincinnati Red Stockings uniforms and captaining two teams of veteran ballplayers for a game to be played by 1860s' rules.[46] A Chicago newspaper account noted the match started much as any two groups of children had done for many years,

> Father Waldo [the old Rockford club's manager], as the chosen umpire, threw the bat into Wright's outstretched hand. Then began the old-fashioned process of measuring to the knob of the handle to determine which captain should have the chance of batting or going into the field. Wright won and called his men in from the field, while Captain Spalding and his men took their various positions."[47]

It rained heavily that day, but the crowd that turned out had braved the elements for a good cause, celebrating a pivotal figure of the game. The contest lasted only a few innings as the storm increased in intensity and washed out the match with Spalding's team leading Wright's 4–0.

In that brief interval, fans watched as middle-aged Albert's first pitch was delivered to the equally senior lead-off batter George, an underhand fastball, shot "like a bullet" to a spot waist-high which had been indicated by the hitter as his preference.[48] Undoubtedly the years melted away for more than a few spectators as they recalled memories stretching back almost three decades before when Spalding and Wright battled as young men in lively contests in the early days of the game. How thrilling it had been for those two, immersed in the excitement of the moment, bringing out the best in each other as those observing the action cheered with abandon. How far it all had come since that time, the making of base ball as the sport of the land.

Epilogue

Baseball's Significance: A Tale of Two Presidents

In late December 1902, as President Theodore Roosevelt aggressively took a sweeping swing with an ash club one afternoon, it might have been assumed he was practicing his batting technique for the coming baseball season. This couldn't have been further from the truth. Teddy was in a makeshift exercise area in the White House, engaged with a trusted aide and friend, General Leonard Wood, Roosevelt's former Spanish-American War commander, in an obscure game referred to as "single stick."[1] The only shared commonality of these two sports was that most of the sticks employed in each were made of ash, but they were used for much different purposes. Baseball's ash bat was utilized to hit the ball and begin the action of the game. In single stick, a piece of ash, about forty inches long and as thick as a man's thumb, was employed by each of two opponents to defend themselves against the wallops of the other while trying to land their own attacking blows with it.[2]

It was a sport that was born from the bloody violence of sword fighting centuries ago, reduced to a two-man game in the 1700s and mainly practiced by the English or French military. Contestants were usually clad in protective fencing masks and padded chest, arm, and neck apparel, battling each other virtually nonstop with these clubs, obtaining vigorous exercise in the process.[3] Roosevelt had recently discovered it and couldn't get enough.

An engraving of Roosevelt and Wood appeared in early 1903 in the popular magazine *Harper's Weekly*. The caption under the picture said the two "were getting their exercise by having bouts of single stick in the upper rooms of the Executive Mansion. In these days of vigorous Americanism it pleases the people to think that the head of the nation plays as hard as he works."[4] It's impossible to imagine any American president from those days to these willfully engaged in any form of physical combat, even for exercise and encased in heavily padded clothing.

On that late December day, one of Wood's blows raised a noticeable welt above the left eye of the president. Newspapers across the country picked up on the incident over the ensuing days, elevating the bruise to a potentially serious injury and focusing on the danger of the activity, claiming "[Roosevelt] was nearly blinded by being struck over one eye with a stick."[5] Of course, the president made light of the situation, the swelling subsided, and the matches continued. This new, stimulating activity exemplified Roosevelt's credo to live "the strenuous life."

As a child, when the cerebral Theodore was told by doctors that his asthmatic poor health would forever keep him from enjoying a robust life, Roosevelt had dedicated his efforts to build himself physically as well as mentally. His father had gently explained it to him, "Theodore, you have the mind but you have not the body, and without the help of the body the mind cannot go as far as it should . . . you must *make* your body."[6] Given this guidance by a parent whom he worshiped, the sickly boy began to engage in calisthenics and gymnastics on a regular basis to build a stronger, more healthy body.

Growing to manhood, Teddy included boxing and wrestling in his college activities at Harvard. As a young adult, he lived a rugged existence for a time in the Badlands of the Dakotas, riding the range on horseback, hunting, herding cattle, and clearing timber. These challenges, living a life that sometimes bordered on physical extremes, were as important to him as his thirst for knowledge. He was forever attempting to reach his own impossibly high standards of the manly person he chose to make of himself and to project to the world. From this perspective, sports were a test of strength, stamina, determination and, above all, courage.

In this regard, Roosevelt seemed to detest baseball. His daughter Alice snorted that "Father and all of us regarded baseball as a mollycoddle game. Tennis, football, lacrosse, boxing, polo, yes—they are violent, which appealed to us. But baseball? Father wouldn't watch it, not even at Harvard."[7] History professor Ryan Swanson, in his book on Roosevelt and athletics in America, explained, "Roosevelt preferred athletic pursuits that caused its participants physical discomfort. The collisions and striking of boxing and football; the physical fatigue of tennis or a long tramp through the forest—these were the types of activities that Roosevelt favored."[8] In line with this mindset, baseball didn't measure up. He damned the national game with faint praise whenever questioned about why he never attended a professional contest in his almost eight years as president. In Teddy's view, the game just wasn't physically challenging enough to be given much consideration. Besides, he was supposedly unable to play it due to his poor eyesight.[9]

Yet, despite his outward disdain for baseball, Roosevelt appears to have harbored a desire for at least one of his sons to become more involved in the sport. In a March 8, 1908, note Teddy wrote to his thirteen-year-old son Archie about his three-years-younger brother Quentin, the president confided,

Yesterday morning Quentin brought down all his Force School baseball nine to practice on the White House grounds. It was great fun to see them, and Quentin made a run. . . . I like to see Quentin practising baseball. It gives me hopes that one of my boys will not take after his father in this respect, and will prove able to play the national game!"[10]

It was an interesting and very private admission Roosevelt was making, expressing pride in Quentin's accomplishments in a sport that Teddy just could not master, at the same time acknowledging the game as part of the country's heritage.

One person who could certainly agree with this last sentiment was the man who succeeded Teddy as president, William Howard Taft. Far from Roosevelt's dislike for baseball, Taft had just the opposite opinion. Perhaps this originated from being born and raised in Mt. Auburn, Ohio, a well-to-do suburb of Cincinnati, where, as a boy of eleven he would have witnessed the vaunted Red Stockings play in their undefeated season of 1869. Harry Ellard, son of Harry Wright's Cincinnati teammate George Ellard, wrote of the Mt. Auburn Baseball Club and Taft,

He was often lured away from his favorite books to indulge in a game of ball with the other members of the Mt. Auburn club, where he shone as a good batsman and excellent outfielder . . . he was known among his youthful companions as "Lub" Taft.[11]

Being heavier than the others may have slowed Taft down a bit, accounting for the nickname, short for lubber, a large, sluggish fellow. He more than made up for this by putting his bulk into smashing the ball, a highly valued talent not wasted on his teammates as they coaxed him onto the playing field. Once he arrived at Yale for college, the moniker "Lub" was quickly shed for another, "Big Bill," awarded him by his classmates. It was a sign of respect for the over-6-foot, 235-pound youth who would focus more on his studies than sports, becoming a scholar as well as a friend to virtually everyone in his class.[12]

When Taft became president, his enthusiasm for baseball translated into attending Washington Senators matches periodically as well as occasionally arranging to see games while traveling across the country on business. Famously, Taft initiated the tradition of the current president throwing out the first ball to begin each season, starting it all on April 14, 1910, when he forcefully pegged the orb from the stands to the Senator's ace, Walter Johnson. A newspaper headline captured the goings-on, "Taft Tosses Ball—Officiates at the Opening Game of the Season—Victory for Washington—Crowd Cheers President's Fine Delivery of the Sphere."[13] Not to be outdone, Johnson fired a one-hit shutout, the home team winning 3–0. Johnson's satisfaction in delivering such a great pitching performance was topped off by receiving an autograph from the president on the ball used in the game.[14]

It was at this time that Taft was credited with what would become another staple of baseball across the country, termed the "seventh-inning stretch." Supposedly, at the same opening game of the 1910 season, Taft rose during the middle of the seventh inning. The spectators, seeing the president get up from his seat, surmised that he was about to depart and out of respect for the man and his office, rose with him. The real reason Taft had stood appears to have been to stretch his legs after sitting through almost seven innings of the game. Thus, at that moment, another custom was enshrined in the sport.

Intriguingly, some trace this convention to a letter penned over forty years earlier. In an 1869 note discovered from Harry Wright to a friend in Cincinnati, Howard Ferris, Wright described this practice already being a part of Red Stockings' games. Harry wrote, "The spectators all rise between halves of the seventh, extend their legs and arms and some- times walk about. They enjoy the relief afforded by relaxation from a long posture upon the benches."[15] Perhaps this is exactly what Taft was doing, the Cincinnati native's reflexive memory bringing him back to the seventh-inning break the Queen City's spectators supposedly took while watching ballgames those many years ago.

A variation on this theme is noted in an article in 1911 on Taft as a baseball fan enjoying a Washington Senators game. "In the seventh inning at Washington, if the home club is behind, every fan in the bleachers and stands gets on his feet for luck, and whenever he is present President Taft is no exception but nearly always stands until the inning is ended."[16] A similar newspaper description was given of Taft as he attended a game in Pittsburgh on May 29, 1909, "In the seventh inning Mr. Taft stood up in his seat to bring luck to the home team, just as the loyal Pittsburg [*sic*] fans did."[17] If Taft didn't invent the practice, he certainly was a faithful practitioner of it.

And that was the point about Taft and baseball. He thoroughly enjoyed the game and knew its intricacies and traditions from playing the sport as a boy and watching it as an adult. As president, when he attended a professional game while traveling, he would often decline the special seating reserved in his honor at the stadium, insisting on being placed in the stands like any other fan to follow the action, free from the pomp and circumstance of the presidential box.

Every so often, he even participated in a friendly ballgame with other politicians. Such was the case on July 6, 1908, when he was campaigning for the Republican nomination for president and arrived late to a contest between the press and a group of statesmen gathered at Hot Springs, Virginia. With the match tied and two on in the eighth inning, he was brought in to bat and hit "a rather hot one, straight into the hands of his son Charley, who was the shortstop of the correspondents." Charley's catch put his father out and initiated a double play, but during the action the other baserunner scored and broke the tie, Taft's team going on to victory, 14–11.[18]

The only sport he enjoyed more than baseball was golf. As historian and author Doris Kearns Goodwin described it, "Taft had no interest in hunting, boxing, or playing polo, no affinity for the often violent contests of strength and endurance, those manifestations of male prowess that so obsessed Roosevelt. His one passion was for the game of golf, which Roosevelt found excruciatingly dull and slow."[19] Roosevelt and Taft agreed on many things when Teddy was president and Taft his secretary of war, but golf was not one of them. Roosevelt's advice to Taft on the sport was not to be photographed while playing it.[20] He feared it would be seen by many of the voting public as an elitist game as well as a colossal waste of time.

While in the Oval Office, Taft would continue his golf addiction, sometimes even letting his picture be taken while playing. One newspaper favorably compared "Big Bill's" success with a driver off the tee to Pittsburgh's batting champion Honus Wagner feasting on a curve ball served up to him at just the right height.[21] Taft routinely powered his drives over two hundred yards or more, a passable distance for an amateur even today, being assisted by his sheer weight. This was a physical attribute that he hoped to keep under control as he walked the golf course multiple times a week, attempting to be "in the first-rate condition his office demands."[22] It was a constant struggle for Taft throughout his presidency, his weight ballooning to close to three hundred fifty pounds during his time in office.

It appears that what watching baseball or playing golf provided for Taft was a contentment he could not otherwise achieve in the crush of daily life, especially as president. With these sports he could enjoy himself, relax in the moment, cheering the skillful play on the diamond or focus on steadying his golf swing before it impacted the ball on the course, all without any interference from the affairs of state that swirled around every other part of his day.[23] These sports provided hours of time beyond the confines of his office and its duties, untroubled as he immersed himself in the games he loved.

Someone who shared Taft's attachment to golf was George Wright. During the 1890s he had become enamored with it, playing often, sometimes even to the exclusion of his first sport's love, cricket. Once he retired from baseball in the early 1880s, from his Boston home he steadily frequented the respected Longwood Cricket Club in nearby Brookline for a match. However, as the decade progressed, George's preferences shifted toward the new sports he was promoting, especially tennis and golf. This mirrored the public's attitude as well, such that by 1900 Longwood decided to no longer sponsor cricket on its grounds due to the relative lack of interest in the game.[24] The club subsequently grew as a hotbed for tennis in the Boston area.

When Wright turned sixty in 1907 he decided to sponsor the first of what would become an annual fall tradition of "old-timers days" at his golf club outside of Boston for invitees from many sports who had taken up golf at the end of the last century.[25] This included tennis, lacrosse, cricket, and baseball players who, as they aged, had given themselves over to chasing a little white ball across an expanse of thousands of yards for an afternoon's enjoyment. During the festivities of the second golf gathering of this type the following year, George even related a cricket story that amazingly tied golf into the picture. As he remembered it, a cricket player had once brought some golf clubs and balls from Scotland to Hoboken's Elysian Fields "and the cricketers used to swat the balls across the fields."[26] The "Royal and Ancient Game" had perhaps been played in some form in America long before George had introduced it to New Englanders in 1890.

Every so often, the local newspapers would feature Wright and his devotion to golf as he sponsored his annual matches as well as played almost daily himself well into his eighties. Francis Ouimet, the famous young American amateur golfer who won the U.S. Open in Brookline, Massachusetts, in 1913 versus heavily favored English professionals Harry Vardon and Ted Ray, lived in Brookline and worked at Wright & Ditson. In his autobiography, Ouimet noted that George "did as much for developing the game of golf in this country as any man."[27] To this end, in 1897 Wright hired transplanted Scotsman and expert golfer Alex Findlay as Wright & Ditson's "Golfer in Chief" to design golf courses in the Northeast as well as golf clubs that the company manufactured and Findlay successfully demonstrated.[28]

Besides golfing, attending baseball games, and frequenting Florida and the West Coast on golfing vacations, George continued as president of Wright & Ditson, albeit with some diminished responsibilities dating to Spalding's buyout of Wright in 1892. His sons, Beals and Irving, were making national headlines themselves as tennis stars during the early decades of the 1900s, but as their playing days ended, they took management positions in their namesake company too, continuing the presence of the Wright family.

Many years before, the Wrights had moved from Sagamore Street to a larger place on Savin Hill in Dorchester, and now the substantial home slowly emptied. George's wife Abbie passed away in the spring of 1913.

His brother Sam Jr., who lived his final years with them as a bachelor, died there at seventy-nine of a cerebral hemorrhage in May 1928, his brother holding a private gathering in his honor at the home.[29] George's two boys had married and moved on, as had one daughter, Georgiana, leaving the other daughter Elizabeth to take care of George. They remained in the sprawling residence, visited periodically by family and friends. Irving's son George fondly recalled the chance he had to meet Babe Ruth when his grandfather took him into the locker room after a game, even getting an autographed ball in the process.[30] Beals's daughters Elizabeth and Dorothy often came to Boston to spend time with their grandfather. Over fifty years later, granddaughter Elizabeth shared her memories of these stays, interviewed by a reporter as part of a special issue on Cincinnati baseball.

> She recalled his smile, his warmth, his crooked fingers. "They were claw-like," she remembers. George Wright's fingers were knotted and gnarled from two decades of catching line drives and ground-ball smashes with his bare hands. . . . "His hands were quite crippled. . . . I remember him always working a small rubber ball in his hands and fingers to try to keep them limber." [She] spent summers with her sister at her grandfather's home. Her parents [Beals was her father] were divorced. She didn't see her father much. "My grandfather was my father. My memory of him is that I loved him dearly."[31]

Like his wife and brother Sam Jr. before him, George would live out his days at the family home, passing away at ninety years old on August 21, 1937. By a few short months he missed his election into the Baseball Hall of Fame later that year.

One of George's last official baseball activities came when he served on the Mills Commission, the brainchild of his good friend and business associate, Albert Spalding. The commission had been assembled in 1905 to bring finality to the long-standing disagreement over the origins of baseball that simmered between Spalding and Henry Chadwick, the longtime editor of *Spalding's Official Base Ball Guide*. Chadwick good-naturedly insisted the sport was derived from the English children's game of rounders, while Spalding adamantly claimed that baseball's roots lay strictly in American soil.

Spalding suggested that former ballplayers Wright and Al Reach be included on the commission along with a trio of former National League presidents; the group's chairman, A. G. Mills; Nick Young; and Morgan Bulkeley. Also included was another player and former president of the

Washington club, Arthur Gorman. All were good friends of Spalding's, representing a heavily stacked deck in his favor. Spalding himself laid down the challenge to Chadwick in a forceful editorial in the opening pages of his *Official Base Ball Guide of 1905*, stating his reasoning and concluding in part, "I am now convinced that Base Ball did not originate from Rounders any more than Cricket originated from that asinine pastime."[32] No one could doubt where Albert stood on the subject. In contrast, George rarely participated in the commission's work at all, gladly letting Spalding's passion concerning the issue carry the day.

On December 30, 1907, after almost three years of the commission's existence, Mills finally wrote an official pronouncement to committee secretary James Sullivan. It was short and to the point, stating that baseball had its origin in the United States and that Abner Doubleday developed it at Cooperstown, New York, in 1839.[33]

Many leads had been followed by Mills and a few others on the committee, all interesting but most with little real substance. Then Spalding heard of a letter to a newspaper from a mining engineer in Denver, Abner Graves, who claimed he had been an eyewitness to the young Abner Doubleday as he used a stick to sketch in the ground a diamond and explain the rules of baseball in 1839 in a field in Cooperstown, New York. Graves said he played the game with Doubleday's guidance, and both Spalding and Mills gave this story their utmost respect and confidence, as was stated in *Spalding's Official Baseball Guide of 1908*, where the pronouncement of Mills noted above was published in March 1908 for the world to digest.[34]

Announcing the findings in Spalding's guidebook gave it the stamp of approval that many were seeking. However, almost as soon as this conclusion was presented to the public, it began to be refuted by others who could forcefully disagree based on evidence about which the commission was unaware or had disregarded. Typical was longtime baseball writer Horace Fogel, who claimed the Olympics of Philadelphia were in existence in 1833 with a set of by-laws and a constitution, six years prior to Doubleday's alleged creation. According to Fogel, they had been crossing the Delaware River and playing ball over in Camden, New Jersey, as early as 1831.[35]

Over the years, the naysayers became more vocal. Graves's account noted he was a "playmate" of Doubleday in 1839 when the game was invented. Yet, he would have been five years old at that time, and

Doubleday, then nineteen, was attending school at West Point Military
Academy. Additionally, in all his future years, Doubleday would never
mention baseball in any of his writings, personal or professional. The
sum of these facts weighed rather conclusively against Doubleday being
baseball's inventor.

Spalding's willingness to conclude that baseball had been invented in a
field in Cooperstown, New York, by a future military war hero appears to
be just another case of Albert Spalding, baseball promoter extraordinaire.
He had spent much of his life marketing baseball as a homegrown sport
of rustic origins and character-building proportions. He had participated in
arranging a trip to England, then sponsored a worldwide tour, to exhibit
the game as America's own. Now, with Abner Graves's letter in hand,
Spalding couldn't resist the urge to sell the proposition to the American
public. After all, Spalding firmly believed that the game had played a
major role in shaping American values, if not his own, and as such its
derivation must be American in nature.[36]

By then, his longtime association with the game as star player, National
League magnate, and business mogul, often referred to by some as the
"Father of Baseball," had established credentials too overwhelming to
ignore when he proclaimed his version of the events as gospel. True, the
sport was most certainly American in origin, an amalgamation of various
games of ball and bat, honed further by organized groups that played for
recreation, civic pride and in varying degrees of professionalism across
much of the country, especially in the Northeast. Was it invented in a flash
of sporting brilliance by a nineteen-year-old in 1839? Hardly.

Spalding had pulled a fast one on the American public. Like many of
P. T. Barnum's hoaxes, there was enough of a kernel of truth to the story
that, along with the sheer bluster of Spalding's delivery, it was swallowed
whole by a baseball audience largely unschooled in the game's history.
The crowds wanted to believe this tantalizing origin myth, for it provided
them even more to root for, an All-American game created by an All-
American hero.

In this vein, over time the public would learn that Spalding had misled
them concerning his personal life. When Spalding's wife, Josie, died in
1899, he remarried in 1901 to his childhood sweetheart, Elizabeth Mayer.
By 1902, he had for the most part exited his active roles in baseball management and running his sporting goods business. In 1900, and again in

1904, Spalding served as president of the US Olympic Committee, his company providing equipment and uniforms for the games. The Spaldings moved to Point Loma, California, neighboring San Diego, where his wife became quite active in a somewhat mystical group located there known as the Theosophical Society. Spalding himself devoted time to active support of civic and cultural projects in the area as it grew, even becoming involved in an unsuccessful run for the US Senate in 1910.[37] As it would eventually become known, in contrast to the moralistic image he carefully nurtured for display as he railed against gambling and drinking in baseball, Albert had carried on an adulterous affair with "Lizzie" for years, including fathering a son by her whom he eventually adopted after his first wife passed away.

Through it all, besides recreation, sports in America served many purposes for many people. One president identified his participation in the country's games as meaningful only if he could courageously face their physically violent nature, while another valued his chosen sports as refuge from the daily political clashes he had to endure. Some middle-class gentlemen had taken to sport as a relaxing pastime from their office monotony, while many workers had used it as an opportunity to briskly shake off the drudgery of their grinding manual labor.

For most of the country, playing sports was the great equalizer, no game more so than the national game, baseball. One portion of a diverse society after the next embraced it; English, Irish, Germans, Jews, African Americans, Hispanics, deaf and "dumb," loners and lubbers, the list of baseball participants was endless. All viewed baseball as the activity in which they needed to participate to be accepted in America. It didn't really matter to them where the game was invented or by whom. What was important was that if they participated in baseball and played by its rules, then they were indeed American, belonging to the larger, glorious whole. George Wright's and Albert Spalding's efforts, as pioneering superstars of the game and then leaders in supplying the implements to play it, were shining examples of what might be accomplished if they chose to play ball.

A few years before he died in 1915, Spalding completed his detailed history of the sport, *America's National Game*. It was autobiographical in nature as he told of its development, characteristically including a somewhat embellished view of his part in its professional growth. At its publishing in 1911, in his formal manner, Albert personally inscribed a note of tribute in the volume he sent to George. The two had known each other for over forty years, both giving their very best to the game they cherished and marketed so enthusiastically to the rest of the country.

To my old comrade
and life long friend
George Wright
whose extraordinary
skill as a ball
player has never
been excelled.
with the compliments
of
A.G. Spalding
New York
Oct. 10, 1911[38]

Acknowledgments

As I complete this book on early American baseball as viewed by two seminal characters in its formation, I am struck by just how much there still is to learn about its profound history. Of the game itself, but also of the players, managers, owners, umpires, promoters, journalists and myriad others who contributed to its development and maturation. The stories being unearthed as my own goes to publication will continue to add to the richness and depth of our knowledge of this wonderful pastime, the men who made it their passion and their livelihoods, and its cultural significance.

Much of this work continues through the organization that brings together those with a dedication to understanding and chronicling the game, the Society for American Baseball Research (SABR). My own investigations have benefitted greatly from the opportunity to learn about various topics impacting my story through input from fellow SABR members, especially Richard Hershberger, Jon Popovich, Bob Tholkes, and John Thorn.

I could not have come this far without the editorial input of a good friend and SABR associate, Ben Alter. I'm grateful for his willingness to review my manuscript and provide insights on its structure as well as content. Likewise, having SABR nineteenth-century research committee cochair Peter Mancuso read and comment on this book helped keep me from straying too far off base in my work. I thank both gentlemen for their patience and guidance.

Two individuals who graciously gave of their time and knowledge were Bruce Garland and Denny Wright. Bruce is an avid collector of baseball memorabilia, especially related to George Wright. He reviewed his extensive collection with me and encouraged my taking pictures of items of interest, two of which appear in the images section of the book. And Denny, George Wright's great grandson, candidly shared with me fleeting glimpses of personal family history that are fading with the years. This helped me to gain a better understanding of the man behind his great grandfather's smile.

Researching this story has been imperative in finding the information and images critical to its telling. Much appreciation goes to those in libraries, historical societies, museums, and other institutions who have provided much-needed support in my efforts. These include staff at the New York Public Library, especially related to the A. G. Spalding Baseball Collection and Harry Wright Papers, the Cleveland Public Library, the New Haven Public Library, the Rhode Island Historical Society, the Chicago History Museum, the Byron (Illinois) History Museum, and the National Baseball Hall of Fame (specifically Tom Shieber and Cassidy Lent).

Many thanks go to two special teammates in my efforts, Rowman & Littlefield editor Christen Karniski and my agent, Susan Canavan of Waxman Literary, both of whom provided expert direction on how to move this project forward. And, of course, my gratitude would not be complete without mentioning my constant guiding light, my wife, Debbie, who patiently listened as the narrative took shape and provided viewpoints on the content that led to a better story.

Notes

CHAPTER 1

1. Richard Hershberger, *Strike Four: The Evolution of Baseball* (Lanham, MD: Rowman & Littlefield, 2019), xix.

2. Albert G. Spalding, *America's National Game: Historic Facts Concerning the Beginning, Evolution, Development and Popularity of Base Ball* (New York: American Sports Publishing Company, 1911), 117.

3. Spalding, *America's National Game*, 118.

4. "Base Ball: The Great Tournament," *Chicago Tribune*, 26 July 1867, 4.

5. Debra A. Shattuck, "Bats, Balls, and Books: Baseball and Higher Education for Women at Three Eastern Women's Colleges, 1866–1891," *Journal of Sports History* 19, no. 2 (Summer 1992), 98, https://jstor.org/stable/43610534.

6. John Thorn, "The Most Important Game in Baseball History?," *Our Game*, 15 December 2011, https://ourgame.mlblogs.com/the-most-important-game-in-baseball-history-3a17133a6d43.

7. Frank Ceresi and Carol McMains, "The Washington Nationals and the Development of America's National Pastime," *Washington History* 15, no. 1 (Spring/Summer 2003), 26–41, https://jstor.org/stable/i40003134.

8. Spalding, *America's National Game*, 109–11.

9. *Chicago Tribune*, 26 July 1867, 4.

10. *Chicago Tribune*, 4.

11. *Cedar Falls Gazette*, 2 August 1867, 2.

12. Philip H. Dixon, "September 28, 1865: The First Fixed Baseball Game," in *Inventing Baseball: The 100 Greatest Games of the 19th Century*, Bill Felber, ed. (Phoenix, AZ: Society for American Baseball Research e-book, 2013).

13. "The Nationals at Home," *National Republican*, 1 August 1867, 3.

14. Spalding, *America's National Game*, 119.

15. *The National Republican*, 1 August 1867, 3.

16. Thorn, "The Most Important Game?"

CHAPTER 2

1. David W. Anderson, Bert Gumpert, and Emily Gumpert, "Abner Doubleday," Society for American Baseball Research, https://sabr.org/bioproj/person/abner-doubleday/.

2. "Out-Door Sports," *Daily Dispatch*, 12 April 1861, 1.

3. Debbie Schaefer-Jacobs, "Civil War Baseball," *O Say Can You See? Stories from the Museum*, 2 August 2012, National Museum of American History, https://americanhistory.si.edu/blog/2012/08/civil-war-baseball.html.

4. Schaefer-Jacobs.

5. Patricia Millen, "Item 1863.11, On the Battlefront, the New York Game Takes Hold, 1861–1865," *Our Game*, 7 November 2012, https://ourgame.mlblogs.com/on-the-battlefield-the-new-york-game-takes-hold-1861-1865-71228bc958d7.

6. John Thorn, "The Game That Got Away," *Our Game*, 3 July 2012, https://ourgame.mlblogs.com/the-game-that-got-away-a385699cd936.

7. "The Base Ball Match," *New Orleans Daily Crescent*, 20 February 1860, 1.

8. "Ball of the Orleans Base Ball Club," *New Orleans Daily Crescent*, 31 January 1860, 1.

9. Bruce Allardice, "Baseball: The Confederacy's 'National Pastime,'" Emerging Civil War, 16 April 2022, https://emergingcivilwar.com/2022/04/16/baseball-the-confederacys-national-pastime/.

10. Horace L. Traubel, "Notes from Conversations with George W. Whitman, 1893: Mostly in His Own Words," in *In Re Walt Whitman*, Horace L. Traubel, Richard Maurice Bucke, and Thomas B. Harned, eds. (Philadelphia: David McKay, 1893), 35–39.

11. John Rickards Betts, "The Technological Revolution and the Rise of Sport, 1850–1900," *Mississippi Valley Historical Review* 40, no. 2 (September 1953), 231.

12. "Base Ball," *Brooklyn Daily Times*, 18 June 1858, 2.

13. Lowell Edwin Folsom, "America's 'Hurrah Game': Baseball and Walt Whitman," *Iowa Review* 11 nos. 2–3 (Spring–Summer 1980), 72, https://doi.org/10.17077/0021-065X.2576.

14. Christopher Devine, *Harry Wright, Father of Professional Baseball* (Jefferson, NC: McFarland & Company Paperback, 2003), 24.

15. Stephen D. Guschov, *The Red Stockings of Cincinnati: Base Ball's First All-Professional Team and Its Historic 1869 and 1870 Seasons* (Jefferson, NC: McFarland & Company, 1998), 31.

16. "George Wright Recalls Triumphs of 'Red Stockings,'" *New York Sun*, 14 November 1915, 6, 4.

17. "Cricket," *New York Clipper*, 25 April 1891.

18. Priscilla Astifan, "Baseball in the 19th Century," *Rochester History* 52, no. 3 (Summer 1990), 19, referenced in Chris Landers, "The 19th Century's Cure for the Offseason Blues? They Used to Play Baseball on Ice," *Cut4*, MLB.com, 3 December 2017, https://mlb.com/cut4/when-america-played-baseball-on-ice -c262554914.

19. "Ball Play," *New York Clipper*, 19 January 1861.

20. "Ball Play: Grand Base Ball Match on the Ice, Atlantic vs. Charter Oak," *New York Clipper*, 16 February 1861.

21. "Ball Play: Brooklyn vs. New York on Ice, Atlantic vs. Gotham, The Champions the Victors," *New York Clipper*, 21 January 1865.

22. "Ball Play: Brooklyn vs. New York."

23. Guschov, *The Red Stockings of Cincinnati*, 8.

24. "Ball Play," *New York Clipper*, 14 March 1868, 8.

25. "Base Balls," *Brooklyn Daily Eagle*, 3 February 1884, 7.

26. "The Equipment," 19c Baseball, 4, https://19cbaseball.com/equipment-4 .html.

27. "Ball Play," *New York Clipper*, 14 March 1868.

28. Harry Ellard, *Baseball in Cincinnati: A History* (Cincinnati: Johnson & Hardin, 1907), 83.

29. John Thorn, "Jim Creighton," Society for American Baseball Research, 2012, https://sabr.org/bioproj/person/jim-creighton.

30. Brian McKenna, "Dickey Pearce," Society for American Baseball Research, 2012, https://sabr.org/bioproj/person/dickey-pearce.

31. Donald Dewey and Nicholas Acocella, *The New Biographical History of Baseball* (Chicago: Triumph Books, 2002), 330.

32. Spalding, *America's National Game*, 119.

33. Spalding, 122–23.

34. Daniel E. Ginsburg, *The Fix Is In: A History of Baseball Gambling and Game Fixing Scandals* (Jefferson, NC: McFarland & Company, 1995), 5.

35. Will Irwin, *Collier's Weekly*, 8 May 1909, quoted in Spalding, *America's National Game*, 97.

36. Bill McMahon, "Al Spalding," Society for American Baseball Research, 2012, https://sabr.org/bioproj/person/al-spalding/.

37. "Death of Spalding Blow to Sport and Business World," *Newark Evening Star*, 18 September 1915.

38. Michael E. Lomax, *Black Baseball Entrepreneurs, 1860–1900, Operating by Any Means Necessary* (Syracuse, NY: Syracuse University Press, 2003), 21.

39. Lomax, 12.

40. "Victory of a Washington Colored B. B. Club," *Evening Star*, 20 July 1867, 3.

41. Philip S. Fonar, "The Battle to End Discrimination against Negroes on Philadelphia's Streetcars: (Part II) The Victory," *Pennsylvania History* 40 (October 1973), 4.

42. Jerrold Casway, "Octavius Catto and the Pythians of Philadelphia," *Pennsylvania Legacies* 7, no. 1 (May 2007), 5–9.

43. Lomax, *Black Baseball Entrepreneurs*, 21.

44. *The Ball Players' Chronicle*, 19 December 1867, from John Thorn, "The Drawing of the Color Line," *Our Game*, 12 November 2012, https://ourgame.mlblogs.com/the-drawing-of-the-color-line-1867-3ebec9782bb0.

CHAPTER 3

1. Devine, *Harry Wright*, 44.

2. "1868 'Clipper Prize' Medal Presented to George Wright with George Wright Letter of Provenance," Heritage Auctions, 17 August 2019, https://sports.ha.com/itm/baseball-collectibles/others/1868-clipper-prize-medal-presented-to-george-wright-with-george-wright-letter-of-provenance/a/50016-56051.s.

3. Fairfax Downey, "He's Always Kept His Eye on the Ball," *Everybody's Magazine* 55, no.1 (August 1926), 90.

4. Ellard, *Baseball in Cincinnati*, 92.

5. Brian McKenna, "Asa Brainard," Society for American Baseball Research, 2012, https://sabr.org/bioproj/person/asa-brainard/

6. Charles F. Faber, "Fred Waterman," Society for American Baseball Research, 2015, https://sabr.org/bioproj/person/fred-waterman/

7. Bill Lamb, "John Hatfield," Society for American Baseball Research, https://sabr.org/bioproj/person/john-hatfield/

8. "Base Ball: The Clipper Gold Medal—The Winners and Their Averages," *New York Clipper*, 2 January 1869, 2.

9. "The Cincinnati Club," *New York Clipper*, 9 January 1869, 3.

10. "George Wright—Baseball Hall of Fame," National Baseball Hall of Fame, https://baseballhall.org/hall-of-famers/wright-george.

11. "George Wright—Baseball Hall of Fame."

12. Devine, *Harry Wright*, 43.

13. Ellard, *Baseball in Cincinnati*, 149.

14. Thorn, "George Wright."

15. "Base-Ball: George Wright's History," *Chicago Tribune*, 24 November 1878, 7.

16. Devine, *Harry Wright*, 15.

17. Devine, 34.

18. "The National Pastime, Tour of the Nationals: The Second Match," *Brooklyn Union*, 19 July 1867, 1.

19. "The National Pastime, Tour of the Nationals."

20. Downey, "He Always Kept His Eye in the Ball," 91.

21. Wm. A. Phelon, "The Team That Never Was Licked, Relics of the Famous Cincinnati Red Stockings of 1869 Bring Back Recollections of the Old Days," *Baseball Magazine*, January 1917, 70.

22. Downey, "He Always Kept His Eye on the Ball," 91.

23. "About Us," Peck & Snyder, https://peckandsnyder.com/pages/about-us.

24. Jerry Houseman, "Peck and Snyder: The Company," as reprinted in *Sports Collectors Daily*, 17 February 2010, https://sportscollectorsdaily.com/peck-and -snyder-the-company.

25. "Ball Play," *New York Clipper*, 14 March 1868, 8.

26. "Ball Play: The Tour of the Nationals Club of Washington Northward— Second Day's Play," *New York Clipper*, 14 July 1866, 4.

27. Henry Chadwick, *Ball Player's Chronicle*, 25 July 1867.

28. "H. Lillywhite Jr.," *New York Clipper*, 25 April 1857, 7.

29. "H. Lillywhite Jr.," 7.

30. "Cricket Material," *New York Clipper*, 10 May 1862, 8.

31. "Cricket Material," 3.

32. Aaron B. Champion, "Whence They Came—Who They Were—Where They Went—What They Did, and How They Did It," *Saxby's Magazine*, August 1887, as quoted in John Thorn, "The Original Reds," *Our Game*, 4 June 2019, https://ourgame.mlblogs.com/the-original-reds-541b6c21a7c5.

33. Bulletin of the Bureau of Labor Statistics, United States Department of Labor, *History of Wages in the United States from Colonial Times to 1928* (Washington, DC: U.S. Government Printing Office, 1929), No. 499, https:// libraryguides.missouri.edu/pricesandwages/1870-1879.

34. Bruce I. Bustard, "Spirited Republic, Alcohol's Evolving Role in U. S. History," *Prologue* (Winter 2014), 16, https://archives.gov/files/publications/ prologue/2014/winter/spirited.pdf.

35. Ellard, *Baseball in Cincinnati*, 145.

36. "Base Ball: The Professionals of 1870, Review No. 4," *New York Clipper*, 11 February 1871, 5.

37. "Base Ball of the Past: The Red Stockings of Cincinnati," *New York Sun*, 2 January 1887, 11.

38. Devine, *Harry Wright*, 46.

39. Guschov, *The Red Stockings of Cincinnati*, 32.

40. "Base Ball: Opening Day of the Cincinnati Club," *New York Clipper*, 24 April 1869, 2.

CHAPTER 4

1. Guschov, *The Red Stockings of Cincinnati*, 44.

2. John Erardi, "Trips by the 1869 Cincinnati Team Made the Game Famous," *National Baseball Hall of Fame*, https://baseballhall.org/discover/trips -by-the-1869-red-stockings-made-baseball-famous.

3. "Sports and Pastimes, Base Ball: 'Haymakers' vs. Cincinnati's," *Brooklyn Union*, 9 June 1869, 3.

4. "Base Ball: The West vs. The North—Cincinnati vs. Mutual, of New York," *Brooklyn Union*, 16 June 1869, 2.

5. Base Ball: The West vs. The North."

6. Ellard, *Baseball in Cincinnati*, 158.

7. "Cincinnati vs. Irvington," *New York Dispatch*, 20 June 1869, 5.

8. "Cincinnati vs. Irvington."

9. Ellard, *Baseball in Cincinnati*, 161.

10. Ellard, 162.

11. Ellard, 165.

12. Devine, *Harry Wright*, 44.

13. Guschov, *The Red Stockings of Cincinnati*, 71.

14. Darryl Brock, "The Journey to Find the 1869 Cincinnati Red Stockings: Keynote Speech to the Sixth Annual NINE Spring Training Conference, 13 March 1999," *Nine: A Journal of Baseball History and Culture* 9, nos. 1–2 (Fall 2000–Spring 2001), 23–34.

15. Brock.

16. Brock.

17. Guschov, *The Red Stockings of Cincinnati*, 68.

18. Alfred H. Spink, *The National Game* (St. Louis, MO: National Game Publishing Co., 1910), 236.

19. Brock, "The Journey to Find the 1869 Cincinnati Red Stockings."

20. Brock.

21. Guschov, *The Red Stockings of Cincinnati*, 36.

22. Devine, *Harry Wright*, 44.

23. "Opening of the Recreation Grounds," *Alta California*, November 26, 1868, quoted in Angus MacFarlane, "Pioneer Park: San Francisco's Forgotten Ball Park," FoundSF, https://foundsf.org/index.php?title=Pioneer_Park:_San_Francisco%27s_Forgotten_First_Ball_Park.

24. "Opening of the Recreation Grounds."

25. Angus MacFarlane, "Baseball Goes East: The 1876 San Francisco Centennial's Magical Mystery Tour," *Base Ball* (Fall 2013), as quoted in John Thorn. "The Knickerbockers: San Francisco's First Base Ball Team?," *Our Game*, 14 May 2013, https://ourgame.mlblogs.com/the-knickerbockers-san-franciscos-first-base-ball-team-864ab16fc3f8.

26. "Indian Hostilities," *Chicago Tribune*, 21 September 1869, 1.

27. "Indian Attack on Railroad Surveyors," *Chicago Tribune*, 8 September 1869, 1.

28. Richard H. Wilshusen and Neil Lovell, "Battle of Summit Springs," Colorado Encyclopedia, 16 February 2021, https://coloradoencyclopedia.org/article/battle-summit-springs-0.

29. Wilshusen and Lovell.

30. Wilshusen and Lovell.

31. John J. Hallahan, "Cincinnati in 1869 Played without a Defeat," *Boston Daily Globe*, 31 August 1919, E9.

32. Hallahan, E9.

33. Hallahan, E9.

34. Darryl Brock, "During Baseball's Stone Age, a Road Trip Created a Whole New Ball Game," *Sports Illustrated*, 23 June 1986, https://vault.si.com/vault /1986/06/23/43876-toc.

35. *Daily Alta California*, 25 September 1869.

36. *San Francisco Chronicle*, 26 September 1869.

37. Brock, "During Baseball's Stone Age."

38. "Base Ball: The Season's Averages—The Cincinnati Club," *New York Clipper*, 18 December 1869, 5.

39. Thomas W. Gilbert, *How Baseball Happened: The True Story Revealed* (Boston: David R. Godine Publishing, 2020).

40. "Base Ball: The Season's Averages," 5.

41. "Base Ball: The Season's Averages," 5.

42. "Base Ball: The Season's Averages," 5.

43. "Base Ball: The Season's Averages," 5.

44. W. A. Phelon, "Reds of '69, Unbeaten in 92 Games, Hold Unique Place," *Washington Times*, 8 January 1926, 24.

CHAPTER 5

1. "Pianos, Organs and Music—at Peter's Music Store," *Brooklyn Daily Eagle*, 13 June 1870, 1.

2. "Base Ball: Red Stockings vs. Mutuals," *Brooklyn Daily Times*, 14 June 1870, 1.

3. "The Atlantics Triumphant: A Glorious Victory for Brooklyn," *Brooklyn Daily Eagle*, 15 June 1870, 2.

4. George Bulkley, "The Day the Reds Lost," *National Pastime*, 1983, as quoted in John Thorn, *Our Game*, 27 November 2017, https://ourgame.mlblogs .com/the-day-the-reds-lost-eb6bd8dd54a9.

5. Andrew J. Schiff, *The Father of Baseball: A Biography of Henry Chadwick* (Jefferson, NC: MacFarland & Company, 2008), 6.

6. Bulkley, "The Day the Reds Lost."

7. "Base Ball: The Cincinnati Club in the Metropolis, Their Defeat by the Atlantics," *New York Clipper*, 25 June 1870, 5.

8. "Base Ball: The Cincinnati Club in the Metropolis."

9. "Base Ball: The Cincinnati Club in the Metropolis."

10. "Base Ball: The Cincinnati Club in the Metropolis."

11. Bulkley, "The Day the Reds Lost."

12. Bulkley.

13. "Base-Ball: The Cincinnati Club in the Metropolis."

14. Ellard, *Base Ball in Cincinnati*, 189.

15. "Champion Matches," *Brooklyn Daily Eagle*, 15 June 1870, 2.

16. "Base Ball: Great Game at Rockford, Illinois," *New York Clipper*, 29 October 1870, 5.

17. Alex Gary, "History Lesson: 150 Years Ago, Rockford Was a Major League Baseball City," *Rockford Register Star*, 20 April 2021, https://rrstar.com /story/sports/2021/04/20/150-years-ago-rockford-was-a-major-league-baseball -city.

18. Adrian C. Anson, *A Ball Player's Career, Being the Personal Experiences and Reminiscences of Adrian C. Anson* (Chicago: ERA Publishing Co.,1900), 7–10.

19. Anson, 43.

20. Roger H. Van Bolt, "'Cap' Anson's First Contract," *Journal of the Illinois State Historical Society (1908–1984)* 45, no. 3 (Autumn, 1952), 268, https://jstor .org/stable/40189226.

21. Spalding, *America's National Game*, 125

22. "Base Ball: The Base Ball Convention," *New York Clipper*, 10 December 1870, 5.

23. "Base Ball: Cincinnati vs. Forest City of Rockford," *New York Clipper*, 9 July 1870, 3.

24. "Base Ball: Cincinnati vs. Forest City of Rockford, Second Game," *New York Clipper*, 16 July 1870, 5.

25. "Base Ball: Cincinnati vs. Forest City—a Tie Game—Score: 16–16," *New York Clipper*, 23 July 1870, 5.

26. Eric Miklich, *The Rules of the Game, a Compilation of the Rules of Baseball (1845–1900)* 19c Base Ball (2005), 23, https://19cbaseball.com/rules/ the-rules-of-the-game.pdf.

27. "Base Ball:—Cincinnati vs. Forest City—a Tie Game—Score: 16–16."

28. "Base Ball: Haymakers vs. Red Stockings," *New York Clipper*, 20 August 1870, 3.

29. Devine, *Harry Wright*, 76.

30. Guschov, *The Red Stockings of Cincinnati*, 122.

31. Devine, *Harry Wright*, 76.

32. Denny Wright, phone conversation with author, 28 May 2023.

33. Jim Gates, "Esteban Bellán Charted the Way for Latino Ballplayers," Baseball Hall of Fame, https://baseballhall.org/discover/esteban-bellan-charted -the-way-for-latin-american-ballplayers

34. Gates.

35. "Base Ball: White vs. Black," *New York Clipper*, 8 October 1870, 5.

36. "Base Ball: White vs. Black."

37. Lomax, *Black Baseball Entrepreneurs*, 29.

38. Gilbert, *How Baseball Happened*, 323–31.

39. *New York Sun*, 15 October 1911, as quoted in Guschov, *The Red Stockings of Cincinnati*, 133.

40. Ellard, *Base Ball in Cincinnati*," 204, 210.

41. John Liepa, "The Cincinnati Red Stockings and Cal McVey, Iowa's First Professional Baseball Player," *Iowa Heritage Illustrated* 87, no. 1 (Spring 2006): 15, https://doi.org/10.17077/1088-5943.1523.

42. Liepa, 15.

CHAPTER 6

1. David McCullough, *John Adams* (New York: Simon & Schuster, 2001), 61.

2. "U.S. Census Bureau History: The Battle of Bunker Hill," U.S. Census Bureau, June 2015, https://census.go v/history/www/homepage_archive/2015/june_2015.html.

3. Edward L. Glaeser, "Reinventing Boston: 1640–2003," National Bureau of Economic Research, December 2003, 24, https://nber.org/system/files/working_papers/w10166/w10166.pdf.

4. Charlie Bevis, "Ivers Adams," Society for American Baseball Research, 2016, https://sabr.org/bioproj/person/ivers-adams/.

5. "The Boston Base-Ball Club," *Boston Daily Advertiser*, 21 January 1871, 4.

6. "Base Ball—The Red Stockings," *New York Clipper*, 3 December 1870, 3.

7. "Triumphs of Old Red Stockings," *New York Sun*, as appeared in *Washington Post*, 21 November 1915.

8. Spalding, "America's National Game," 141–43.

9. "Base Ball: The Red Stockings," *New York Clipper*, 10 December 1870, 3.

10. Mark Lamster, *Spalding's World Tour: The Epic Adventure That Took Baseball Around the Globe—and Made It America's Game* (New York: Public Affairs, 2006), 19.

11. Lamster, 13.

12. Peter Levine, *A. G. Spalding and the Rise of Baseball: The Promise of American Sport* (New York: Oxford University Press, 1985), 10.

13. David Nemec, "Henry C. Schafer," Society for American Baseball Research, 2016, https://sabr.org/bioproj/person/henry-c-schafer/.

14. *The Boston Journal*, 20 February 1871, as referenced in "Base Ball : The Boston Club," *Brooklyn Daily Eagle*, 23 February 1871, 3.

15. William J. Ryczek, *Blackguards and Red Stockings: A History of Baseball's National Association, 1871–1875*, revised edition (Jefferson, NC: McFarland & Company, 2016), 16.

16. Ryczek, 16.

17. Richard Hershberger, "1871 Winter Meetings: The Winter of Three National Associations," as published in *Base Ball's 19th Century "Winter"*

Meetings, 1857–1900, ed. Jeremy K. Hodges and Bill Nowlin (Phoenix, AZ: Society for American Baseball Research, 2018).

18. Hershberger.

19. Harry Wright, letter to Nick Young, 26 April 1871, Correspondence, Microfilm Reel 13, Harry Wright Papers (HWP), A. G. Spalding Baseball Collection (AGSBC), Manuscripts and Archives Division, The New York Public Library.

20. Ryczek, *Blackguards and Red Stockings*, 17.

21. Harry Wright, letter to Nick Young, 21 April 1871, Correspondence, Microfilm Reel 13, HWP, AGSBC.

22. "Albert Spalding," Baseball Reference, https://baseball-reference.com/players/s/spaldal01.shtml.

23. "Base Ball: Professionals of 1870, Review, No. 4," *New York Clipper*, 11 February 1871, 5.

24. "Base Ball: Professionals of 1870."

25. "Base Ball: The Players of 1872—Pitching and the Pitchers," *New York Clipper*, 28 December 1872, 5.

26. Sam Crane, "Fifty Greatest Ball Players in History," *New York Evening Journal*, 1 December 1911.

27. Crane.

28. Levine, *A. G. Spalding*, 16.

29. Crane, "Fifty Greatest Ball Players," December 1911.

30. Crane.

31. "Barnes Deserves Place among Game's Immortals," *Detroit Times*, 12 February 1915, 7.

32. "Base Ball: Boston vs. Lowell," *New York Clipper*, 22 April 1871, 5.

33. "Ross Barnes," Baseball Reference, https://baseball-reference.com/players/b/barnero01.shtml.

34. "Willie Keeler," Baseball Hall of Fame, https://baseballhall.org/hall-of-famers/keeler-willie.

35. Wright, letter to Chadwick, 2 January 1875, Correspondence, Microfilm Reel 13, HWP, AGSBC.

36. "Base Ball—Professionals of 1870," *New York Clipper*, 1 April 1871, 5.

37. Wright, letter to Chadwick, 2 January 1875, Correspondence, Microfilm Reel 13, HWP, AGSBC.

38. *New York Sunday Mercury*, 2 April 1871.

39. Devine, *Harry Wright*, 90.

40. Wright, letter to H. B. Philips, 11 March 1878, Correspondence, Microfilm Reel 13, HWP, AGSBC.

41. "Base-Ball: The Great Championship Game at Washington," *New York Tribune*, 6 May 1871, 1.

42. "Base Ball: Base Ball Gossip," *New York Clipper*, 25 February 1871, 2.

43. "Sports and Pastimes—Base Ball: Boston v. Haymakers," *Brooklyn Daily Eagle*, 10 May 1871, 3.

44. "Games and Pastimes—Base Ball: George Wright's Accident," *Chicago Tribune*, 14 May 1871, 3.

45. "Games and Pastimes—Base Ball: George Wright's Accident," 3.

46. "Sporting News—Base Ball," *Brooklyn Times Union*, 11 May 1871, 2.

47. Wright, letter to Young, 10 May 1871, Correspondence, Microfilm Reel 13, HWP, AGSBC.

48. Wright, letter to Young, 17 June 1871, Correspondence, Microfilm Reel 13, HWP, AGSBC.

49. "Sports and Pastimes—Base Ball: Boston, Mass., June 20," *Brooklyn Daily Eagle*, 21 June 1871, 2

50. "Sporting Advertisements," *New York Clipper*, 8 April 1871, 5.

51. "Amusements—The New Boston Base Ball Club," *Boston Evening Transcript*, 24 April 1871, 4.

52. "1873 Baseball Scorecard, Bostons vs. Philadelphias," *Boston Athenaeum Digital Collections*, https://cdm.bostonathenaeum.org/digital/iiif/info/p13110coll5/3614/full/full/0/default.jpg.

53. "1876 Baseball Scorecard, Boston vs. Hartford," Boston Athenaeum Digital Collections, https://cdm.bostonathenaeum.org/digital/iiif/p13110coll5/3626/full/full/0/default.jpg.

54. Devine, *Harry Wright*, 101.

55. "1875 Boston Red Stockings Statistics," Baseball Reference, https://baseball -reference.com/teams/BOS/1875.shtml.

56. Devine, *Harry Wright*, 121.

57. John Thorn, "Diamond Visions: Baseball's Greatest Illustration Act, Part 5," *Our Game*, 20 November 2015, https://ourgame.mlblogs.com/diamond -visions-baseballs-greatest-illustration-art-part-5-c8fce267267f.

58. Thorn.

59. George Wright, *Record of the Boston Base Ball Club Since Its Organization* (Boston: Rockwell & Churchill Press, 1874).

60. George Wright, *George Wright's Book for 1875* (Hyde Park, MA: Norfolk County Gazette Office, 1875).

61. Thorn, "Diamond Visions."

62. Henry Chadwick, *Beadle's Dime Base-Ball Player: Compendium of the Game, Comprising Elementary Instructions of This American Game of Ball* (New York: Irwin P. Beadle & Co., 1860).

CHAPTER 7

1. John Thorn, "The Base Ball Guides," *Our Game*, 18 May 2020, https://ourgame.mlblogs.com/the-base-ball-guides-5ef2aa168263.

2. Levine, *A. G. Spalding*, 17.

3. Wright, letter to A. G. Fitzgerald, 5 January 1874, Correspondence Microfilm 13, HWP, AGSBC.

4. Wright, letter to James M. Ferguson, 5 January 1874, Correspondence Microfilm 13, HWP, AGSBC.

5. Wright, letter to James M. Ferguson.

6. Devine, *Harry Wright*, 105.

7. Spalding, *America's National Game*, 175.

8. Spalding, 175–76.

9. Eric Miklich, "The 1874 Boston Red Stockings World Tour," as published in *Boston's First Nine, the 1871–1875 Boston Red Stockings*, ed. Bob LeMoine and Bill Nowlin, assoc. ed. Len Levin (Phoenix, AZ: Society for American Baseball Research, 2016), 333.

10. A. G. Spalding, "The Trip to Europe," letter to the editor, *Philadelphia City Item*, 19 April 1874, Newspaper Clippings 1874–75, Microfilm Reel 12, A. G. Spalding Scrapbooks (AGSS), A. G. Spalding Baseball Collection (AGSBC), Manuscripts and Archives Division, New York Public Library.

11. "Base Ball: Great Game between the Boston and Athletic Clubs Yesterday," *Philadelphia Inquirer*, 16 July 1874, 2.

12. Tim Murnane, "Tim Murnane's Account of the 1874 Base Ball Trip to Europe," *Boston's First Nine*, 343.

13. Wright, *George Wright's Book for 1875*, 24.

14. "The American Base-Ball Players in Liverpool," *Liverpool Post*, 31 July 1874.

15. "The American Base-Ball Players in Liverpool."

16. "Base-Ball at Manchester," *London Telegraph*, 3 August 1874.

17. Miklich, "The 1874 Boston Red Stockings World Tour," *Boston's First Nine*, 338.

18. Spalding, *America's National Game*, 183.

19. Anson, *A Ball Player's Career*, 78.

20. Wright, *George Wright's Book for 1875*.

21. Wright.

22. Spalding, *America's National Game*, 186.

23. Levine, *A. G. Spalding*, 20.

24. "Early Chicago, 1833–1871," *Illinois State Archives*, https://ilsos.gov/departments/archives/teaching_packages/early_chicago/doc23.html.

25. "Base Ball: White Stockings vs. Athletics," *Chicago Tribune*, 8 October 1871, 3.

26. "The Chicago Fire of 1871 and the 'Great Rebuilding,'" *National Geographic*, https://nationalgeographic.org/article/chicago-fire-1871-and-the-great-rebuilding/.

27. "Everything: The White Stockings," *Chicago Tribune*, 14 October 1871, 2.

28. Spalding, *America's National Game*, 208.

29. Lamster, *Spalding's World Tour*, 21.

30. Spalding, *America's National Game*, 201.

31. Levine, *A. G. Spalding*, xiv.

32. Spalding, *America's National Game*, 201.

33. Spalding, 203.

34. Lamster, *Spalding's World Tour*, 22.

35. Spalding, *America's National Game*, 203.

36. Michael Haupert, "Chicago Cubs Team Ownership History, 1876–1919," as published in *BioProject: Team Ownership Histories*, Society for American Baseball Research, https://sabr.org/bioproj/topic/chicago-cubs-team-ownership-history-part1/.

37. Haupert.

38. Spalding, *America's National Game*, 205.

39. "Out-Door Sports: A Strong Team for Chicago, Next Year—Boston Will Suffer," *Boston Globe*, 21 July 1874, 5.

40. *Boston Globe*, as appeared in "Base-Ball: Boston's Dissatisfaction," *Chicago Tribune*, 28 July 1875, 5.

41. "Spalding, Barnes, McVey, White," Baseball-Reference.

42. Spalding, *America's National Game*, 208.

43. Levine, *A. G. Spalding*, 25.

44. Michael Haupert, "William Hulbert and the Birth of the National League," *Baseball Research Journal* (Spring 2015), https://sabr.org/journal/article/william-hulbert-and-the-birth-of-the-national-league/.

45. Jack Bales, *Before They Were the Cubs: The Early Years of Chicago's First Professional Baseball Team* (Jefferson, NC: McFarland & Company, 2019), 88.

46. "Baseball: 'National League of Professional Clubs,'" *New York Clipper*, 12 February 1876, 2.

47. "Sporting: Western Baseball Emporium," *New York Clipper*, 8 April 1876, 5.

48. "Sporting: Western Baseball Emporium."

49. Haupert, "Chicago Cubs Team Ownership," *BioProject: Team Ownership Histories*.

CHAPTER 8

1. "1884 Boston (Bostons, Red Stockings, Beaneaters, Red Caps) National League, Threads of Our Game, 10 September 2022, https://threadsofourgame.com/1884-boston/.

2. "Out-Door Sports: Base-Ball—First Championship Game," *Boston Post*, 24 April 1876, 3.

3. "Baseball: The Centennial Campaign," *New York Clipper*, 5 February 1876, 5.

4. "George Wright," Baseball-Reference, https://baseball-reference.com/players/wrightgeorge.shtml.

5. "Base Ball: The Red Stockings Tour of New York—the Grand Match with the Amateur Stars," *New York Clipper*, 25 June 1870, 2.

6. David L. Fleitz, *More Ghosts in the Gallery* (Jefferson, NC: McFarland & Company, 2007), 12.

7. George V. Tuohey, *A History of the Boston Base Ball Club* (Boston: M. F. Quinn & Co., 1897), 199.

8. "Baseball: The Players of 1876, the Short-Stops," *New York Clipper*, 3 February 1877, 2.

9. Tuohey, *A History of the Boston Base Ball Club*, 198.

10. "Sporting News: Interview with Al Spalding, Captain of the Centennial Chicagos," *Chicago Tribune*, 28 November 1875, 13.

11. "Games and Pastimes: BaseBall—Spalding's Opinion of the League." *Chicago Tribune*, 13 February 1876, 12.

12. "Games and Pastimes: BaseBall—Spalding's Opinion of the League."

13. Madeline Bilis, "Throwback Thursday: When the First Telephone Call Was Made," *Boston Magazine*, 10 March 2016, https://bostonmagazine.com/news/2016/03/10/first-telephone-call/.

14. "Scalpers: The U.S. Troops Suffer a Disastrous Defeat on Little Horn," *Illinois State Journal*, 3.

15. "The Centennial Nines," *New York World*, as referenced in "Sporting News: Base-Ball," *Chicago Tribune*, 28 November 1875, 12.

16. "Chicagos, 5; Bostons, 1," *Boston Globe*, 31 May 1876, 1.

17. "Chicagos, 5; Bostons, 1."

18. "The Open Field: The Bostons again Conquered by the Chicagos, 8 to 4," *Boston Globe*, 5 June 1876, 1.

19. Anson, *A Ball Player's Career*, 96.

20. "Spalding," Baseball-Reference.

21. "Barnes," Baseball-Reference.

22. "The Actives Defeat the Quicksteps," *Reading Times*, 12 May 1876, 4.

23. "Varieties," *The Pittsburgh Post*, 2 August 1876, 3.

24. Spink, *The National Game*, 384–85.

25. Stephen Eschenbach, "Home-Plate Security," *Harvard Magazine* (July–August 2004), https://harvardmagazine.com/2004/07/home-plate-security-html.

26. Fred Thayer, letter to Albert Spalding, 18 May 1911, as quoted in Spalding, *America's National Game*, 478–79.

27. "In the Suburbs: Cambridge—Harvard Notes," *Boston Globe*, 20 January 1877, 8.

28. William T. Reid, '01, "Baseball at Harvard," in *The H book of Harvard Athletics, 1852–1922*, ed. John A. Blanchard (Cambridge, MA: Harvard Varsity Club, 1923), 188.

29. Reid, 190.

30. *Providence Dispatch*, as quoted in "Base-Ball: Non-League Items," *Chicago Tribune*, 27 May 1877, 7.

31. *Norristown Herald*, as quoted in *Newport Daily News*, 6 February 1877, 1.

32. Spalding, *America's National Game*, 477.

33. "Base-Ball: The Tournament," *Chicago Tribune*, 18 September 1877, 2.

34. John F. Green, "Pete Hotaling," Society for American Baseball Research, https://sabr.org/bioproj/person/pete-hotaling/.

35. Larry DeFillipo, "July 3, 1877: Louisville's Charley Snyder Becomes the First Major Leaguer to Wear a Catcher's Mask," Society for American Baseball Research, https://sabr.org/gamesproj/game/july-3-1877-louisville's-charley-snyder-becomes-the-first-major-leaguer-to-wear-a-catcher's-mask.

36. "Summer Pastimes: The Bostons Beat the Cincinnatis," *Boston Globe*, 22 August 1877, 5.

37. George Wright, letter to Albert Spalding, 17 May 1911, as quoted in Spalding, *America's National Game*, 479.

38. "Sporting: Peck & Snyder's New B.B. Goods," *New York Clipper*, 2 June 1877, 8.

39. "Sporting: Peck & Snyder's," *New York Clipper*, 25 August 1877, 8.

40. "Sporting: Thayer's Pat. B. B. Mask," *New York Clipper*, 11 May 1878, 8.

41. "Notes and Comments," *Sporting Life*, 20 August 1883, 6.

42. Peter Morris, *A Game of Inches, The Stories behind the Innovations That Shaped Baseball* (Chicago: Ivan R. Dee, 2006), 299.

43. "Cummings the First 'Curve Pitcher,'" *Chicago Tribune*, 18 March 1895, 11.

44. Bales, *Before They Were the Cubs*, 109.

45. "Baseball: Reviewing the Season—The Base-Playing of 1877," *New York Clipper*, 29 December 1877, 2.

46. *Cincinnati Commercial*, 29 June 1870, as referenced by David Arcidiacono in "1870c.7, First Catcher's Glove? About 1870, Perhaps," *Protoball*, https://protoball.org/1870c.7.

47. Jim Daniel, "#GoingDeep: The Evolution of Baseball Gloves," Baseball Hall of Fame, https://baseballhall.org/discover/going-deep/the-evolution-of-baseball-gloves.

48. Spalding, *America's National Game*, 475.

49. Spalding, 476.

50. Levine, *A. G. Spalding*, 77.

51. "Sporting: Base-Ball—*The League Book*," *Chicago Tribune*, 3 March 1878, 7.

52. A. G. Spalding and Lewis Meacham, ed., *Spalding's Official Base Ball Guide* (Chicago: A. G. Spalding & Bro. 1878).

53. Spalding and Meacham.

54. Spalding and Meacham.

55. Levine, *A. G. Spalding*, 73.

56. "Bond," Baseball-Reference, https://baseball-reference.com/players/bondtommy.shtml.

57. "Death of the Father of Harry Wright," *Boston Globe*, 20 December 1877, 5.

58. "Death of Old Sam Wright," *New York Clipper*, 29 December 1877, 3.

59. Devine, *Harry Wright*, 135.

60. "Sam Wright, Short-stop," *New York Clipper*, 15 May 1880, 5.

61. "Baseball: The League Convention and Its Work," *New York Clipper*, 23 December 1876, 3.

62. "Baseball: Crooked Play," *New York Clipper*, 10 November 1876, 2.

63. Spalding, *America's National Game*, 226–27.

CHAPTER 9

1. John Thorn, "Paul Hines and the Unassisted Triple Play," *Our Game*, 5 May 2015, https://ourgame.mlblogs.com/paul-hines-and-the-unassisted-triple-play-220f56473f1a.

2. "Wright Recalls Triumphs," *New York Sun*, 14 November 1915, 40.

3. "Baseball: Boston vs. Providence," *New York Clipper*, 18 May 1878, 3.

4. "Ball Games: The Bostons again Defeated at Providence," *Boston Globe*, 9 May 1878, 2.

5. Richard Hershberger, "Revisiting the Hines Triple Play," *Baseball Research Journal*, Spring 2016, Society for American Baseball Research, https://sabr.org/journal/article/revisiting-the-hines-triple-play.

6. "Base Ball: Hines' Triple Play," *St. Louis Globe-Dispatch*, 9 May 1878, 3.

7. Spink, *The National Game*, 262.

8. "Paul Hines," Baseball-Reference, https://www.baseball-reference.com/players/h/hinespa01.shtml.

9. "John Ward," Baseball-Reference, https://www.baseball-reference.com/players/w/wardjo01.shtml.

10. Fred Stinson and Richard Waldbauer, "The Providence Grays as a Franchise," paper presented at the Society for American Baseball Research (SABR) symposium at Brown University, Providence, Rhode Island, 6 July 1984, courtesy of Rhode Island Historical Society (RIHS).

11. Richard Waldbauer, "A Social History of the Providence Grays," paper presented at the SABR symposium, Brown University, Providence, Rhode Island, 6 July 1984, courtesy of RIHS.

12. Mike Roer, *Orator O'Rourke: The Life of a Baseball Radical* (Jefferson, NC: McFarland & Company, 2005), 71.

13. "Nationals and New Bedfords," *Washington Post*, 17 July 1878, 4.

14. William D. Perrin, "Line Drives, Then and Now, V," *Providence Journal*, June–July 1928, in *Days of Greatness, Providence Baseball, 1875–1885* (Cooperstown, NY: Society for American Baseball Research, 1984), 8, courtesy of RIHS.

15. Jon Popovitch, "Wright & Ditson, Official Sporting Goods Provider to Baseball's Renegade Labor Leagues," paper presented at SABR 19th Century Baseball Research Conference, 20–21 April 2018.

16. "Baseball: Baseball Notes," *New York Clipper*, 8 March 1879, 3.

17. "Baseball: Later Baseball Notes," *New York Clipper*, 22 March 1879, 3.

18. "New Advertisements: Providence Base Ball Association Season of 1879," *Providence Morning Star*, 1 April 1879, 1.

19. Waldbauer, "Social History of the Providence Grays."

20. "Baseball: Baseball Notes," *New York Clipper*, 12 April 1879, 5.

21. "The National Game: Opening of the League Season of '79," *Providence Morning Star*, 2 May 1879, 1.

22. "Out-Door Sports: The Struggle for the League Pennant," *Providence Evening Press*, 20 June 1879, 1.

23. "Base Ball," *Providence Morning Star*, 23 June 1879, 1.

24. "Base Ball," *Providence Morning Star*, 14 April 1879, 1.

25. "Base Ball," *Providence Evening Press*, 28 April 1879, 2.

26. Stefan Fatsis, "Mystery of Baseball: Was William White Game's First Black," *Wall Street Journal*, 30 January 2004, 1.

27. "Local News." *Providence Evening Press*, 24 June 1879, 2.

28. John Thorn, "Pioneers: William Edward White," *Our Game*, 10 April 2023, https://ourgame.mlblogs.com/pioneers-william-edward-white-f87a9ad1ca8d.

29. Thorn.

30. Denny Wright, phone conversation with author, 28 May 2023.

31. "New Advertisements," *Providence Morning Star*, 23 June 1879, 1.

32. "Baseball: Providence vs. Boston," *New York Clipper*, 5 July 1879, 3.

33. "Baseball: The League Championship," *New York Clipper*, 27 September 1879, 2.

34. "Stick and Sphere," *Boston Globe*, 24 September 1879, 4.

35. "EX-TYNG-UISHED," *Providence Evening Press*, 26 September 1879, 1.

36. "Triumphs of Old Red Stockings," *New York Sun*, as reprinted in *Washington Post*, 21 November 1915, MS3.

37. "Baseball: Providence vs. Boston—The Deciding Contest." *New York Clipper*, 4 October 1879, 3.

38. "Baseball: The League Arena—The Providence Club Wins the Championship," *New York Clipper*, 4 October 1879,

39. "Baseball: The League Arena."

40. "Baseball: The League Arena."

41. "Base-Ball Nines Playing Cricket," *New York Times*, 16 October 1879, 3.

42. "Baseball: Baseball Notes," *New York Clipper*, 3 January 1880, 2.

43. "Baseball: Baseball Notes," *New York Clipper*, 15 November 1879, 5.

44. "Rowing Machines," *Boston Globe*, 30 November 1879, 2.

45. "This Kind of Argument Is the Veriest Kind of Twaddle," Baseball History Daily, https://baseballhistorydaily.com/tag/tommy-beals/.

46. John M. Ward, "Is the Base-Ball Player a Chattel?" *Lippincott's Magazine* 40 (August 1887), 310–19, https://explorepahistory.com/odocument.php?docId =1-4-5.

47. Ward.

48. David J. Gordon, "Competitive Balance in the Free Agent Era: The Dog That Didn't Bark," *Baseball Research Journal* (Fall 2020), https://sabr.org/journal /article/competitive-balance-in-the-free-agent-era-the-dog-that-didnt-bark/.

49. "Baseball: Baseball Notes," *New York Clipper*, 28 February 1880, 5.

50. "Base Ball," *Providence Daily Journal*, 9 January 1880, 1.

51. Hallahan, "Season without a Defeat," *Boston Globe*, 31 August 1919, E9.

52. Richard Hershberger, "The First Baseball War: The American Association and the National League," *Baseball Research Journal* (Fall 2020), https:// sabr.org/journal/article/the-first-baseball-war-the-american-association-and-the -national-league/.

53. Barney Terrell, "1883–84 Winter Meetings: The Union Association," in *Base Ball's 19th Century "Winter" Meetings, 1857–1900*. Society for American Baseball Research.

54. Popovich, "Wright & Ditson," SABR 2018, 19th Century Baseball Research Conference.

55. Lomax, *Black Baseball Entrepreneurs*, 43.

56. "Sporting: Chicago, 7; Toledo, 6," *St. Louis Globe-Democrat*, 11 August 1883, 4.

57. John R. Husman, "Moses Fleetwood Walker," Society for American Baseball Research, https://sabr.org/bioproj/person/fleet-walker/.

58. "Cap Anson: Baseball Hall of Fame," National Baseball Hall of Fame.

59. Husman, "Moses Fleetwood Walker."

60. Husman.

61. Lomax, *Black Baseball Entrepreneurs*, 83.

62. R. A. R. Edwards, *Deaf Players in Major League Baseball, A History, 1883 to the Present* (Jefferson, NC: McFarland & Company, 2020), 4.

63. Edwards, 14.

64. "William Hoy," Baseball-Reference, https://baseball-reference.com/ players/hoybilly.shmtl.

65. Lawrence S. Ritter, *The Glory of Their Times* (New York: The MacMillan Company, 1966), 23, 54.

CHAPTER 10

1. Spalding, *America's National Game*, 4.

2. "Obituary: William A. Hulbert, President of the Chicago Base-Ball Club and of the National League," *Chicago Tribune*, 11 April 1882, 6.

3. Haupert, "Chicago Cubs Team Ownership History."

4. "Baseball: The Chicago Club," *New York Clipper*, 6 May 1882, 3.

5. "Sporting News: Base-Ball," *Chicago Tribune*, 13 February 1881, 12.

6. "Cutlery: A. G. Spalding & Bro.," *Chicago Tribune*, 26 April 1882, 1.

7. "Bicycles," *Daily Inter Ocean*, 29 April 1882, 1.

8. Spalding and Meacham, *Spalding's Official Base Ball Guide*, 1878.

9. A. G. Spalding, ed., *Spalding's Official Base Ball Guide* (Chicago: A. G. Spalding & Bro. 1879).

10. "Spalding's Complete Manual of Boxing, Club Swinging and Dumbbell Exercise," *New York Clipper*, 30 December 1882, 13.

11. "The Fire Record: Spalding & Bros.' Sporting-Goods House Damaged to the Extent of $80,000," *Chicago Tribune*, 27 October 1884, 6.

12. "To Sportsmen!!," *New York Times*, 29 March 1885, 16.

13. Albert Spalding, *Rise to Follow* (New York: Henry Holt and Company, 1943), 21

14. Arthur Bartlett, *Baseball and Mr. Spalding, The History and Romance of Baseball* (New York: Farrar, Straus and Young, 1951), 146.

15. Levine, *A. G. Spalding*, 73.

16. Spalding, *Rise to Follow*, 20.

17. Barlett, *Baseball and Mr. Spalding*, 103.

18. Spalding, *America's National Game*, 265.

19. Anson, *A Ball-Player's Career*, 128.

20. "King Kelly," Baseball-Reference, https://baseball-reference.com/players/kellyking.shtml.

21. Levine, *A. G. Spalding*, 30.

22. Mike Kelly, *Play Ball: Stories of the Ball Field* (Boston: Press of Emery & Hughes, 1888), 6.

23. "Sporting Events: Chicago Shows Boston How Base-Ball Ought to Be Played," *Chicago Tribune*, 21 May 1881, 6.

24. Anson, *A Ball-Player's Career*, 115.

25. Spalding, *America's National Game*, 516.

26. Marty Appel, *Slide, Kelly, Slide: The Wild Life and Times of Mike "King" Kelly, Baseball's First Superstar* (Lanham, MD: The Scarecrow Press, Inc, 1999), xiv.

27. Haupert, "Chicago Cubs Team Ownership History."

28. Spalding, *America's National Game*, 525.

29. Spalding, 515.

30. Spalding, 527.

31. Levine, *A. G. Spalding*, 84.

32. "Spalding's Australian Tour," *Daily Inter Ocean*, 25 March 1888, 5.

33. "Baseball: Baseball Notes," *New York Clipper*, 7 February 1880, 5.

34. "Base-Ball in Australia," *Chicago Tribune*, 25 March 1888, 2.

35. Levine, *A. G. Spalding*, 99.

36. Lamster, *Spalding's World Tour*, 44.

37. Henry Chadwick, ed., *Spalding's Official Base Ball Guide* (Chicago: A. G. Spalding & Bros., 1890), 120.

38. Levine, *A. G. Spalding*, 101.

39. "Live Washington Topics: A Great Day for Chicago at the White House," *Sun*, 9 October 1888, 2.

40. Levine, *A. G. Spalding*, 101.

41. Jerry Kuntz, "The Rise and Many Falls of Professor Bartholomew," email to Tom Shieber, National Baseball Hall of Fame, 19 April 2010.

42. Harry Clay Palmer, *Sights Around the World with the Base Ball Boys* (Philadelphia: Edgewood Publishing Company, 1892), 21.

43. Lamster, *Spalding's World Tour*, 40.

44. "Al Spalding in Town," *Boston Globe*, 30 August 1888, 5.

45. "A Renowned Cricket-Player," *San Francisco Examiner*, 16 November 1888, 4.

46. "News from John Ward," *Boston Globe*, 13 November 1888, 3.

47. "News from John Ward," 3.

48. "Spalding's Scheme," *World*, as reported in *Daily Inter Ocean*, 21 November 1888, 2.

49. "Notes of the Trip and Travelers," *Daily Inter Ocean*, 30 December 1888, 9.

50. Palmer, *Sights Around the World*, 20.

51. Anson, *A Ball-Player's Career*, 148–50.

52. Thomas W. Zeigler, "Basepaths to Empire: Race and the Spalding World Baseball Tour," *Journal of the Gilded Age and Progressive Era*, April 2007, 187, https://jstor.org/stable/25144475.

53. Palmer, *Sights Around the World*, 84–85.

54. Spalding, *America's National Game*, 256–57.

55. Palmer, *Sights Around the World*, 82–83.

56. Ryan, 1888–89 trip diary.

57. "Baseball as She Is Played," *Sydney Morning Herald*, 17 December 1888, 3.

58. Chadwick, *Spalding's Official Base Ball Guide*, 122–23.

59. Chadwick, 123.

60. "Baseball: The American Baseballers," *Adelaide Observer*, 5 January 1889, 19.

61. "Even the Sphinx Smiled," *Boston Globe*, 5 March 1889, 9.

62. "The Spalding Tourists," *New York Clipper*, 9 March, 1889, 9.

63. Palmer, *Sights Around the World*, 198–212.

64. Lamster, *Spalding's World Tour*, 188.

65. Palmer, *Sights Around the World*, 213–14.

66. Lamster, *Spalding's World Tour*, 215.

67. Anson, *A Ball-Player's Career*, 262.

68. Spalding, *America's National Game*, 263.

69. Palmer, *Sights Around the World*, 239.

CHAPTER 11

1. John Thorn, "The Krank: Baseball's Rarest Book," *Our Game*, 10 August 2015, https://ourgame.mlblogs.com/the-krank-baseball's-rarest-book-8c36ef3b73eb.
2. *Weekly Arizona Miner*, 23 September 1881, 1.
3. "Base Ball: A Base Ball 'Crank,'" *Providence Evening Press*, 28 June 1883, 4.
4. "Thomas William Lawson," 19c Baseball, https://19cbaseball.com/perfect-game-baseball-cards.html.
5. Thomas W. Lawson, *The Krank: His Language and What It Means* (Boston: Rand Avery Company, 1888), 3–5.
6. Lawson, 3.
7. David Shulman, "On the Early Use of Fan in Baseball," *American Speech* 71, no. 3 (Autumn 1996), 328, https://jstor.org/stable/455556.
8. Denny Wright, phone interview with author, 15 June 2023.
9. "Not Love All," *Boston Globe*, 1 August 1888, 4.
10. "Many Great Players," *Boston Globe*, 31 July 1887, 5.
11. Valentine Gill Hall, *Lawn Tennis in America* (New York: D. W. Granbury & Co., 1889), 36–37.
12. Downey, "He's Always Kept His Eye on the Ball," 92.
13. "Recent Deaths: Mr. Henry A. Ditson," *Boston Evening Transcript*, 21 November 1891, 9.
14. "Lawn Tennis," *Journal of American Pastimes*, May 1881, 1.
15. "History of the Tennis Ball," International Tennis Federation, November 2019, https://itftennis.com/media/2280/balls-history-of-tennis-balls.pdf.
16. "History of the Tennis Ball," 5.
17. "The National Lawn-Tennis Association Convention," *New York Clipper*, 10 March 1883, 3.
18. "Athletics: The Tennis Convention," *New York Clipper*, 19 March 1887, 9.
19. J. Parmly Paret, *Lawn Tennis, Its Past, Present, and Future* (New York: The Macmillan Company, 1904), 84.
20. "Athletics: Lawn Tennis," *New York Clipper*, 7 April 1888, 8.
21. Downey, "He Always Kept His Eye on the Ball," 92.
22. "Beals Wright," International Tennis Hall of Fame, https://tennisfame.com/hall-of-famers/inductees/beals-wright.
23. "Irving Wright," DB 4 Tennis, https://db4tennis.com/players/male/irving-wright.
24. Denny Wright, phone interview with author, 15 June 2023.
25. William T. Tilden II, *The Art of Lawn Tennis* (New York: George H. Doran Company, 1921), 54.

26. J. Parmly Paret, *Methods and Players of Modern Lawn Tennis*, ed. S. Wallis Merrihew (New York: American Lawn Tennis, 1915), 82–83.

27. *The Field*, quoted in "Beals C. Wright through English Eyes," *Outing Magazine* 59, no. 6 (March 1912), 682.

28. "Baseball: The American College Association," *New York Clipper*, 22 March 1884, 3.

29. "Baseball: Boston Gossip," *New York Clipper*, 22 March 1884, 2.

30. "Uniforms," *Journal of American Pastimes*, May 1881, 4.

31. "Athletic: The Harvard University Football Uniform," *New York Clipper*, 10 November 1883, 9.

32. "Base Ball: The Champion Trade Nine," *Boston Globe*, 21 January 1883, 8.

33. "Mirror of City Life: The Commercial Base Ball Club," *Boston Globe*, 15 February 1883, 1.

34. Andrew Walsh, "The Gem City Polo Club and the First Roller Polo League," Dayton Vistas, 2 April 2018, https://daytonvistas.com/1880s-gem-city -polo-club-first-roller-polo-league/.

35. Stephan Hardy, "'Polo at the Rinks': Shaping Markets for Ice Hockey in America, 1880–1900," *Journal of Sport History* 33, no. 2 (Summer 2006), 170, https://img1.wsimg.com/blobby/go/7fae685c-999f-4d27-bda7-79d5f3cef78e/downloads/Polo.pdf?ver=1658661221887.

36. Walsh, "The Gem City Polo Club."

37. *Henley's Manual of Roller Skating* (Richmond, IN: M. C. Henley, 1885), 135–36.

38. *Henley's Official Polo Guide* (Richmond, IN: M. C. Henley, 1885), 1–88.

39. Hardy, "'Polo at the Rinks,'"163.

40. *Wright & Ditson's Polo Guide* (Boston: Wright & Ditson, 1885), 28–29.

41. "Baseball: From the Hub," *New York Clipper*, 13 December 1884, 10.

42. "Baseball: From the Hub," *New York Clipper*, 10 January 1885, 10.

43. Hardy, "'Polo at the Rinks,'" 163.

44. *Wright & Ditson's Polo Guide*, 1–83.

45. Hardy, "'Polo at the Rinks,'" 167–68.

46. Downey, "He Always Kept His Eye on the Ball," 89.

47. Downey, 89.

48. Bunker Hill, "Eastern Department: New England Notes," *American Golfer*, December 1912, 145.

49. Bunker Hill, "Eastern Department," 144.

50. "Initial Game of Royal Golf," *Boston Globe*, 13 December 1890, 6.

51. Brian DeLacey and Maxwell M. Carey, "America's Public Links Cradle, Boston's Franklin Park," *MassGolfer* (Fall 2000), 14, https://cityofbostongolf .com/images/documents/Franklin_Park_HISTORY_2015_v3.pdf.

52. "Second Trial of Royal Golf," *Boston Globe*, 29 March 1891, 6.

53. Denny Wright, phone interview with author, 15 June 2023.

54. Hardy, "'Polo at the Rinks,'" 168.

CHAPTER 12

1. "Elmira's Great Ball Game," *New York Sun*, 3 July 1887, 1.

2. "Elmira's Great Ball Game."

3. Henry Guy Carleton, "Twain as Umpire," *Boston Globe*, 3 July 1887, 1.

4. Henry Guy Carleton, extracts from "Twain as Umpire" as quoted in "Mark Twain's Rulings: He Makes Decisions Which Revolutionize Base Ball," *Great Falls Tribune*, 16 July 1887, 4 .

5. "Elmira's Great Ball Game," 2.

6. David Arcidiacono, *Major League Baseball in Gilded Age Connecticut* (Jefferson, NC: McFarla.nd & Company, 2010), 96.

7. "New Advertisements: Two Hundred and Five Dollars Reward," *Hartford Courant*, 20 May 1875, 3.

8. Weston Ulbrich, "Mark Twain, the Hartford Baseball Crank," Greater Hartford Twilight Baseball League, 15 April 2021, https://ghtbl.org/twain.

9. Mark Twain, *A Connecticut Yankee in King Arthur's Court* (New York: Charles L. Webster & Company, 1889), 519.

10. A. G. Spalding, "The Banquet to Baseball Braves: Arrangement of Guests," *New York Star*, 9 April 1889, Newspaper Clippings, Microfilm Reel 12, AGSS, AGSBC.

11. Spalding.

12. "Baseball: Welcoming Home the Tourists," *New York Clipper*, 13 April 1889, 12.

13. "Base Ball: Many Ovations," *Sporting Life*, 17 April 1889, 2.

14. DeWolf Hopper and Wesley Winans Stout, *Once a Clown, Always a Clown: Reminiscences of DeWolf Hopper* (Boston: Little, Brown, and Company, 1927), 85.

15. CurzonRoad, "Baseball: De Wolf Hopper Recites 'Casey at the Bat' (1909)," YouTube, https://www.youtube.com/watch?v=1G2HN_1DRUo.

16. Palmer, *Sights Around the World*, 277.

17. "Baseball: Annual Meetings—National League," *New York Clipper*, 1 December 1888, 9.

18. Leonard Koppett, "During the Brotherhood Revolt the Mood in Baseball Wasn't Fraternal," *Sports Illustrated* Vault, 1 June 1981, https://vault.si.com/vault/1981/06/01/yesterday-during-the-brotherhood-revolt-the-mood-in-baseball-wasn't-fraternal.

19. Jonathan Garlock, "Knights of Labor History and Geography 1869–1899," Mapping American Social Movements Project, University of Washington, https://depts.washington.edu/moves/knights_labor_map.shtml.

20. "A Hellish Deed," *Chicago Tribune*, 5 May 1886, 1.

21. Ward, "Is the Base-Ball Player a Chattel?"

22. "Baseball," *New York Clipper*, 24 September 1887, 8.

23. "Baseball: Stray Sparks from the Diamond," *New York Clipper*, 8 June 1889, 9.

24. Koppett, "During the Brotherhood Revolt."

25. Spalding, *America's National Game*, 285.

26. "Extra: League-Brotherhood Gossip," *New York Evening World*, 25 June 1889, 1.

27. "Baseball: Stray Sparks from the Diamond," *New York Clipper*, 5 October 1889, 11.

28. "Baseball: Stray Sparks from the Diamond," *New York Clipper*, 2 November 1889, 9.

29. "Now for a New League," *New York Sun*, 5 November 1889, 6.

30. Koppett, "During the Brotherhood Revolt."

31. Koppett.

32. "League Lost $231,000," *Boston Globe*, 23 November 1890, 17.

33. Spalding, *America's National Game*, 288.

34. David Voigt, "The Players' League War: 1890," as quoted in John Thorn, "David Voigt's History of Baseball, Part 3," *Our Game*, 21 January 2016, https://ourgame.mlblogs.com/david-voigts-history-of-baseball-part-3-7136c5d59776.

35. Gary Richardson and Tim Sablik, "Banking Panics of the Gilded Age, 1863–1913," Federal Reserve History, 4 December 2015, https://federalreservehistory.org/essays/banking-panics-of-the-gilded-age.

36. "A Bold Stroke: Spalding Bros. Absorb the Reach Co," *Sporting Life*, 4 September 1889, 1.

37. "A Bold Stroke."

38. National Archives, "Sherman Anti-Trust Act (1890)," Milestone Documents, https://archives.gov/milestone-documents/sherman-anti-trust-act.

39. "Henry Ditson Dropped Dead," *Boston Weekly Globe*, 17 November 1891, 3.

40. John Thorn, "Who Was George Wright? Part Three," *Our Game*, 22 September 2016, https://ourgame.mlblogs.com/who-was-george-wright-part-three-55376c85a4f9#.1s0hlwq5m.

41. "Removal," *Sporting Life*, 10 March 1894, 3.

42. Jamaica Plain Historical Society, "Jamaica Plain's Connections to the History of Baseball," *Jamaica Plain News*, 12, April 2021, https://jamaicaplainnews.com/2021/04/12/jamaica-plains-connections-to-the-history-of-baseball/268782.

43. Devine, *Harry Wright*, 164.

44. "William Henry Wright," *New York Clipper*, 12 October 1895, 9.

45. "In Memoriam," *Sporting Life*, 12 October 1895, 2.

46. "Honor Wright: Memorial Fund Games in Many Cities," *Boston Globe*, 14 April 1896, 9.

47. "Veterans Play Ball," *Chicago Chronicle*, 14 April 1896, 1.
48. "Veterans Play Ball."

EPILOGUE

1. "Whacked the President with a Single Stick," *New York Times* 30 December 1902, 5.
2. "Game of Singlesticking Made Popular by President Roosevelt," *Washington Times*, 1 March 1903, Magazine Features, 4.
3. "Game of Singlesticking."
4. "Engraving: 'The Strenuous Life in the White House' . . . engraving from *Harper's Weekly*, February 21, 1903," *Biblio*, https://biblio.com/book/engraving -strenous-life-white-house-engraving/d/1321115006.
5. "President Takes Up Singlestick Play," *St. Louis Republic*, 30 December 1902, 9.
6. Doris Kearns Goodwin, *The Bully Pulpit: Theodore Roosevelt, William Howard Taft, and the Golden Age of Journalism* (New York: Simon & Schuster, 2013), 39.
7. Michael S. Rosenwald, "The President Who Hated Baseball," *Washington Post*, 27 October 2019, https://washingtonpost.com/history/2019/10/26/president -who-hated-baseball/.
8. Ryan Swanson, *The Strenuous Life* (New York: Diversion Books, 2020), 195–96.
9. Rosenwald, "The President Who Hated Baseball."
10. Joseph Bucklin Bishop, ed., *Theodore Roosevelt's Letters to His Children* (New York: Charles Scribner's Sons, 1919), 222–23.
11. Harry Ellard, "'Lub' Taft, Outfielder," *Baseball Magazine* 2, no. 2 (December 1908), 20.
12. Goodwin, *The Bully Pulpit*, 29.
13. "Taft Tosses Ball," *Washington Post*, 15 April 1910, 2.
14. J. Ed. Grillo, "World Famous Fans: Men of National Prominence and Their Views on the National Game," *Baseball Magazine* 7, no. 5 (September 1911), 7.
15. Lilia F. Brady, "Nothing But the Facts: Take Me Out to the Ballgame," *Cincinnati Magazine*, April 1982, 111.
16. Grillo, "World Famous Fans," 7–8.
17. "Taft Guest of Pittsburg: Busy Day, with Good Ball Game in It," *Sun*, 30 May 1909, 1.
18. "Timely Hit of William H. Taft," *Cincinnati Enquirer*, 7 July 1908, 6.
19. Goodwin, *The Bully Pulpit*, 136.
20. John Fisher, "In Golf, President Taft Finds a National Treasure," *Sports Illustrated*, 12 December 2019, https://si.com/golf/news/feature-2019-12-09-in -golf-president-taft-finds-a-national-treasure.

21. "The Critical Moment for Mr. Taft," *New York Sun*, reprinted in *American Golfer* 3, no. 1 (November 1909), 62.

22. "Where Is Taft? Asks Beverly, Mass., in Vain," *New York Times*, 22 August 1909, 44.

23. Fisher, "In Golf, President Taft Finds a National Treasure."

24. "Blow to Cricket: No Games This Year on the Longwood Grounds," *Boston Globe*, 6 April 1900, 9.

25. "Eastern Department—New England Notes," *American Golfer* 1, no. 2 (December 1908), 63.

26. "Eastern Department—New England Notes," 64.

27. Francis Ouimet, *A Game of Golf: A Book of Reminiscences* (Boston: Houghton Mifflin Company, 1932), 45.

28. "Feature Interview with Richard B. Findlay," Golf Club Atlas, June 2012, https://golfclubatlas.com/feature-interview/richard-b-findlay.

29. "Deaths: Wright," *Boston Globe*, 7 May 1928, 11.

30. Denny Wright, phone interview with author, 15 June 2023.

31. John Erardi, "Granddaughter Fondly Remembers Early Reds Star," *Cincinnati Enquirer*, 10 July 1988, 145, J-8.

32. A. G. Spalding, "What Is the Origin of Base Ball?" in Henry Chadwick, ed., *Spalding's Official Base Ball Guide for 1905* (New York: American Sports Publishing Company, 1905), 9.

33. Henry Chadwick, ed., *Spalding's Official Base Ball Guide for 1908* (New York: American Sports Publishing Company, 1908), 48.

34. Chadwick, 42.

35. Bert Dodge, "Pitchers Springing Few New Curves This Year: Fight Over Origin of Baseball," *Newark Evening Star*, 26 March 1908, 6.

36. Levine, *A. G. Spalding*, 112.

37. Levine, 88, 125–34.

38. A. G. Spalding, inscription to George Wright on inside front cover of *America's National Game*, 10 October 1911, from the personal collection of Bruce Garland, photographed by the author, 15 September 2023.

Bibliography

Acocella, Nicholas, and Donald Dewey. *The New Biographical History of Baseball.* Chicago: Triumph Books, 2002.

Anson, Adrian C. *A Ball Player's Career: Being the Personal Experiences and Reminiscences of Adrian C. Anson.* Chicago: ERA Publishing Co.,1900.

Appel, Marty. *Slide, Kelly, Slide: The Wild Life and Times of Mike "King" Kelly, Baseball's First Superstar.* Lanham, MD: The Scarecrow Press, Inc, 1999.

Arcidiacono, David. *Major League Baseball in Gilded Age Connecticut.* Jefferson, NC: McFarland & Company, 2010.

Bales, Jack. *Before They Were the Cubs: The Early Years of Chicago's First Professional Baseball Team.* Jefferson, NC: McFarland & Company, 2019.

Bartlett, Arthur. *Baseball and Mr. Spalding: The History and Romance of Baseball.* New York: Farrar, Straus and Young, 1951.

Bishop, Joseph Bucklin, ed., *Theodore Roosevelt's Letters to His Children.* New York: Charles Scribner's Sons, 1919.

Blanchard, John A., ed. *The H Book of Harvard Athletics, 1852–1922.* Cambridge, MA: Harvard Varsity Club, 1923.

Bucke, Richard Maurice, Thomas B. Harned, and Horace L. Traubel, eds. *In Re Walt Whitman.* Philadelphia: David McKay, 1893.

Chadwick, Henry, ed. *Spalding's Official Base Ball Guide for 1908.* New York: American Sports Publishing Company, 1908.

Devine, Christopher. *Harry Wright, Father of Professional Baseball.* Jefferson, NC: McFarland & Company, 2003.

Edwards, R. A. R. *Deaf Players in Major League Baseball, A History, 1883 to the Present.* Jefferson, NC: McFarland & Company, 2020.

Ellard, Harry. *Baseball in Cincinnati: A History.* Cincinnati: Johnson & Hardin, 1907.

Felber, Bill, ed. *Inventing Baseball: The 100 Greatest Games of the 19th Century.* Phoenix, AZ: Society for American Baseball Research, 2013.

Fleitz, David L. *More Ghosts in the Gallery.* Jefferson, NC: McFarland & Company, 2007.

Gilbert, Thomas W. *How Baseball Happened: The True Story Revealed.* Boston: David R. Godine Publishing, 2020.

Ginsburg, Daniel E. *The Fix Is In: A History of Baseball Gambling and Game Fixing Scandals.* Jefferson, NC: McFarland & Company, 1995.

Goodwin, Doris Kearns. *The Bully Pulpit: Theodore Roosevelt, William Howard Taft, and the Golden Age of Journalism.* New York: Simon & Schuster, 2013.

Guschov, Stephen D. *The Red Stockings of Cincinnati: Base Ball's First All-Professional Team and Its Historic 1869 and 1870 Seasons.* Jefferson, NC: McFarland & Company, 1998.

Hall, Valentine Gill. *Lawn Tennis in America.* New York: D. W. Granbury & Co., 1889.

Henley's Manual of Roller Skating. Richmond, IN: M. C. Henley, 1885.

Henley's Official Polo Guide. Richmond, IN: M. C. Henley, 1885.

Hershberger, Richard. *Strike Four: The Evolution of Baseball.* Lanham, MD: Rowman & Littlefield, 2019.

Hodges, Jeremy K., and Bill Nowlin, eds. *Base Ball's 19th Century "Winter" Meetings, 1857–1900.* Phoenix, AZ: Society for American Baseball Research, 2018.

Hopper, DeWolf, and Wesley Winans Stout. *Once a Clown, Always a Clown: Reminiscences of DeWolf Hopper.* Boston: Little, Brown, and Company, 1927.

Kelly, Mike. *Play Ball. Stories of the Ball Field.* Boston: Press of Emery & Hughes, 1888.

Lamster, Mark. *Spalding's World Tour: The Epic Adventure That Took Baseball Around the Globe—and Made It America's Game.* New York: Public Affairs, 2006.

Lawson, Thomas W. *The Krank: His Language and What It Means.* Boston: Rand Avery Company, 1888.

LeMoine, Bob, and Bill Nowlin, eds., Len Levin assoc. ed. *Boston's First Nine, the 1871–1875 Boston Red Stockings.* Phoenix, AZ: Society for American Baseball Research, 2016.

Levine, Peter. *A. G. Spalding and the Rise of Baseball, The Promise of American Sport.* New York: Oxford University Press, 1985.

Lomax, Michael E. *Black Baseball Entrepreneurs, 1860–1900: Operating by Any Means Necessary.* Syracuse, NY: Syracuse University Press, 2003.

McCullough, David. *John Adams.* New York: Simon & Schuster, 2001.

Morris, Peter. *A Game of Inches: The Stories behind the Innovations That Shaped Baseball.* Chicago: Ivan R. Dee, 2006.

Ouimet, Francis. *A Game of Golf: A Book of Reminiscences.* Boston: Houghton Mifflin Company, 1932.

Palmer, Harry Clay. *Sights Around the World with the Base Ball Boys.* Philadelphia: Edgewood Publishing Company, 1892.

Paret, J. Parmly. *Lawn Tennis, Its Past, Present, and Future.* New York: The Macmillan Company, 1904.

Paret, J. Parmly, and S. Wallis Merrihew, eds. *Methods and Players of Modern Lawn Tennis.* New York: American Lawn Tennis, 1915.

Ritter, Lawrence S. *The Glory of Their Times.* New York: The MacMillan Company, 1966.

Roer, Mike. *Orator O'Rourke: The Life of a Baseball Radical.* Jefferson, NC: McFarland & Company, 2005.

Ryczek, William J. *Blackguards and Red Stockings: A History of Baseball's National Association, 1871–1875,* Revised Edition. Jefferson, NC: McFarland & Company, 2016.

Schiff, Andrew J. *The Father of Baseball—A Biography of Henry Chadwick.* Jefferson, NC: MacFarland & Company, 2008.

Spalding, Albert. *Rise to Follow.* New York: Henry Holt and Company, 1943.

Spalding, Albert G. *America's National Game: Historic Facts Concerning the Beginning, Evolution, Development and Popularity of Base Ball.* New York: American Sports Publishing Company, 1911.

Spink, Alfred H. *The National Game.* St. Louis, MO: National Game Publishing Co., 1910.

Swanson, Ryan. *The Strenuous Life: Theodore Roosevelt and the Making of the American Athlete.* New York: Diversion Books, 2020.

Tilden, William T. II. *The Art of Lawn Tennis.* New York: George H. Doran Company, 1921.

Tuohey, George V. *A History of the Boston Base Ball Club.* Boston: M. F. Quinn & Co., 1897.

Twain, Mark. *A Connecticut Yankee in King Arthur's Court.* New York: Charles L. Webster & Company, 1889.

Wright, George. *George Wright's Book for 1875.* Hyde Park, MA: Norfolk County Gazette Office, 1875.

Wright, George. *Record of the Boston Base Ball Club Since Its Organization.* Boston: Rockwell & Churchill Press, 1874.

Wright & Ditson's Polo Guide. Boston: Wright & Ditson, 1885.

Index

AA. *See* American Association
Adams, Ivers Whitney, 76–77, 85
Adams, John, 75
Adams, Samuel, 75
Adelaide, Australia, 159
Alcock, C. W., 95–96
Alcohol: Brainard's consumption of, 44, 77; Kelly's consumption of, 150–51; players' consumption of, 43–44, 81, 101, 150–51; spectators' consumption of, 101, 106, 137; US consumption of, 43
All-Americas, 154, 180; Australian Tour, 154, 158; World Tour, 159–60
Allison, Doug, 45,77, 86, 127, 128; as catcher, 33; catcher's mouth guard used by, 40; Cincinnati Red Stockings, 33–34; glove used by, 118; Providence Grays, 126; triple play, 126; Washington Olympics, 77
American Association (AA), 120, 137, 139, 163, 174, 186–87
American centennial, 110, 113
American College Association, 169
American Museum, 152
American Publishing Company, 179
American Revolution. *See* Revolutionary War

America's National Game, 203
Anson, Adrian Constantine, 69–70, 111–12, 114, 127, 136, 137, 141, 150, 180–81; Australian Tour, 154–55; as ball player, 136, 148, 149; Chicago White Stockings, 103; compensation to, 70, 103; England Tour, 97, 98, 99; Forest Citys of Rockford, 70; as manager, 136, 137, 144, 148; Marshalltown, 69; nicknames of, 69, 136; Philadelphia Athletics, 97–98, 103; racism of, 99, 138–40, 157; World Tour, 156, 161
Anson, Henry, 69–70, 180
Anson, Sturgis, 69–70
Atlanta Braves, xi
Auckland, New Zealand, 158
Australian Tour, 153–156; Albert Goodwill Spalding's idea of, 153; All-Americas, 154; Australia, 153, 155, 158–59; balloonist on, 154; Chicago White Stockings, 154–59; Harry Wright's idea of, 153; Hawaii (Sandwich Islands), 153, 157–58; New Zealand, 153, 158
Ayers, F. H., 167

Wright, Abbie (maiden name Coleman), 88, 121, 134, 199

Wright, Beals, 134, 199, 200; tennis champion, 168–69

Wright, Dan, 36–37, 155

Wright, Denny, 72, 131, 164–65, 168, 174

Wright, Dorothy, 200

Wright, Elizabeth: daughter of George, 121, 200

Wright, Elizabeth: granddaughter of George, 200

Wright, George, 47, 50, 52, 54–55, 75, 85, 91, 146, 160, 169, 180, 203; Australian Tour, 155–57, 164; as ball player, xi, 5, 7, 11, 17, 35–38, 39, 45, 46, 64, 65–66, 67, 69, 74, 76, 82, 83, 84, 109, 110–11, 118, 119–20, 121, 123, 125, 129, 131, 133, 136, 190–91, 204; Barnes assessment by, 83; "Base Ball Attitudes" with Barnes, 90; Base Ball Emporium, 129; books authored by, 89–90, 91; Boston Red Stockings joined by, 76–77; California visit by, 58, 155; catcher's mask, 116–17, 120; catcher's mouth protector, 39, 117; Chadwick assessment of, 84–85; Cincinnati Red Stockings joined by, 30, 34; Clipper Gold Medal, 31, 35, 72; during Civil War, 16–17; as club owner, 138; compensation of, 42–43, 78; as cricketer, 17–18, 20, 98, 134, 155–56, 198; death of, 200; early years of, 4–5, 11; England Tour, 96, 97, 98, 160; as golfer, 174, 198–99; golf promotion by, 173–74, 175; grandson of George, 200; hand protection of, 40; Harry Wright in business with, 20–21; ice base ball, 18–19; ice hockey promotion by, 173, 175; injuries of, 70–72, 86–87, 134, 200; as manager, 76, 128, 129, 133, 136; marriage of, 88; Mills Commission, 200–201; New York

Gothams, 17; nicknames of, xii, 17; Philadelphia Olympics, 20; product endorsement, 89; professionalism, 5, 10; Providence Grays, 123; record of (1869), 60–61; reserve system issues, 136; roller polo promotion by, 172, 175; sole sports equipment business owner, 88, 121, 128–29; sports equipment business. *See* Wright & Ditson, Wright & Gould; sports guides by, 120, 138, 167–68, 172, 175; tennis promotion by, 165–68; triple play, 125–26; Unions of Morrisania, 4; university contacts of, 169; Washington Nationals, 4–5; William Edward White, 130–31; World Tour, 160, 174

Wright, Georgiana, 121, 200

Wright, Harry, 5–6, 36, 47, 52, 53, 61, 68, 75, 99–100, 103, 106, 114, 121, 151, 169, 195, 196; Albert Goodwill Spalding's relationship with, xii, 78, 94–95; as ball player, xi, 5, 32, 37–39, 44, 69, 71, 77; Barnes assessment by, 83–84; Base Ball Telegraph of, 41; Boston Red Stockings assembled by, 77–78; Cincinnati Red Stockings assembled by, 30, 33–34; Civil War years, 16–17; as club secretary, 80–81, 87; compensation of, 42–43, 78; conditioning advice from, 86; as cricketer, 20; cricket goods sold by, 42; domination of NA by, xii, 89, 151; England Tour, xii, 91, 93–95, 96, 97, 153; final years of, 189–90; George Wright in business with, 20–21; Harry Wright Day, 190–91; ice base ball, 18–19; L. H. Mahn in business with, 189–90; as manager, xi, 5, 32, 35, 39, 43–45, 46, 51, 65, 71, 74, 76–77, 78, 80, 84, 86, 87, 121, 123, 131–33, 136, 189–90; Schafer's assessment by, 85; support of George's business by, 88; Sam Wright Jr.'s assessment by, 121–22

About the Author

Jeffrey Orens is a writer of historical nonfiction with an exceptional eye for overlooked gems in history. He has written for historical journals and is a member of the Society for American Baseball Research (SABR), publishing articles on nineteenth-century baseball as well as presenting at SABR's nineteenth-century baseball conference in Cooperstown, New York. He is the author of *The Soul of Genius: Marie Curie, Albert Einstein, and the Meeting That Changed the Course of Science*, an in-depth look at one of the most exciting periods of science through the lives of the two most well-known scientists in the world. He lives with his wife, Deborah, in Fairfield, New Jersey.